About Prison

MICHAEL G. SANTOS

With an introduction by
George F. Cole

THOMSON
™
WADSWORTH

Australia • Canada • Mexico • Singapore • Spain
United Kingdom • United States

THOMSON

WADSWORTH

Senior Executive Editor, Criminal Justice: *Sabra Horne*
Editorial Assistant: *Paul Massicotte*
Marketing Manager: *Dory Schaeffer*
Marketing Assistant: *Neena Chandra*
Advertising Project Manager: *Stacey Purviance*
Project Manager, Editorial Production: *Jennie Redwitz*
Print/Media Buyer: *Karen Hunt*

Permissions Editor: *Kiely Sexton*
Production Service: *UG / GGS Information Services, Inc.*
Copy Editor: *Lura Harrison*
Cover Designer: *Yvo Riezebos*
Cover Image: *Steven Puetzer/Photonica*
Compositor: *UG / GGS Information Services, Inc.*
Text and Cover: *Webcom*

Printed in Canada
1 2 3 4 5 6 7 07 06 05 04 03

For more information about our products, contact us at:
Thomson Learning Academic Resource Center
1-800-423-0563

For permission to use material from this text, contact us by:
Phone: 1-800-730-2214   **Fax:** 1-800-730-2215
Web: http://www.thomsonrights.com

Library of Congress Control Number:
200310774

ISBN 0-534-62355-7

Wadsworth/Thomson Learning
10 Davis Drive
Belmont, CA 94002-3098
USA

Asia
Thomson Learning
5 Shenton Way, #01-01
UIC Building
Singapore 189969

Australia/Newzealand
Thomson Learning
102 Dodds Street
Southbank, Victoria 3006
Australia

Canada
Nelson
1120 Birchmount Road
Toronto, Ontario M1K 5G4
Canada

Europe/Middle East/Africa
Thomson Learning
High Holborn House
50/51 Bedford Row
London WC1R 4LR
United Kingdom

Latin America
Thomson Learning
Seneca, 53
Colonia Polanco
11560 Mexico D.F.
Mexico

Spain/Portugal
Paraninfo
Calle/Magallanes, 25
28015 Madrid, Spain

Contents

Foreword

This is a guidebook to understanding prison written by Michael Santos, a man who has been in federal prison for over 15 years. Mr. Santos is a man who ought to know something about making the best of a prison stay—during his stint for a drug crime conviction he has become a successful writer, contributing his work to popular journals and college textbooks, and most recently developing the text you now hold in your hands. This book is the culmination of a decade of thinking and writing about prison from the inside. When he entered prison in 1987, Mr. Santos' life was in crisis. He has transformed that crisis into contribution, for his work serves to teach the free world about prison life and now to inspire people who face confinement with ways to make it through their sentenced time.

About Prison is a new addition to the *Wadsworth Contemporary Issues in Crime and Justice Series*. As editor of that series, I am delighted to introduce Michael Santos' book, *About Prison*, to this year's list. The Wadsworth Series publishes books that address important issues in crime and justice in ways that go well beyond the coverage provided by typical classroom textbooks. It is the aim of this series to deepen our understanding of important questions facing criminology and criminal justice, and the series has, over the years, published some of the most important books on current topics of interest to the field. This book now joins that prestigious list.

WHO SHOULD READ THIS BOOK?

The book is written with a particular target audience in mind: The person facing a prison sentence. For this reader, the book provides an invaluable service. It offers guidance about the problems a person will face in prison and some of the ways those problems can be overcome. Mr. Santos tells his own story of going to prison and dealing with its challenges, but he does a lot more than that. He talks about how a person can develop a philosophy of his or her time in prison. He talks about the significant ways in which prison is different from life outside, but he also talks about how a person can make a life inside, despite these travails. In this way, this book is a contribution that fills a void in the literature on prisons. It is a book about being in prison, written by a person in prison, written for people in prison. I hope that many of those who face time behind bars will take advantage of the lessons contained within these pages.

But others should read this book, even if they will never be in a prison. Why? Because prisons have grown to be a dominant aspect of contemporary American culture, with a steady annual increase in prisoners for a generation. In a mere 30 years, the prison population in the United States has grown from 200,000 to 1.2 million. Among poor men of color, prison is increasingly a paramount fact of life. If present circumstances continue, more than one quarter of today's black pre-school males can expect to spend time behind bars at some time in their adulthood. Our nation's incarceration rate is at or near the top of the list among nations of the world, and at the very top among industrialized Western societies. At no time in history has there been this kind of change in incarceration policy in a "free" nation. It is not too extreme to say that no understanding of contemporary America is possible unless the national love affair with prisons is a part of that understanding.

This book does more than recount one person's experience with prison then, and it also does more than offer a guide for those who might end up in the author's situation. It describes what several hundred thousand Americans face every year: going into a prison. It details the challenges, paradoxes, banalities, and peculiarities of being a prisoner that are everyday life for over a million of our fellow citizens. And by doing this, the book helps the many of its readers who will never be put in this position to imagine what they might do—what they might *have* to do—in order to make it through the ordeal.

This book transports those of us who are far removed from prison life into the world of the prison in ways that enable us to gain commonality with those of us who will become people behind bars. By bridging this gap, the book offers insights into the broader society that embraces the repeated exposure of its citizens to this tribulation. It accomplishes this aim by the power of one small voice, the personal story of one of the witnesses to this mass imprisonment society from the vantage point of the inside. One story of survival, one story of a kind of triumph.

None of this is to say that Mr. Santos believes the sentence he now serves has worked out for the best. He will tell you that he often feels deeply wronged by the enormity of the penalty he must suffer, and the inability of the system to take account of the changes in his life. He knows that the crimes he committed were wrong, but he wonders if the comparative waste of what might turn out to be half his life behind bars is a just consequence for his actions and a wise investment of social resources. This is a view that is hard to dispute.

Yet his purpose in writing this book is in no way to plead his case. Here, he wants merely to tell his story and that of a few others in order to promote whatever wisdom might be gained by those who read it—especially those who might face similar challenges. In that spirit, I congratulate you for using this book and encourage you as you consider its implications.

Todd R. Clear
Series Editor

Introduction

In September 1992 I received a letter from a prisoner at the U.S. Penitentiary in Atlanta. This was not unusual. Because I teach and write about corrections I often receive letters from inmates either telling me that my textbook "tells it like it is" or asking for assistance. This letter, however, was different. It was from Michael Santos, a 23-year-old first-time nonviolent drug offender in his fifth year of a forty-five year sentence. Not only was I shocked by the severity of the punishment, but I was impressed with the way Mr. Santos was doing his time. During those five years at USP, Atlanta, he had earned a bachelor's degree and was working on a master's. He asked me to comment on the papers he was writing as part of his graduate program. From this initial contact has blossomed a warm and enduring friendship.

For a prisoner to earn two college degrees while incarcerated is rare. Among the more than 1.3 million prisoners in the United States, 65 percent have less than a high school education and only 12 percent have some college education or more. Although most state and federal prisons have educational programs for inmates who lack high school equivalency, there are very few institutions where college courses are offered. The Comprehensive Crime Act of 1994 banned federal funding to prisoners for post-secondary education and Pell grants for tuition assistance were eliminated. Some state legislatures passed similar laws under pressure from people who argue that tax dollars should not be spent on the college tuition of prisoners when law-abiding students must pay their own way. Yet studies have found that inmates who take courses are less likely to recidivate.

Michael Santos is a gleaner. He is undoubtedly one of the very few state or federal prisoners who has tried to better himself through higher education during his long period of incarceration. Today, without college courses, a good library, or access to a typewriter—let alone a computer—Santos has continued his education through correspondence courses, independent study, and writing. His work is found in several criminal justice anthologies and textbooks including the Wadsworth publications *The American System of Criminal Justice* and *American Corrections*. *About Prison* is his first book but it will be followed by *Profiles from Prison* (Greenwood/Praeger) and *What if I Go to Prison?* (available through www.MichaelSantos.net.)

Over the years I have visited Michael on numerous occasions at the Federal Correctional Institutions in McKean, Pennsylvania and Fort Dix, New Jersey and we are in monthly contact through telephone calls and letters. I have been rewarded, not only by knowing an outstanding individual, but also by gaining a better understanding of what it is like to be incarcerated. Through conversations with Michael I have learned how he and other prisoners stay out of trouble, deal with the prison bureaucracy, keep fit, and maintain a positive attitude.

Mr. Santos is an excellent writer who describes prison life from a human perspective. He brings to the reader compelling descriptions of prison society, the interactions between prisoners and officers, the lack of privacy, the role of gangs, the prison economy, and the ways long-term inmates view their future. Readers will gain a perspective of incarceration from someone who has experienced it from the "inside."

George F. Cole
Professor Emeritus of Political Science
University of Connecticut

Preface

In 1987, when I was 23, I began my life as a federal prisoner. Prior to my incarceration, I didn't know anything about living in confinement. As I write this book, however, in 2003, I have begun serving my sixteenth year behind these fences. The time I've served (and the insights and understandings I unearth day by day), coupled with the studies I've completed during my incarceration, qualify me to describe life inside the federal prison system.

This is a book about my life in prison. As such, I believe the strength of this book comes from the reader seeing firsthand what prison life is really about. My hope is that this book will be used as a resource in classes that deal with the modern correctional system and as a supplement to discussions of the correctional system and prison and jail management. Students learn a lot about how prisons work and how the correctional system is created. But they don't learn about the people inside those prisons. My book is about those people. My hope is that this book will provide a face and a story to replace the anonymous individuals presented in so many corrections books. From one point of view, the American correctional system is about the people in the system— the prisoners *and* the workers. Here are those people.

Despite having no history of violence, I've served a significant portion of my sentence in a maximum-security prison. I've lived a few years as a medium-security prisoner, and I've spent the past seven years confined in the low-security prison at Fort Dix, New Jersey. Through this book, I hope to help others learn about the abnormal way of life that exists behind these walls and fences.

I've made a conscious effort not to sensationalize this story, not to make prison seem worse or better than it actually is. My goal has been to report accurately and to keep my story real. I've described my own experiences and observations of living virtually my entire adult life as a federal prisoner in various security settings.

But not all prisoners serve their time in the same way I've served mine. Accordingly, I provide various dialogues, vignettes, and profiles of other prisoners with whom I've been confined. In describing these prisoners, I frequently use their voices, hoping to provide the reader with a more complete and authentic picture of the growing subculture that exists within the Federal Bureau of Prisons. I apologize if the occasional harshness of prisoner language offends sensitive readers; prison isn't for the sensitive. Where other prisoners wanted me to use their names, I've done so. Where they didn't, I've created pseudonyms. Their stories, however, are as close to the truth as I'm able to verify and report.

The federal prison system promises to continue its unprecedented growth. When I began serving this sentence, the Bureau of Prisons held fewer than 40,000 prisoners. Today, the federal prison population exceeds 160,000 people; taking into account prisoners in various state prison systems, our nation now confines approximately 2 million offenders.

To accommodate these rapidly growing correctional systems, many universities now design courses to help future prison administrators prepare for careers in corrections. I'm hoping some of these correctional personnel find what I've written here in *About Prison* helpful as they acquire impressions and understandings of life behind prison fences.

Ultimately, I hope *About Prison* influences future correctional professionals to contemplate the goals of confinement and question the wisdom of policies that result in "us-versus-them" environments. Rather than creating societies of deprivation—which is an accurate characterization of prisons in our nation—administrators might consider supporting policies that would provide prisoners with opportunities to accept responsibility; to redeem themselves; and, finally, to earn their freedom. Instead of warehousing prisoners for decades at a time, correctional personnel might think about supporting policies that will influence offenders to examine their system of values and accept the fundamental responsibility of living at one with law-abiding communities.

My release date is not scheduled to surface until August of 2013. During the remaining years I have to serve, I am committed to continuing my efforts to reach out to the broader society and help citizens understand the prison system and the people that it holds. It is one of the ways I am working to redeem myself. I welcome the opportunity to interact with citizens and urge readers to share their thoughts or questions about long-term confinement with me.

Although I do not have direct access to the Internet, I have a support system that maintains a Web site for me at www.MichaelSantos.net. Besides offering extensive content on my experiences and observations as a man in prison, my site features a "Dialogues" section with an open forum where I invite professors, university students, correctional professionals, and all visitors to post their comments or questions. I respond to those comments or questions as they are posted on my site's forum so that others may follow our open dialogue. I respond not only from my own perspective, but speak directly with other prisoners to present their views as well.

The Web site represents one of the ways I reach out of these fences to prepare myself for a law-abiding life upon release, and one of the few ways citizens can communicate directly with the people their tax dollars are paying to confine. I encourage all readers to participate in the efforts I make to reconcile with society. After all, in the end, I think prisons should do more than warehouse human beings. An open dialogue may help. I would be grateful for an opportunity to learn from those who choose to express their thoughts, and encourage readers to communicate, either through my Web site, or by writing me at the following address.

Michael G. Santos
10115 Greenwood Avenue N
PMB 184
Seattle, WA 98133

URL: www.MichaelSantos.net
Email: info@MichaelSantos.com

ACKNOWLEDGMENTS

The federal prison system is about confinement, and trying to grow within these walls elicits a relentless flow of obstacles. Over the past sixteen years, I've had a significant amount of help in navigating my way through these obstacles, and I need to thank all who have helped me grow.

First and foremost, I want to salute my sister Julie who has made great personal sacrifices to help me from the day I was arrested. More than anyone, she has served every day of this sentence with me, and I'll always be grateful for her love and steadfast support. Julie has been that rare paragon of loyalty, an essential feminine presence in my life, and a guide to my evolving conscience.

I'm also grateful for the support I received from my mother, Frances Sierra; my father, Julio Santos; and my younger sister, Christina. All of them helped me find the resources to educate myself during my confinement and gave me the strength to move forward.

Besides my immediate family, I also must expressly thank my mentors. Dr. R. Bruce McPherson not only has helped me develop my writing skills, he has been a constant role model to me, exposing me to art, literature, and the importance of developing balance, temperance, and good character. He has helped me become a better person.

Professor George Cole, too, has been a faithful source of support since I first contacted him back in 1992 when Professor John DiIulio recommended that I write him to learn from one of America's top penologists; my relationship with George made this book possible, and his assistance has yielded a palpable result.

Other academic mentors who have supported and helped me learn during my confinement include Professors Norval Morris, Marilyn McShane, Francis Cullen, Tara Gray, Tim Flanagan, Todd Clear, Mary Bosworth, and Leo Carroll. I'm grateful for their guidance and for giving me the opportunity to learn from them.

I want to express my appreciation to those within the Bureau of Prisons who opened doors for me and allowed me to pursue my academic goals. I'm grateful to those who treated me like a human being and not just like a prisoner. In USP Atlanta, some of those people include Lynn Stephens, Dennis Griffin, Phil Little, Walt Wells, and Quintella Forbes. At FCI McKean, those people include Dennis Luther, Craig Apker, and Celia Barto. At Fort Dix, I especially want to thank Bernard Grant, from the UNICOR factory, and the members of my unit team, including Unit Manager Jones, Case Manager Petriello, Counselor Wiget, and my work-detail supervisor, Counselor Hood. I also want to thank the custody staff, especially Lieutenant Marts, for not interfering with the efforts I am making to grow through writing. Finally, in the BOP's central office, I must thank Ms. Sylvia McCollum, who has encouraged my writing since my correspondence with her began in the late 1980s.

I live in a community of prisoners. The hundreds of friends I have made behind these fences have helped me serve my time and encouraged me to remain committed to my goals. From my years in USP Atlanta, I especially want to acknowledge my friendships with Dan and Paul Robinson and with Mark Howard. At McKean, with Joe Hargrave, Wayne Davis, and Mark Durall. And at Fort Dix, with Tom Cappa, Jerry Cohen, Pete Hockford, and Bob Brennan. I also want to applaud Joe Reddick and Seth Ferranti, two fellow prison writers. I'm grateful for all these friendships, as they've made my imprisonment easier to bear.

Finally, I embrace the Axelrod family, Sabra Horne, Skeydrit Bahr, Celine Gendron, Francoise Hembert, Betty Seaver, Janice Singer, and especially, Carole Gerard. These people came into my life after prison gates closed behind me; they never judged me for the bad decisions I made as a younger man. Instead, they've shown me love and encouraged my efforts to mature and find the depths of my humanity.

Acquaintances assist people like me as if they were crutches. But family, mentors, and friends do more than that. They empower me to hope, to walk and then run, to find the sun, to discover myself. I am privileged to have these relationships, and I hope my family, mentors, and friends find this book not totally unworthy of the influence they've had on me.

On a personal note, I thank all readers for this opportunity they've given me to participate in their lives. And I wish them Godspeed.

Michael G. Santos
August 2003

1

Entry into the Criminal Justice System

It was all quite new to me when I was arrested in August 1987. First, there were the guns pointed at my head during the arrest. The DEA agents then attempted to convert me into an informant. After declining to cooperate in the investigation against me, I was booked into the federal holding facility in Miami. A court appearance followed, during which I learned that I had been indicted by a grand jury on charges that carried the possibility of life without parole. Because I was accused of being the kingpin of a criminal organization, the judge would not grant bail. The charges against me meant that I was both a flight risk and a danger to the community. These were my first experiences in the criminal justice system.

I spent my first year as a "pretrial" prisoner, learning what follows the loss of freedom. Through my own experiences and my conversations with other prisoners, I observed the system and how others lived through it.

BEGINNINGS

Sometime in late 1986, I realized that I needed a lawyer. Although I wasn't facing imminent legal problems—at least I didn't expect to—I recognized I should make preparations for the future. I knew I was responsible, at least partially, for organizing a network of people who distributed cocaine. The people in the network were all friends of mine, people with whom I had attended school since the fifth grade. Once the distribution scheme was in place, my friends waited eagerly for the multiple kilograms I would send from Miami.

I was 23, and, although I neither considered myself a criminal nor associated with people who adhered to criminal lifestyles, I understood that my actions over the past 12 to 15 months could lead to my being charged with some kind of criminal conduct. In retrospect, it sounds absurd that I failed to acknowledge my own or my friends' criminality. Although none of us carried weapons, stole, or intimidated anyone, we broke the law every day by facilitating the illegal distribution of large quantities of cocaine. It was too simple, and I will describe my role in it all as we progress through the story. The point is that I deluded myself into believing that because I didn't actually handle the cocaine, or didn't participate in the hand-to-hand distribution, I wasn't vulnerable to prosecution. The term "criminal," I foolishly convinced myself, defined only murderers, rapists, armed robbers, and others who preyed upon society. Denying my own culpability as a criminal was just another manifestation of my own sense of self-importance. I was living a life that was the personification of arrogance.

At the time I realized I needed a lawyer, I was living in Florida. Raised in Lake Forest Park, a small suburb just north of Seattle, I had graduated from Shorecrest High School in 1982. When I was a small child, maybe 5 or 6, my father started an electrical contracting firm. He and my mother built this business with expectations that when I grew older I would take it over. On weekends and during summer vacations, I worked with my father—and I hated every day of it. Both of my parents were hard workers, with my mother doing the books and my father working the field. I was always looking for a way to escape any aspect of the work.

From the time I was in elementary school, I was the kind of kid who had a flip answer for everything. And the sarcasm didn't leave me as I grew through my school years; neither did the arrogance. After graduation I worked in the family firm for a few years, but I certainly didn't expect to make a life for myself working as a contractor. Just before I turned 22, I saw an opportunity to emancipate myself from the responsibilities associated with my father's business. Without thinking of the risk it presented to my family or me, I took advantage of the opportunity.

MY LEAP INTO CRIME

For seven years before I made the leap into crime, I had been close friends with Alex. He was two years ahead of me when I began at Shorecrest, had his own car, and was a good athlete and popular. I looked up to him and we formed a friendship. Alex's father owned a small company, too, and as I worked for mine, Alex worked for his father whenever his schedule allowed. After graduation, Alex began working there full time. He also started supplementing his income by selling small quantities of cocaine.

Those were the mid 1980s. Somehow, at least in the crowd with which we ran, cocaine had a sense of glamour to it. *Scarface* was popular in the theaters, and those who distributed cocaine had a swashbuckling way about themselves. The people to whom Alex sold cocaine weren't too different from us—people from the suburbs who were hooked on Seattle nightlife. There were no addicts, and we didn't see any crime associated with it. Alex dealt enough to supplement his income and to leave him with enough cocaine to have his own supply for free.

We were both active in the Seattle nightclub scene, and over time we got to know the owners of several of the city's most popular clubs and restaurants. Those relationships meant we didn't wait in long admission lines, and, once inside, we never had a problem with preferred seating. By the time I was 22, my father had given me much more responsibility in his company. I was the VP, working in contract administration and finance. The position gave me access to the company bank accounts, but it also required long hours of drudgery. What I really enjoyed was acting the big shot at The Vogue, Cutters, The Regrade, or some of the other 1985 hot spots in Seattle. I never looked forward to work the following day.

It was in that atmosphere that I spoke with Alex about becoming his partner. Alex had been dealing for so long that his scheme was moving along with the precision of his gaudy Swiss watch, and despite his having been selling for several years, there was not even a hint of legal problems. Since I had access to capital, I proposed that I would finance a large purchase of cocaine. Instead of his selling ounces and earning a few thousand each month, I suggested we could sell kilograms and make tens of thousands each week. He agreed.

My father trusted me implicitly, and I betrayed him. We had been speaking about buying a new dump truck and excavator for a large highway job we had under contract. I fabricated a story about a company that had the type of equipment we were looking for and told my father I knew the company was going out of business. I said I wanted to make the owner a cash offer for his equipment, convincing my father that such a move could shave at least 10 percent off the purchase price. So, my father didn't object when I made a large cash withdrawal from the company's account. But, of course, I wasn't going to buy any construction equipment, or even attempt to make an offer. For me, it was just a ruse that would give me temporary access to the cash I needed to fund a 10-kilogram purchase of cocaine. With Alex's distribution scheme in place, I expected to resell it all over a weekend. And we did.

I took the cash out of the bank on Friday. We purchased the 10 kilograms over the weekend, and by Monday we had cashed out. With the proceeds from the sale, I deposited the money back into my father's company account on Monday; I told my dad that the owner of the equipment didn't accept my offer. Alex and I split the $100,000 that we made over the weekend. Those middleman profits I made enabled me to quit my father's firm and move to Key Biscayne, Florida. Wanting to set myself up, I leased a breathtaking oceanfront condominium. Then I started placing myself in circles that

I expected could help me make the contacts I needed to facilitate the new venture Alex and I had begun in Seattle.

Instead of educating myself or pursuing a career—goals to which most people my age were aspiring—I used my early profits to fund my newly created position in my partnership with Alex. My role was to locate the sources of supply, negotiate a deal, and then make the purchases. In Miami, that was about as complicated as finding salmon in a Seattle fish market. Using a combination of cash and credit, I purchased the cocaine in 10-kilogram increments for $27,000 per kilogram. John, another one of my long-time friends offered to transport the cocaine from Florida to Seattle for $1,000 per kilogram. He brought it to Alex, who then made it available to the Seattle clients we had cultivated, for $40,000 per kilogram. After expenses, one successful trip would net Alex and me about $60,000 each, and John would earn $10,000. It wasn't too sophisticated, but it worked.

From the time I moved to Florida, I sent up to 30 kilograms of cocaine a month to Seattle. Although I arranged and paid for the cocaine's purchase, worked closely with John in orchestrating its transportation to Seattle, and had been instrumental in organizing the network that became capable of distributing those kilograms, I never acknowledged my level of culpability. Naively and erroneously, I assumed that because I didn't place myself near the cocaine, I couldn't be convicted of any criminal wrongdoing. At 23, and earning six figures in a good month, it became easy to convince myself of anything.

Little did I know that the steps I had taken to distance myself from each transaction rendered me guilty of committing the U.S. government's most notorious drug offense. Because I had organized and led a group of at least five people who distributed cocaine on more than three occasions, involving substantial amounts of money, I was guilty of operating a Continuing Criminal Enterprise (CCE), in violation of Title 18 of the United States Code, Section 848. The charge would give my sentencing judge the discretion to sentence me to a term of not less than ten years and up to life imprisonment. Whatever term he chose, the statute would prevent me from access to parole. At 23, I was a cocaine kingpin.

ARREST

My problems with the criminal justice system began when Alex was arrested. He had hired Salvatore to store the cocaine in Seattle, and Salvatore made some blunders that resulted in the Drug Enforcement Agency (DEA) placing his apartment under surveillance. That surveillance resulted in them nabbing Alex just after he had picked up a kilogram for delivery. When Alex was arrested, of course, I didn't know how much the DEA knew. I decided to hire a lawyer in Florida just in case.

Paco, the supplier, from whom I had been purchasing cocaine in Miami was no amateur, of that I was sure. He was from Colombia but lived in a spectacular waterfront home on Key Biscayne. I first met him at Regine's, a swank private disco in Coconut Grove. We saw a lot of each other, and it wasn't long before Paco became my primary source of supply. He had cocaine available to him by the hundreds of kilograms, so my needs were never a problem. After Alex was busted, I asked Paco to recommend a good lawyer for me. Paco introduced me to Henry, a well-known East Coast criminal defense attorney who had built a practice representing people charged with involvement in organized crime and drug offenses. After my initial consultation with Henry, I agreed to retain him so he would be available to represent me in the event I encountered legal problems.

On August 11, 1987, within six months of the time I initially retained Henry, my neatly designed wall collapsed. It was a sunny Florida afternoon as I walked toward my apartment. I saw three men in dark clothing standing outside my door. Visceral instincts told me there was a problem, as I lived in a secure building and did not recognize the people waiting for me. My initial thought was to turn around, walk to my car, drive to an airport, and leave whatever problems awaited me behind. But I was tired of leading this secret life, this life of deception and lies. So, instead of running, I chose to keep walking, to confront whatever problem awaited me from the three men whom I reasoned were not there to make friends.

When I moved closer, each man pulled a pistol from his jacket, pointed the gun at my head and screamed orders.

"Put your hands in the air!"

"Don't move!"

"You're under arrest!"

The men were agents of the DEA, and they told me I was being arrested pursuant to a federal grand jury indictment charging me with operating a Continuing Criminal Enterprise. It's the most powerful drug charge in the government's arsenal. At that moment I knew my life was changing forever.

The agents threw me against the wall, slammed handcuffs on my wrists, and recited the Miranda warning I had heard so many times on television: "You have the right to remain silent. Anything you say can and will be used against you in a court of law . . . ." The guns, the handcuffs, the Miranda warning all seemed kind of theatrical, surreal. But my arrest was happening, and it was happening quickly. The agents led me through the complex of my building, in full view of all my neighbors, down to the underground parking garage and into their waiting Ford LTD.

Somewhere along the way the government agents began questioning me, advising "You can work with us and save yourself."

I told them I chose to exercise my right to remain silent; I wanted to speak with my attorney. To my relief, the agents left me alone in my thoughts as we drove to a DEA office for some initial processing.

As we made the drive, my mind scattered. I had no idea what awaited me as I began this new and unfamiliar journey through the criminal justice system. On the one hand, I felt relief that my experiences of living a secret life soon were going to end; on the other, I worried about the unknown awaiting me.

I had never been arrested before, never spent time in prison. Nevertheless, I was on my way to life in seclusion. Although I had been lying to myself and others for nearly two years about my true activities, deep inside I knew I was guilty of the crimes with which I was being charged. Still, I kept telling myself the words my defense attorney had told me just weeks before: "There is a big difference between an indictment and a conviction." I maintained a long-shot hope we would emerge victorious after a trial and my life would then return to me—those were the deluded hopes of a man about to be condemned.

We arrived at the DEA offices in a nondescript office park. I was led to an area where my picture was taken and I was fingerprinted. Despite my assertion about wanting to remain silent until I spoke with my attorney, the agents pursued their questioning. Recognizing me for what I was—young, inexperienced, and, despite the serious charges against me, unsophisticated—the agents tried to engage me in any kind of dialogue.

"You know you're facing a minimum of ten years in prison," one would say.

"But no one who's been convicted of running a CCE ever gets 10 years," another added.

"The judge can give you life, and, most of the time, that's what CCEs get."

"You ought to think about what you're doing."

"We can help you."

"If you work with us, you could sleep in your own bed tonight."

"You're just making it harder on yourself by not talking."

Their comments came one after the other. I heard what the agents were saying, but I felt as if I were in enemy territory and that I couldn't trust them. An hour earlier they had been pointing guns at my head; such behavior didn't convince me the agents were on my side.

My mind was clouded, and it was hard to appreciate the seriousness of what was going on. I sat there without saying anything. Out of frustration, I suppose, the agents eventually locked me in a small room.

Looking around the room, it was smaller than my closet at home. Yet, it had a little bench and a curious toilet/sink combination configured out of stainless steel. I remember looking around the room and thinking that this was what confinement was all about. Just sitting there, alone, out of touch with the world and unable to concentrate on anything. I waited in that room for about an hour, maybe a bit longer, wondering what was going to happen next. Hardly any time had passed, and it was hard for me to really accept that this arrest had happened. Even so, I wasn't optimistic that the problems would go away quickly. Although I was willing to spend whatever I had to fight the charges, deep inside I knew that I was guilty. In fact, I had been waiting for an end to the twisted life I'd been living. I was embarrassed at the predicament I had put myself into, and despite the "I'm innocent" rhetoric, I was afraid. Until only a few hours ago, I had played as if I were a rock star, but now as I sat in the tiny cell, I was afraid that my life was about to become insignificant—and I was afraid of going to prison. Whatever was going to happen, in the few hours I had spent in custody, it was clear that I no longer controlled my own life. I was no more than an object passing through a vast, indifferent system.

One of the agents finally came by and asked me whether I had reconsidered and would agree to talk with him and the others. I told the agent I wanted to talk with my attorney. He said I was making a mistake but let me make a phone call.

I called Henry and told him I had been arrested and was in the custody of the DEA. It was a short conversation. He told me I shouldn't say anything without him being present and we disconnected. Soon thereafter, the agents drove me to the Metropolitan Correctional Center in Miami (MCC Miami). I didn't know anything about where they were taking me. I was in restraints the entire time and realizing quickly that my life had already changed. Probably forever.

MCC MIAMI

The Metropolitan Correctional Center, a facility of the Federal Bureau of Prisons, had been built about ten years prior to the time I arrived. It wasn't designed to intimidate. This surprised me somewhat, because the only time I had seen prisons before was on television or in films. They always looked big and imposing from the outside. Mean. This facility, on the other hand, didn't look so frightening. The neatly manicured lawns and pastel colors of the building gave the appearance of a large office complex. At least at that point, I thought the building looked kind of serene. I had heard about country club prisons, and I thought that maybe it wasn't going to be so bad. My initial reaction to the place calmed my fears a bit. But only for a minute, because immediately I was struck by the high, double, chain-link fences surrounding the perimeter. Coils of glistening razor wire topped and separated the fences; they reminded me that I was indeed entering a prison. It was about 5:00 in the afternoon when the DEA agents delivered me.

The agents and I walked from their car to the front door of the facility. In retrospect, I now realize that was the last time I walked outside of a prison or a related institution without steel cuffs and a chain binding my ankles. Once inside, the agents passed me to the guards as if they were delivering a package. The DEA had done its deed in capturing me, and now it was up to the prison system to hold me. The guards, who worked for the Bureau of Prisons (BOP), didn't treat me as if I were a human being. Although this was all new to me, they process new bodies into the system every day. While the DEA agents removed their restraints, and the BOP guards fastened me in theirs, the officers from different branches of government chatted and joked as if no one else were present. The feeling that I was a nonentity was being reinforced. I was more like an inanimate object that they were checking into inventory than someone who shared a common humanity with them. The guards led me to a small holding cell where they removed my handcuffs and locked me inside. I was alone in the room but the environment had changed. This was no temporary holding cell like the relatively peaceful one at the DEA offices. Indeed, outside my cell, pandemonium reigned.

The cell had no windows or bars through which I could see, so I couldn't identify the sources of all the noise. It was deafening. Steel slamming against steel. Hundreds of voices all screaming at once. After leading a rather tranquil life on South Florida beaches for the past year or so, the noise, coupled with the unknown of what was to come, inspired anxiety and fear.

After what seemed like an excessive wait, a guard opened a trap door within the steel door of the holding cell. He passed through a paper bag containing two pieces of stale white bread, a slice of baloney, an orange, and a plastic container holding some extrasweet Kool-Aid®. Dinner. The trauma of being arrested had depleted my appetite, though. I didn't eat.

I wondered about my parents, my sisters. How were they going to react to this devastating news? I felt so ashamed. Yet there I sat, hands holding my face as I stared at the concrete and steel meeting in the corners of my cell. I was facing charges carrying the possible penalty of life without parole. "This can't be possible," I thought. How does a 23-year-old deliver this news to a family that has had no previous experience with the criminal justice system? I had no answer.

The End of Privacy

A guard soon came to interrupt my self-pity. He ordered me up and out of the cell. I was led to a station where another guard took my photograph and fingerprinted me. The guard then took me to yet another room.

"Strip," he said.

The guard stood in front of me as I began taking off my clothes. He didn't say anything. He just stood about 2 feet in front of me and looked. Intensely. When I stopped at my underwear, he spoke.

"Strip naked," he said.

After removing my drawers, the guard told me to hold my hands out, then turn them over. I remember thinking, "What's this guy doing, inspecting me?" He certainly was. He told me to lift my arms, pull back my ears, run my fingers through my hair, and spread my lips apart. Then he told me to lift.

"Lift what?" I asked.

"Don't get smart with me, God damn it! Lift your balls!" He barked.

I wasn't being sarcastic, I just didn't know what he was talking about. Anyway, I lifted my genitals, wondering what he possibly thought I could be hiding under there.

The guard ordered me to turn around.

"What the hell is this?" I thought.

"Lift the bottom of your feet," he commanded.

I lifted my knees and raised my feet off the ground. This aggravated him further, though I didn't know why.

"Let me see the bottom of your feet!" he demanded.

I showed him, wondering whether he wanted to look between my toes.

"Bend over," he said.

"You've got to be kidding," I responded.

"Just do what I'm telling you."

I bent over.

"Spread 'em," he said.

So I moved my legs apart.

He said, "If you don't stop fucking around with me I'm callin' the lieutenant."

"Look man," I said. "I don't know who or what the lieutenant is. And I'm not fucking around with you or anyone. This is all a little new to me. I just came in here and don't know what you're talking about."

That dialogue lessened his intensity. "Spread the cheeks of your ass," he said. "I need to look up your hole." And thus began my introduction to the dehumanizing life of being a prisoner.

After the humiliating strip search, the guard confiscated all my clothes and gave me a one-size-fits-all green jumpsuit, a pair of boxer shorts, unmatched socks, and a pair of cloth slippers. I was led to a much larger holding tank, the place from where a significant amount of the noise had been coming.

The rectangular holding tank had three concrete walls and was separated from the hallway with another wall of round, evenly spaced steel bars that one associates with old jail cells. Inside the cell, a steel bench ran along the three walls; the stainless-steel toilet/sink contraption stood conspicuously in the corner.

Although the room was much larger than any of the other closet-sized cells in which I'd been confined, somewhere between forty and fifty prisoners were crammed inside it. The noise was unbearable. The men were screaming to communicate in several different languages, and guards were screaming above them outside the cages so they could be heard. It was a madhouse. I was sure that continued exposure to the Bedlam-like atmosphere could drive a person insane. I wondered how bad things must be in the job market for someone to choose to work in such an environment.

Despite the chaotic atmosphere, some prisoners, I noticed, were actually sleeping through it. The cell was so crowded I had to watch where I stepped. All of the bench space had been taken. Most people were standing but some were sitting on the sticky floor. A few men left their troubles behind, apparently, by stretching out on the filthy floor, closing their eyes, and sleeping through the insanity.

I felt like an idiot, standing there among all those strangers, people with whom I thought I had nothing in common. It's true we were all prisoners of the federal government, but while we were crammed into that crowded holding cell, our identities had been stripped from us and each individual clung atavistically to any available space.

About 11:00 P.M. the guards must have finished processing their paperwork because that's when they came by the cell, shouting, "Listen up! When I call your last name, step to the front of the cell." In groups of about ten, we were led in different directions. Most of the prisoners were led to the housing units. They obviously had been assigned previously. I was a new prisoner and had not yet been classified. Accordingly, I was led with a small group to a special housing unit for high-security prisoners.

Walking into the special housing unit was an eerie experience. I saw scores of other prisoners wandering around the unit's common area. They were shooting pool, talking, or just watching us new arrivals come through the door. Not knowing anyone, I just walked with my group to the unit officer's station. The guard gave me a bedroll containing a blanket, sheets, and a towel, then assigned me to a room.

"Lockdown's in an hour," he shouted over the din of the cellblock. "You can shower or use the phone."

Since early that afternoon, I had been moving through the most traumatic experience of my life. Guns were pointed at me, I was arrested and put in restraints, and then carried as if I were a package in a strange car. Oversized law enforcement officers threatened me with life imprisonment and then locked me in a series of cages. Then, I was led into cells with hundreds of others who were locked up. I had no idea what to expect next. I felt the stench of my body, and I wanted to shower. Doing so, however, would mean that I couldn't tell my family what had happened. I realized that I'd have to carry that filth on me through the night, because I needed to call my parents; I needed to tell them about this abrupt change to my life—and to theirs.

The Beginning of Shame

Despite the unit holding well over one hundred prisoners, only two phones were available. I waited in line for nearly an hour and finally was able to make a call. My mother answered, and I told her to put my father on the extension line. When they both were on, I told them that I had been arrested and that I was in jail. As soon as I mentioned the word "arrested," my mother began sobbing on the phone, as if she were expecting this dreaded call. I didn't know how to respond to her tears. But it wasn't only her, as I could hear how the news broke my father, too. They were both crying, not asking why I was in jail. Despite the explanations I tried to provide for my lifestyle, deep inside, they knew I was involved in something wrong. Whenever they tried to inquire, to admonish me, or anything of the sort, I cut off the conversation. They had been dreading this call but were not totally surprised by it. In some ways, the call may have been a relief. At least I was alive.

As always, I tried to project strength while professing innocence of these ridiculous charges against me. But they heard the noise in the background and, perhaps, cracks in my voice. They were not interested in my tales of innocence or in my legal strategy to contest the charges. There were no questions from my parents during that call about why I had been arrested. I was their only son and they were afraid for me. It was as if by then, they knew that I would not be forthcoming with the truth and they didn't want to waste time with more of my lies. All they wanted was an assurance. Between their tears, the only questions they wanted me to answer were whether I was okay and how they could help me. Like any loving parents, they only wanted to save me from the currents that were about to carry me away, if not drown me. I had no words to comfort them.

It was then, perhaps, that I began to face my reality for the first time. The arrest and the processing were one thing, but they were impacting me only. As I listened to my mother crying, and my father sounding helpless, I realized what my behavior had done to them. It was worse knowing that I was only in the first steps of what promised to be a long triathlon of humiliation, embarrassment, and fears. They couldn't have been surprised at what I was doing. The secretive life, the profligate spending—it all had to reek of drugs. But how could parents who had tried to provide their children with everything acknowledge that their son was so selfish, so indifferent to the moral code they had tried their best to instill? With that one phone call, too, they knew that I was beyond their reach; they couldn't save me from the problems I had created for myself.

My time on the phone was limited, so I told them that I had to disconnect. I gave them the name of my attorney and suggested they call him for more information. There was nothing more I could say. Since I had no idea what to expect, I had no words that possibly could comfort them. "I love you," was all I could say, but I didn't know when I would call again. My telephone time had expired and I was ordered to report to my room for lockdown.

The room, quite small, held a metal bunk bed attached to the wall. It had a toilet, sink, and two lockers in which prisoners were supposed to store all their belongings. Another prisoner had been assigned to the room before me.

"What!" he said as I opened the door.

"Hi," I said. "The guard told me this was my room."

"This my room. Top bunk yours."

"That's what I meant," I said.

I didn't know whether there was a protocol to follow. He was reading while lying on top of his bed. I made the top bunk and climbed up, happy to lie horizontally after one of the worst days in my life.

"What you doin' here?" My cellmate asked.

"What do you mean?" I responded.

"Why they put you in S-H-U? You get a shot?" He asked.

"I just came in," I answered.

"Word? You come from the streets?"

"I was arrested this afternoon." I said.

"Where you from?" He asked.

"Seattle. But I've been living in Key Biscayne for the past year." I said. "How 'bout you?"

"New Yoke. The city."

"What's S-H-U?" I asked.

"Special Housing Unit. You'll be gone tomorrow."

"What's so special about it?" I asked.

"It ain't special, that's just what it's called." He said. "It's high security."

"Where am I goin' tomorrow?" I asked.

"The compound," he answered.

"What's the compound?" I wanted to know.

"It's better. There's more movement," he answered.

"If it's so good why don't you go?" I asked.

"I can't," he responded. "I have too much violence on my record."

"Great," I thought. "On my first night in prison I'm locked in a cell with a stranger who may be a homicidal maniac." I decided not to inquire about the details.

He said that since I'd just come into the system, the next morning I'd likely be awakened very early and processed for my initial court appearance. The best thing I could do, he suggested, would be to sleep because the next day would be full. Readily accepting his advice, I said goodnight and went to sleep. I won't say I kept one eye open, but it wasn't the soundest rest of my life.

Until that afternoon, I had been living in an oceanfront, gated community of multi-million dollar condominiums. It was safe. Key Biscayne is an island paradise, with a rockless, white-sand beach that is far removed from anything that even resembles difficulty. Yet during those moments before I collapsed into sleep, Key Biscayne felt as far away as the moon. Farther, actually, because I couldn't even see it. Despite the confidence I tried to project, I had doubts of whether I ever would again.

I hadn't slept in a bunk bed since I was a child; yet there I was, locked in a small room that was part of a concrete block in the depths of a federal prison. I was with a stranger, one with whom I expected I had nothing in common. Lying there, he didn't seem particularly threatening, but one couldn't be too certain about a man who said he was too violent to be housed together with prisoners. All I knew was that he was from New York, and, from his diction, he likely was from the streets. If more information would be forthcoming, it would have to wait until the morning, because he was snoring before I passed out from exhaustion.

GOING TO COURT

About 4:00 A.M., I opened my eyes and looked outside the cell's narrow window beside my bunk. I don't know what woke me. I don't think it was the steel-frame bed, and there wasn't any noise at that hour. Perhaps, it was just the strain of what was happening. I looked outside the cell's narrow window beside my bunk, and I saw the chain-link fences, the endless coils of razor wire, and the bright lights shining around the prison's compound. I remember the feeling, a sinking despondency, a fear that my world had changed forever. I wanted to reach out, to catch myself from falling. But it was too late for all that, as I had missed all chances to save myself. I wiped tears from my eyes as I realized that I could grab at nothing but air. I was left in those feelings of self-pity for only a brief period before a guard twisted his key into the huge steel lock of the door and yanked it open.

"Santos," he yelled, "get dressed and report downstairs. You're going to court."

As instructed, I put on my prison garb and went downstairs. Another guard was waiting for other prisoners and me; he led us back to the same large holding cell I had been in the night before. Other prisoners quickly filled the space. The noise, ricocheting off the concrete walls, sounded like the roar of a major league stadium after the home team scored; smoke from the other prisoners' cigarettes burned my eyes.

Guards distributed breakfast: individual paper bags with cereal boxes, a small carton of milk, and a plastic spoon. I was one of the first in the cell, so I had a seat on the steel bench. Still exhausted from the previous day's events, I had no appetite. I gave my bag away and just sat there, feeling lost and completely disoriented.

After breakfast we went through a series of strip searches and clothing exchanges. Then the guards introduced me to the chaining process, where they wrap steel chains around each prisoner's waist, fasten handcuffs around the wrists, and then secure the handcuffs to the chains. After the arm and wrist movement is restricted, the guards use a set of leg irons to limit the prisoner's leg movement. The irons are locked around each ankle, and a chain connecting the steel ankle bracelets prohibits large steps.

After we were all chained, the guards marched about one hundred of us to a fleet of three or four school-type buses. The other prisoners and I marched along as if we were part of a herd. Some of the prisoners who appeared used to the procedure were mocking the guards, cussing at them to loosen their handcuffs. Others were making the sound of cows, "moooo, mooo." It was madness, and I hated being a part of it. But I kept moving along with the rest of them, taking baby steps so the steel chains binding my ankles wouldn't dig into my skin. About three hours passed between the time the guard called me from my cell to the time I made it to my seat on the bus. At about 7:00 A.M., we headed for the federal courthouse.

When we finally arrived, we were led through an underground entrance to a series of large holding cells or "tanks." Again, the prisoners scrambled for space, of which there was not enough; again, the noise rose to painful levels. It was here where all the prisoners waited for our respective court hearings to begin.

About 10:00 A.M., Henry, my attorney, came to explain what was going on. We met in a tiny cubicle. I didn't know what was going on or what to expect. Henry said we were going to make our initial court appearance. The federal prosecutors would argue that I was the same Michael Santos in the indictment, he said. Because I was being charged with serious felony offenses, carrying a potential sentence of life without parole, the prosecutors would insist that the judge order my immediate extradition to Seattle and I should be denied access to bail.

I wanted the meeting with Henry to last longer. It was a welcome respite from the crowded, unbearable madness that reigned in that sardine-style packed holding cell. Before leaving the prison, I was given the same clothes that I had been wearing at my arrest. Versace linen slacks, a Ted Lapidus silk shirt, and cream-colored Python skin shoes; one of the guards had stolen the matching belt. The clothes were sticking to my stinking body, and it was so crowded in that cage that sitting wasn't an option. In that cubicle with Henry, I had a slice of peace, and I was able to talk with someone whom I not only knew but who also spoke English.

My mother and sister were present in the courtroom to show their support, he said, but I wouldn't be able to talk with them. Henry explained that I wouldn't be called into the courtroom until late that afternoon, so I would have to tough it out in the cages all day. The court hearing would be rather brief, he explained. The judge would listen to the legal arguments, then likely order my return to Seattle. He wasn't optimistic about my being granted bail, in any amount.

We weren't together for more than fifteen minutes. And he didn't tell me anything during that meeting to bolster my hope. I was feeling lost, disconnected from my family and everything in the world that mattered. The guards escorted me back to that same holding cage from which I had come, and, impossibly, it seemed even more crowded than when I had left. I had to push my way in so the guard could close the steel bar door and twist his key in the slot to lock it. There I stood, shoulder to shoulder with hundreds of the doomed, unable to stop the assault on my ears. I prayed, asking God for strength to carry me through this struggle and challenge that was to become my life.

A few hours later, I was rescued from the cage again. A representative of the court came to interview me. She was an attractive woman, I remember, and stylishly dressed. I had only been separated from society for a day, but I looked at her with longing, as if she represented a part of life that I would not know again—femininity. Her presence made me feel conscious of my deplorable condition, and the funk that must have emanated from my body. Clearly, she wasn't interested in me as an individual; to her, I was another prisoner, one among hundreds that she processed every week. She wanted to ask about my residence, employment history, and ties to the community. The lady said she needed this information to present to the court in order to help the judge determine whether bail would be appropriate.

Those court proceedings were all so new to me. I couldn't be sure whether I might say something that would jeopardize Henry's defense strategy by talking to the lady from court services. Instead of providing her with the simple, innocuous information she requested, I was distrustful of the entire system. After all, part of the Miranda warning includes the statement "anything you say can and will be used against you . . . ." Conscious of the Trojan horse, I respectfully told the lady from court services that I would speak only in the presence of counsel. She then terminated the interview, and I was again taken from the tranquility of the small interview room and locked back inside the holding tank.

Before the lady came, I had maneuvered myself into a corner with two walls to lean against for support. When I left, that spot was taken quickly by someone else. When I returned to the cage, the only room for me was in the center of the crowd. That's where I stood for the remainder of the day.

I never had an opportunity to speak with my mother or my sisters; they were in the courtroom. In fact, the only people with whom I spoke all day were my attorney and the lady from court services. In the cages, the cacophony of a hundred people screaming made conversation impossible. So, I stood mute, trying to sleep while standing. I thought about how in the hell I ever could have left the promise of my family's company to sell cocaine. Suddenly, I felt so dirty. Although I had played an integral role in the distribution of many, many kilograms of cocaine, it was only while standing in that crowded holding cell that I began to acknowledge to myself that I was a drug dealer. While living the artificial life that I had created for myself, it was a lot easier to pretend I was something else. Despite the self-awareness that was coming to me, I was committed to continuing the charade, to proclaim my innocence to everyone else. I had too much pride to admit to anyone else that I was a criminal, evidence against me notwithstanding.

By 4:00 P.M., I still hadn't been called into court. Finally, Henry came to tell me my hearing had been postponed until the following day because the prosecuting attorney from Seattle was flying to Miami to argue on behalf of the government's case. I'd have to return to MCC Miami and go through the entire admissions procedure. Again.

The marshals fastened the chains to our bodies, and we returned to the Miami holding facility, arriving about 6:00 P.M. Having to be processed once again, I wasn't admitted back to my cell until well after 10:00 P.M. It had been a physically draining experience, beginning before dawn. Knowing that I'd be going through it again on the following day made it worse. I went to my cell, without eating, and slept.

Initial Appearance

The next morning, guards woke me again at 4:00 A.M. I was led to the area where preparations were made for court transfers. It was my second day without eating, but I still had no appetite. I passed on the brown-bag breakfast and went through the chaining process and the rest of the motions eventually leading me to the same holding tank at the federal courthouse.

Late that afternoon I was called in for my first court appearance. The prosecutor from Seattle, Ken Bell, presented the government's case. He outlined the reasons I should be denied bail and extradited to Seattle so I could stand trial. Henry made a contrary argument that I had my family members in the courtroom and no previous criminal history. He told the court that I was prepared to post reasonable bail to guarantee my presence in the proceedings. The judge, however, agreed with the government. The decision meant I'd soon be on my way, via government transport, to Seattle, Washington, my hometown. The hearing lasted fewer than fifteen minutes.

During the proceeding I saw my mother and sister in the courtroom, helpless and crying as they sat listening to the charges against me. We weren't allowed to talk. I was in an area for defendants while they were sitting in the back of the courtroom with the other spectators. But what if I could talk to them? What could I say? How does a son comfort a loving mother and sister who must listen to government prosecutors talk about the possibility of imposing a sanction of life imprisonment without parole?

Although I had family support present, I began to realize that I would be moving through this system alone, as others—people I didn't know at all—would be deciding my fate. As a prisoner, neither privacy nor autonomy were factors in my life. It's one of the ironies of prison that one can be moving alone through the system and yet never have a moment of privacy or a feeling of autonomy. One is not "alone" in the sense of being outside the company of others but, rather, because he is completely outside the presence of those whom he loves. Instead, the prisoner is constantly around strangers, forming transient relationships that can be broken without notice. There is no autonomy because one's life is never one's own. Others who are part of the criminal justice machine dictate our comings and goings.

After my hearing, the marshals transported the other prisoners and me back to MCC Miami, and we spent the next several hours being processed into the facility.

QUESTIONS, QUESTIONS

Upon my return to the unit, the case manager, Mr. Shapiro, called to see me. Mr. Shapiro explained that he was considering transferring me from the high-security unit to the prison's open compound; first, he said, he had to ask me a few classification questions. The high-security unit is an enclosed, self-contained building where prisoners spend at least twenty-three hours of every day. There was little freedom of movement but, being a newly confined prisoner, I didn't know the difference—only what my cellmate had told me during my first night.

"Do you have any objections to transferring to the open compound?" the case manager asked during my mini-classification meeting.

"No," I answered. He checked a box on his form.

"Have you ever worked for law enforcement?" he continued.

"No," I answered.

"Have you ever testified in court?" he asked.

"No," I said.

"Do you have any reason to believe that your life would be in danger if you're transferred to the open compound?"

Wondering what type of environment to which he was transferring me, I answered no to his final question.

"Pack your property," he said. "You're going to the compound."

"I just got here. I don't have any property," I reminded him.

"Then wait by the unit door. An officer will come by to pick you up," he said.

All I knew about the "compound" was that the person in whose cell I slept the previous night told me it was better. Up to that point, my life in confinement had been nothing more than a series of uncomfortable movements. I never had a chance to adjust or to develop a feel for the place. So I was indifferent about this move to the compound. As far as I knew, it was just going to be another experience I had to move through.

C Unit—General Compound

I had been designated to "C" unit. When the guard who had been escorting my group delivered me, another guard, the unit officer, unlocked the door. In prison, I was learning, there were guards all over the place. The guards all wore gray slacks, white shirts, and burgundy ties. I hadn't yet had much interaction with them because all of my time had been spent preparing for court and waiting in holding cells. My first impression was that they were sticklers for what seemed like petty rules to me, but they didn't strike me as being sadistic or particularly abusive. In fact, the encounters I had had with them thus far left me with the feeling of indifference; I didn't give them any more thought than I would the man who works pumping gas.

C Unit was shaped like a bow tie. The narrow portion of the building's design was used for staff offices—the unit team—where a unit manager, case managers, and counselors monitored the inmates assigned to the unit. The staff area also separated the two wider areas of the tie, which were individual inmate housing units. Of course, I was then too new in the system to be giving any thought as to how the architectural design of the prison was supposed to influence prisoner–guard relations. Thoughts on that subject would come to me later.

Two-man inmate rooms equipped with a porcelain toilet and sink, wooden bunk beds, and two lockers lined the outside walls of the bow-tie designed buildings. All areas outside the inmate rooms were common areas, places where inmates congregate, socialize, or wait to be released from the unit.

Since it was late when I arrived, there were few prisoners in the common areas. Most of the other prisoners already had been ordered to their rooms. The unit was dark and quiet, which was a welcome surprise. The guard assigned me to a top bunk in a four-man room. He showed me where the bathroom was located, then left me to settle in for myself. I had no idea what I was doing. I was beginning to realize that although others would control much of my life, there would be a lot of self-service adjusting as a prisoner. Never having been confined before, I felt self-conscious about walking into a strange room occupied by three other men. Living outside, one doesn't exactly plan for such a preposterous situation. Yet, I was about to spend my second night in prison, and it was the second time I had been assigned to such an absurdity. I supposed it was a normal part of the abnormal world I had been thrust into, so I went along with it.

The other three men assigned to the room already were asleep, and the small amount of light made it difficult for me to see. Trying to make my bed in the dark, cramped, unfamiliar quarters was not an option without disturbing the other prisoners around me. Instead, I just draped the sheets across the mattress, climbed onto the bed, and passed out from exhaustion. It must have been close to midnight when I fell into bed.

Early the following morning, the other prisoners in my room awoke and began getting ready for the day. Their movements roused me. One of them said something to me in Spanish. I have dark hair and an olive complexion, so they assumed I spoke Spanish. But I didn't. Since they didn't speak English, we weren't able to communicate beyond a few nods and superficial greetings. They were getting ready for their work details; I needed to get ready for my first day in prison. Since I had no work assignment, I was free for the day—or so I thought.

Not knowing anyone in the prison, or anything about prison rules, I asked the guard if he would direct me to the prison library. I wanted to see what type of mental stimulation I could find. The guard responded by asking where I worked. I explained I had just come in and that no one had spoken with me about work.

"Then you work for me," he said.

The guard told me I couldn't go anywhere until I did some work in "his" unit. He instructed me to find some window cleaner and to gather some old newspapers to clean the unit's windows. Until I was assigned a job, the guard said, I would work as his "unit orderly."

From about 8:00 until 11:00 that morning I performed the stipulated manual labor. By then, everyone in the unit was talking about lunch, "chow" as it was called in prison. Instead of the brown-bag meals given to people in the holding tanks, prisoners on the compound ate in the dining room, the "chow hall." Our unit would be released for chow somewhere between 11:00 and 11:30.

After returning the window cleaner to the supply room, I went to the common bathroom to shower. As a new prisoner, I had no personal supplies and therefore had to use government-issue products. The guard provided me with a bar of soap, a toothbrush, toothpaste, a razor, and some toilet paper.

"Take care of it," the guard warned. "Supplies aren't passed out again 'till Monday."

Another prisoner lent me his rubber sandals for use in the shower, and that loan was a blessing because hundreds of other prisoners assigned to the same housing unit rotated use of the showers; the shower shoes lessened the chance of one becoming infected with a fungus.

Washing Off the Filth

Taking a shower was a luxury I hadn't known since my arrest. My last shower had been at home, two days earlier, but I felt as though I were carrying a lifetime of filth on me. Ever since the DEA had taken me into custody, it seemed as though my life had been dominated by processing. As a prisoner, one loses his or her identity and begins to feel like an inanimate object moving through an assembly line. Clothes are taken away and numbers replace the name. Those who operate the prison machine, the staff, are indifferent to the humanity of the prisoners; other operators of the machine look for opportunities to assert their authority—sometimes maliciously—over the lives they control. I doubt that staff members begin their employment with bad intentions, but just as the prison machine conditions prisoners, it also impacts the staff. Years of seeing human beings in chains and locking them in cages shape the demeanor of many staff members, making them cynical and often calloused. My first shower helped me wash the grime of the prison experience off of my body. If only for those few minutes I stood beneath the water, I was free.

After the shower, I realized some of the practical problems of being new to the prison system. I had no dish in which to keep the single bar of soap I was issued and no convenient place to keep my razor and toothbrush. One of the small metal lockers in my room was assigned to my bed, but it was covered with rust and not too clean. I covered the locker with discarded newspaper I found and placed my limited belongings on top.

The prison operated a commissary, I learned, from which prisoners could use money sent to their accounts to purchase hygiene items, food, and recreational products. Henry had told me it was only a matter of days before the prosecutors would arrange my transfer to Seattle, so I didn't ask anyone to send money to my commissary account. Instead, I used the personal supplies issued by the prison machine.

Chow

After my shower, I dressed and waited with the other prisoners in the unit for the guard to unlock the door so we could walk to the chow hall. I didn't know which of the many buildings enclosed by the prison fences was the dining room, and having been on the compound for only a few hours, I hadn't spoken for any length of time with anyone. I just observed my new environment. The building was relatively clean, and I expected that it had been built within the past ten years. During those first days, I think that I was considering the downside to what could happen to me. I hadn't seen any overt psychopaths running around, and there didn't seem any immediate danger of brutality. Rumors of prison rape seemed a complete fabrication, at least from my earliest observances. My initial take on the prison assuaged a lot of the fear that first passed through me after my arrest. Although there was a lot of talk about life sentences, that didn't seem even remotely possible in my case. If I were convicted, I reasoned, I might have to pass a year or two in confinement but certainly not more than that. If worse came to worse, I figured I could handle what was coming.

Waiting for chow, I quickly noticed, seemed a major event in the prison. Well over one hundred prisoners were gathered in the unit's common area, most in a large cluster directly in front of the door. The guard stood just outside the door and yelled "CHOW!" Like a large herd of cattle, the prisoners began moving toward the dining room. No running was allowed on the compound, so many of the prisoners in front of the herd walked at a brisk clip, moving as fast as they could without running.

I brought up the rear, following the others on my first trip to the prison dining room. When I got there, I associated the environment and the food with that of a cafeteria at any large American high school. The only difference was the makeup of the patrons: all men wearing similar clothing and a conspicuous absence of women.

Eating in the dining room that day, my first day on the compound, I realized that it was the first time in my life I was around such a large group of people without a single woman or child being in the mix. Indeed, among all the prisoners at MCC Miami, not many were younger than I. I wondered how much time would pass before I would come into a more normal mixture of genders. I began preparing my mind to live as a prisoner.

In some ways, during those first days of prison, I think I was waffling on whether my expectations were to be freed after a trial, or whether life behind those fences was going to be my reality for the foreseeable future. So I thought about what I could do during the time I would spend inside if things went badly for me in court. After those days of being shuffled around from holding cell to holding cell, from prison to court proceeding, it's probably no surprise that I was feeling a bit inadequate. The image I had created for myself outside dissolved rather easily, like an ice cube in a cup of hot tea. If I were going to serve time in prison, I hoped there would be an opportunity to make something of my life.

THE RULE OF LAW

After lunch, I walked through the compound in search of the education department. There were no restrictions for walking around at that time. The campus was like a large, fenced-in park with scattered buildings, closely cropped lawns of green grass, palm trees, and even a pond in the center. Except for the razor-wire-topped fences that surrounded the perimeter, the setting was quite scenic.

I found the education department in a building near the dining room. Inside were a few classrooms, a leisure library, and a law library. I had no background in legal research, but my ignorance didn't stop me from looking through the law books and doing what I could to broaden my understanding of the legal system and the charges against me.

Several prisoners were in the law library, and a few inmates were assigned to work there as inmate law clerks. I spoke with a few of them and learned some basic rules about legal research. I began pulling case books and reading about others who had been charged with offenses similar to mine. The cases I chose, however, didn't inspire me. Every one described individuals serving lengthy sentences and whose convictions were affirmed by U.S. appellate courts.

Occasionally, I looked up to study the other prisoners around me. They all seemed so much older, and they all spoke with confidence about the law. I hardly understood what I was reading, but they were talking about legal decisions like others talk about NFL teams. I wondered whether they were lawyers, and, if so, why they were in prison. I felt like I was in a foreign country, one where I neither spoke the language nor understood the customs.

Another prisoner spoke to me. "Just get here?" he asked.

"Yeah. I came in on Wednesday," I answered.

"Where'd you come from?" he asked while flipping through the pages of his book.

"Key Biscayne," I answered.

"Oh, you're just in the system?" he asked.

"Yeah. I was arrested on Wednesday," I said.

"That's surprising," he said. "It usually takes years before a guy finds the law library. My name's Frank Bachner."

"Michael Santos," I responded.

Frank was about forty, clean cut, and of medium build. He looked like a professional of sorts. A lawyer or an accountant. We shook hands.

"Have you been in prison a long time?" I asked.

"I've been here for six months," he said. "But I did three years in the seventies for smuggling pot. Now I'm waiting to stand trial on Continuing Criminal Enterprise charges," he said.

"I'm charged with CCE, too," I said, encouraged to meet someone who seemed to be in the same predicament. I hoped to learn something from Frank.

"You look a lot younger than most 848s," Frank observed, referring to the statute of the U.S. Code. "How old are you?"

"Twenty-three," I answered.

"Twenty-three," he repeated. "Done time before?"

"No," I answered. "This is my first time."

"Terry," Frank called out to another prisoner. "This guy's got 848, too. First offense. He's twenty-three."

"Welcome to Club Fed," Terry said as he turned around. "How'd they catch you?"

"Catch me? They just arrested me," I said. "My lawyer told me I was indicted and I'm going to Seattle for trial."

"Good luck," Terry said. "If you need any help let me know."

"Actually, I do," I said. "I don't know how to find my way through these books."

Frank and Terry then showed me a few things about navigating through law books. Frank told me not to be discouraged. "The Continuing Criminal Enterprise statute is one of the most difficult charges to prove," he said. "And at first glance, you don't fit the kingpin profile."

"That's what my attorney tells me," I responded.

"Well, listen to him," Frank continued. "The government will have a hard time convicting you. Did they catch you with anything?"

"No, nothing," I said.

"You see what I mean?" he said. "Terry and I were just talking about that. The government has a high conviction rate because most of these guys plead guilty even though the government doesn't have anything on 'em. Guys just start rattin' at the first sign of trouble. Stay strong and you'll be fine," Frank said.

Whether Frank was trying to convince himself or me was not clear, but his confidence gave me a boost, and I spent most of my first day on the compound at MCC Miami in the law library. Despite all the strangers around me, I was feeling kind of alone. Reading through all those legal cases gave me a mental escape, and it was interesting for me to read about the legal system. Frank gave me my first exposure to inmate legal advice. Increasingly, I would find that while rich in optimism, it would be dubious in terms of validity.

After my sojourn to the law library, I returned to the housing unit. The guard told me I had a visitor waiting and then showed me the way to the visiting room. Henry, my attorney, was waiting for me.

The visiting room reminded me somewhat of an airport departure area. Instead of carpeting and cushioned seating, however, the visiting room at MCC Miami had the institution tile floors and rigid plastic chairs, all connected in a row facing a single direction. Visitors sat next to each other, shoulder to shoulder, so that after a visit one's neck ached from turning during conversation.

Henry just came to talk, to ease my nerves, and to tell me what I could expect to happen. He also brought me a copy of my indictment, which articulated the charges against me. Henry told me the government would transfer me to Seattle soon, perhaps as early as the following day. Once I arrived in Seattle, he said, I would proceed through a plea hearing at which time I would enter a formal plea of not guilty to the charges, then wait two to four months for the trial. While being held, he said, I should not discuss my case with anyone else, as the prison system was full of "snitches," prisoners looking to reduce their exposure to confinement by providing information to prosecutors about others.

I told Henry that I had not spoken with anyone since I was arrested, but that I had found the law library and begun reading cases about people who had been prosecuted for drug crimes. The results of those published cases didn't inspire me, as most of the people I read about were serving lengthy prison terms.

"Don't read the cases," Henry said. "Most of those defendants had shoddy lawyers. Besides, every case is different and I will fight your case vigorously. Leave the law to me. You just stay strong. Exercise. Read anything but the law. And don't talk with the other prisoners."

Our visit, which lasted less than thirty minutes, left me confident that I had a zealous advocate who would succeed in persuading the members of my jury that I was not guilty of the charges against me. I returned to my room believing the time I was spending in confinement was a temporary hindrance, an experience I had to go through but one that would end soon enough. Clearly, I was deluding myself. Henry encouraged my delusion. His primary objective, as it turned out, was to maximize his legal fees.

I spent the next few hours lying on the top of my bed reading through the twenty-plus page document Henry had given me. My indictment. Beginning with the ominous words *United States of America v. Michael G. Santos*, it put a damper on my premature optimism. I read through each charge, then crossed my hands upon my chest and stared at the ceiling above me, wondering about what was to come.

I realized that the government had a good grasp of everything. My friend and partner, Alex, had cooperated with the government after his arrest. He told the prosecutor about how we started and about every transaction thereafter. I guess it would have been kind of normal for me to have been angry with him or to have felt betrayed. Oddly enough, those weren't the feelings running through me. Although the indictment made it clear that Alex had told the government everything he could, I surmised that he had cooperated out of fear of going to prison rather than out of spite to hurt me. It was my problem, not one that Alex created, but one that I had walked into voluntarily. After my second day in prison, I was just hoping that it would end soon, and I was paying Henry to pull me out of it.

Henry had been adamant about my not discussing the case with others. Yet, I was eager to learn more about the court system, about the prison system, about what I could expect. I couldn't remove from my mind the potential sentence of life without possibility of parole. Henry told me not to concern myself with the sentence, as we were going into this legal battle with the intention of winning; in that case, no sentence would be imposed.

I needed Henry's guidance during those difficult first days of confinement. My mind had been shifting from one extreme to the next. The first night I remember waking up in the dead of darkness crying in my bunk over the life I had left behind. A few days later I was convincing myself that it wasn't so bad and, at worst, I'd spend a few years in prison. Later, I'd read through a few law books and see that many people were serving extremely long sentences for charges that were identical to mine. Other prisoners were telling me to fight, but I didn't really know them. I was truly lost, and I wanted some guidance, some assurance. Henry was telling me in no uncertain terms that "we" were going to win, as long as I let him handle the situation. I liked his use of the word "we," as if he were part of a team with me.

In essence, I was agreeing to accept Henry's counsel and cede all control of my future to the courtroom battle between him and the government prosecutors. Like a character in a work by Kafka, I'd watch others pull the strings that dictated my life. By allowing Henry to dictate the strategy, I not only lost my immediate freedom but also gave up the free will I had to influence my destiny. Giving up even further control over my life would make me a prisoner in earnest.

A 4:00 P.M. census count interrupted my contemplation. These census counts, I learned, occurred several times each day. I had been either in court or sleeping during the counts on the previous days, so I hadn't noticed them. I couldn't miss the 4:00 P.M. count, however, as all prisoners were required to stand by their bunks while the guards—consistent with the dehumanizing rituals of the system—came around to count all prisoners as if we were inventory items in a human warehouse.

The census count took about fifteen minutes to clear, and immediately thereafter, the prisoners swarmed around the officer's station. I didn't know what was going on, but I could tell something major was about to happen. The prisoners all were bustling with anticipation and the noise generated by hundreds of simultaneous conversations in predominantly English and Spanish—accented by a few Asian languages—made it difficult to hear anything.

After fifteen minutes, the guard's scream overpowered the myriad prisoner conversations: "Mail Call! Silence!" As if by magic, the prisoners all quit talking. Once the unit was quiet, the guard, like Santa Claus, began pulling envelopes out of a waist-high canvas mailbag and yelling the recipient's last name.

As the prisoners heard their names, they would respond, "Pass it back!" Through this procedure, the guard distributed several hundred pieces of mail. Knowing that I wouldn't receive mail, I took the opportunity to use the telephone, which at most other times had a line of at least ten people.

After the mail was distributed, the prisoners again gathered around the living unit's door and waited for the guard to release them for dinner. In prison, kitchen workers begin serving dinner about 4:45 in the afternoon, well before the time most Americans return home from work. Despite the childlike supper hour, most of the prisoners made no effort to restrain their impulse to race to the chow hall. The meals, apparently, helped the men break up their day. Instead of going to dinner, once the unit was released, I walked around the yard. On the open compound the prisoners were free to walk around the different areas of the institution as long as they didn't enter others' housing units. I walked to the recreation area, which included a weightlifting pavilion, tennis courts, basketball courts, a softball field, and a running track. One could certainly develop an extensive exercise routine, and a lot of the prisoners spent much of their time in the recreation area.

I returned to the law library and, despite Henry's admonition, resumed my reading of cases. I also spoke with a few prisoners who seemed knowledgeable about the law. When they learned that I had just come into the system and was facing a CCE charge, several tried to offer their legal services for a fee.

The going rate seemed to be about $500 to read my legal work and help me keep an eye on my attorney. Not knowing much about the law, it seemed like it might be a good idea to find someone who could advise me through the legal maze from the inside. After all, I really had no way of evaluating what was being done.

I thought it would be prudent to retain the services of one of these "jailhouse lawyers." Terry, whom I met earlier through Frank, struck me as the most forthright in the group. I had no real way of knowing whether Terry was in fact an honest person. He was in prison, just like I was and he could have been a con man. But, I felt as if I needed more guidance, and he seemed knowledgeable to me. Despite only having looked at my indictment, he assured me the government would have a real struggle persuading the jury to convict me of operating a Continuing Criminal Enterprise. For $500, he said, he would explain the legal papers I received from my attorney and help me understand all of the preparations being made for trial.

After spending the evening talking with Terry, I agreed to send him the $500, and he agreed to help me understand the proceedings as well as the prison system. I was completely oblivious to Henry's earlier statement that I soon would be transferred to Seattle. Instead of thinking rationally, I was intoxicated with Terry's certainty that I would win this case, and I told him I was expecting a visit the following day, at which time I would make arrangements to send him the money. Even if I were transferred, Terry said, he would help me through the mail. And like a fool, comfortable in my ignorance, I went to sleep easier that night knowing I had made another ally to help me with my legal problems.

Terry, who was assigned to my unit, was about thirty-five, twelve years older than I. He had been in prison for six years, he said, which then seemed like an insufferably long time. I couldn't imagine serving that long in prison, and Terry's "wisdom" about the system certainly seemed valuable to me. In reality, I had no way of knowing whether Terry had any authentic qualifications as a lawyer. The only certainty was that he knew more than I knew.

One thing Terry concurred with Henry about was that I shouldn't discuss my case with other prisoners. Terry explained that as a "pretrial detainee" in the system, I would be confined with people who were going to court for one reason or another. A high percentage of these people, he said, were government informants. They were looking for ways to reduce their sentences or exposure to punishment by providing information to government prosecutors about other prisoners.

Without questioning what distinguished Terry from these other prisoners whom I knew nothing about, I agreed not to discuss my case with anyone but him.

HOME TO SEATTLE

Before I had an opportunity to tell my family about the arrangement I had made with Terry, however, the U.S. Marshal Service began my transfer to Seattle. I was awakened again quite early in the morning and processed with scores of other prisoners for transport. Instead of boarding a bus for the courthouse, though, my bus delivered a group of other prisoners and me to the Homestead Air Force Base.

As usual, we traveled on the bus in chains, and I wondered whether they would be removed for our plane ride. Soon after we arrived at the air force base, a Boeing 727 taxied right next to the bus and I had my answer.

As the unmarked plane stopped, between ten and fifteen federal officers—
U.S. marshals and BOP guards—surrounded the plane. Each officer guarded
the plane with a military-style rifle held alertly in front of them. Watching
from my seat on the bus, I saw the plane's rear door open; prisoners began to
walk down the stairs, hands cuffed and connected to the chain around their
waists and ankles linked together with chains similar to the ones binding
my own.

After the prisoners disembarked, other prisoners and I hobbled off the bus
and up the steps of the plane. We were directed by the U.S. marshals, who
operated the prisoner-transport service, to available seats.

I sat next to another prisoner whose wrists were bound in a more complex set of handcuffs. His restraints had a black steel casing around the chain
of the cuffs. I started a conversation with him.

"Where you headed?" I asked.

"Leavenworth," he said.

"My name's Michael," I introduced myself.

"I'm Carlos," he said.

"Where's Leavenworth," I asked.

"Kansas," he responded. "Where you going?"

"Seattle. I'm going up for trial," I said.

"What'd they get you for?" he asked.

"Continuing Criminal Enterprise," I answered.

"That's what I got," Carlos said.

"How long have you been in?" I asked.

"Ten years," he said.

"Ten years!" It sounded like forever, and Carlos didn't look too much
older than I.

"When do you get out?" I asked.

"Don't know. I've got life," he said, as if it were nothing.

"You've got a life sentence?" I asked while my stomach dropped to my
ankles.

"Yeah," Carlos confirmed.

"Was there any violence in your case?" I asked, hoping he would tell me
something to distinguish his case from my own.

"Nope," he answered.

"And all this time you've never had a chance to get out?" I asked.

"Well, I keep filin' in court, but I've never won anything. I'm on my way
back now 'cause I just lost," he said. "Who knows what'll happen."

"Is that why you've got those special handcuffs?" I asked. "They're different from everyone else's."

"Yeah. I get black boxed wherever I go 'cause of the life sentence."

Listening to Carlos tell me about his life sentence, about the ten years he
already had served in confinement, was like receiving an unexpected punch
in the nose. "Could this be happening to me?" I thought to myself. I couldn't
believe he had served a decade in confinement. And for what? He was serving
his life sentence for the same charges on which I was about to stand trial.

I just sank in my seat and tried to disappear for the remainder of the flight. And it was a long one.

We landed in several cities where some prisoners left the transport service and new prisoners joined us. The names of the cities weren't given to those of us waiting on the plane. Like packages, we were just along for the ride, going wherever the marshals led us. In the afternoon, the plane stopped flying and all the prisoners were transported to local prisons for the night. Our journey would resume in the morning. After two of these overnight stops, the plane finally landed in Portland, Oregon, where a few other prisoners and I concluded our flight. When we got off the plane, we were directed to a large van that drove us to Seattle. I was booked into the city jail in Kent, Washington, as a pretrial detainee. It was the same booking procedure that I had gone through everyplace else.

I had been processed in and out of so many law enforcement facilities over the past several days that being admitted into the Kent City jail was nothing new. The one difference is that Kent's jail is a small facility, holding a total of perhaps one hundred and fifty prisoners. It was clean, quiet, and relatively comfortable.

The jail was completely enclosed, meaning there was no recreation yard available like the yard at MCC Miami. When I first arrived I was assigned to Unit C, which held approximately twenty-five prisoners in single-man rooms. Because I was a new prisoner, and all the rooms had already been assigned, I was given a vinyl mattress and told to sleep on the floor in the "dayroom."

The living conditions in C unit were clean but rather barren. Its dayroom was an area for prisoners to spend their time when they weren't required to be locked in their cells. Because C unit was the lowest on the jail's pecking order, or social hierarchy, it featured unfinished concrete floors; the rooms had steel doors, the stainless steel toilet/sink contraptions, and only two hours outside of lockdown status each day for prisoners.

The first weekday after my arrival at the jail, I was roused early in the morning, chained, and transported to the federal courthouse in Seattle. Henry had arranged for Paul, a local attorney, to meet me there. I had neither spoken with nor met Paul before, but he told me that Henry had retained him to act as local counsel for perfunctory court proceedings. Today's hearing, he said, would require me to enter a plea. He explained that the magistrate judge would read each of the counts against me and follow with a question, "How do you plead?" I was to answer, "Not guilty."

Contemplating my conversations with Carlos on the airplane, I harbored reservations about moving forward with this pretense of innocence. I knew I was guilty of every charge against me. Besides my guilty conscience, I was glad the criminal part of my life finally was behind me. I was tempted to put an end to the charade and plead guilty, to let the chips fall where they may. Yet, I had given Henry carte blanche to think for me. His statement was that with the right amount of money I could win, and any discussion of capitulation was a sign of weakness. I didn't realize that failing to explore my options was a much clearer sign of stupidity. Lacking the courage to think for myself,

I obediently followed the decisions I had allowed others to make for me. After all, I thought, I had no experience in these matters.

Again, my court appearance was rather brief, no more than fifteen minutes. The process of being chained, transported to the courthouse, placed in the holding cell to wait for my scheduled appearance, and transported back to the jail, however, was an all-day affair beginning before dawn and concluding at dusk. It was physically exhausting, psychologically draining, and horribly dehumanizing. Yet, I was beginning to get used to it.

A Visitor

After returning to the jail, I learned that I could receive visitors. However, I felt humiliated at my status as a prisoner and was reluctant to receive visitors. I had only been in confinement for a couple of weeks and was still living in a state of denial—refusing to acknowledge my culpability, convincing myself that I didn't belong inside a correctional facility; I wasn't a criminal. I didn't want people to see me in my prison clothes or in a jail's visiting room.

My sister, Julie, had learned about the jail's visiting hours, however, and she surprised me by coming to visit. The guard escorted me to a small booth about the size of a confessional in a Catholic Church. I sat on a steel stool and waited. A plate glass window separated me from the other side of the booth, with a telephone available for me to talk with my visitors.

After a few minutes of waiting in the booth, my sister appeared, radiant in her beauty and completely incongruous in the surrounding ugliness. She came expressing love, warmth, and steadfast support for me, regardless of what happened. Her sincere and unselfish devotion left me weak. I felt unworthy of her commitment to me. Yet, she made it clear that she was ready to make any personal sacrifice, to move mountains on my behalf.

Our visit lasted fifteen minutes before the guard informed us that my visiting time had elapsed. I'm sure I cried a pound of tears during the brief visit and I knew that my family's support rendered me more fortunate than most other prisoners, despite the time I was facing. Julie then was led away and a guard escorted me back to a serious version of hell: life in confinement.

Locked back in my pod, I climbed on top of my bunk to look through the narrow strip window. I wanted to see Julie drive away. I pounded on the window with my fist, but she couldn't hear me and kept on walking. I saw her wiping her eyes, and I thought more about how my predicament was hurting my family. During those first days of confinement, I was too humiliated to invite my parents to come see me. They wanted to come, but I made up some excuses, and before long I was shipped out. Julie didn't give me an opportunity to deceive her; she just showed up at the jail. As I saw her walking away, I realized how much I wanted to hold her. But, a year would pass before I would be given the privilege of a "contact" visit.

Isolation

I passed about a week assigned to the jail's floor before a cell became available for me. When I moved into the cell, and the heavy steel door locked behind me, I realized how completely alone I was. While sleeping on the floor in the unit's dayroom, I had been joined by several other prisoners. Our shared experience gave us an opportunity to talk. None of the other men faced charges as serious as mine. But at that time, I hadn't yet accepted my precarious status.

I had been away from Seattle for over a year, and talking with the other prisoners helped me cope with this change in my life. Once the steel door locked behind me, it was just me, the cell, and emptiness. I missed the company of the dayroom miscreants.

As a prisoner of C unit I was confined to my cell for twenty-two hours each day. I was soon to learn that each place of confinement had different rules. A steel plank served as the bed, and I had a vinyl mattress filled with some combination of air and a foamlike substance. I spent most of my time in bed, reading, or writing letters from the steel desk that was attached to the cement-block wall. I strengthened myself by doing push-ups, but sleep provided the best escape, and I began sleeping at least twelve hours each day.

Thoughts about my future tormented me throughout the day and night. My worries began to have a physical effect on me; I developed a series of boils on my body. One would begin to grow on my arm, swelling up over a matter of days with hot, thick pus. The round swelling, 2 to 3 inches in diameter, was incredibly painful. About ten days after the boil began to grow, the jail's nurse would lance it, bringing me instant relief. But, the relief was short lived; within a few days another boil would begin growing on another part of my body. The nurse said stress was causing those boils.

After a couple of weeks in C unit, I was transferred to B unit, which offered carpeting on the floors, wooden doors on the cells, a wooden desk inside the cell, and perhaps five or six more hours available outside the cell. Prisoners with good behavior graduated from C unit to B unit, and if they maintained good behavior, they would be offered a chance to transfer to A unit, where privileges increased.

The privileges softened the time. While in B unit, I had more opportunities to associate with the twenty-five or so other prisoners assigned to the unit. I learned to play cards and table games. And I used the phone.

I was the only federal prisoner among the group. Most of the others were serving time for crimes like driving under the influence, disturbing the peace, or fighting. I don't think any had more than a few months to serve. Some would come in for a few weeks then get released. I wondered what that felt like, wondered when release would come for me. It was a small jail and had a small library. I wasn't a reader before my arrest, but while in the jail, I looked for the thickest books I could find. One of the first I read was by Michener, a story of Texas. I also read the Bible, from cover to cover, and prayed for God to strengthen me. If I wasn't reading, those table games and the telephone kept my mind off the perils that awaited me.

During the several weeks I passed confined in B unit, I had several visits from my sisters. I still didn't want to see my parents, as the humiliation was just too much to bear. They were in Florida, so there wasn't much danger of them surprising me. I spoke with them over the phone and tried to reassure them of my strength. Maybe I was trying to convince myself. Visits with my sisters were enough for me. I could talk with them and not feel the same guilt I would experience if I were to look at my parents. Even though the visits with my sisters lasted for only a quarter hour, I looked forward to seeing them whenever they came. It didn't matter what we spoke about, I just enjoyed seeing them, even if it was through glass.

Henry flew up to Seattle from Miami to see me a few times as well. He kept me abreast of what was going on in the case, but I didn't understand any of it. And I didn't care. I just wanted him to get me out of prison. Being in a small city jail, I was not going to have access to prisoners who could help me understand the law or the criminal justice system. Unlike the population confined with me at the federal holding center in Miami, the guys confined with me at the Kent jail were serving tiny sentences and wouldn't have any experience with the troubles I was facing.

During the several weeks I passed confined in B unit, I realized that I just had to rely on what Henry told me. I wanted to communicate with Terry, the jailhouse lawyer at MCC Miami, but I neither knew his last name nor his address. I was pretty much on my own.

Finally, I was admitted to the A unit at the Kent City Jail. It was kind of an honor dorm, one that made serving time as easy as possible. Each prisoner had a single-man cell that was clean and well equipped, including its own small television with cable reception. We also had a lot of time available out of our cells, so we had the cherished choice of either spending our time in the company of others or embracing the solitude of our own rooms. I remained in A unit for about five weeks and grew rather used to my tranquil surroundings.

I had my sister order a subscription to a newspaper, and I read several books. During the evening I watched television and forced myself to do several hundred push-ups each night. Other than the boils that would erupt on my legs or arms, I was in a rather tranquil mood during those months I passed in A unit. I knew there would be a few months before the trial, but I was okay. The serenity of the unit made me comfortably numb to the realities of my life.

One morning I was called by the jail administrator and told that I had to make a call to my attorney. When I called Henry he told me the government had reassigned me to a different judge, one in Tacoma, and that I likely would be transferred from the Kent City Jail to a much larger facility in Pierce County.

Sure enough, later that afternoon two U.S. marshals came by to transport me to the Pierce County Jail in Tacoma. I didn't understand why my case was transferred from Seattle to Tacoma, as I had rarely been to that city. Whatever the reason, I didn't expect the change to be favorable.

PIERCE COUNTY JAIL

The marshals delivered me to the Pierce County Jail sometime in November 1987. From the second I walked toward the area for admissions, "booking," I realized this jail was far different from any other place I had been confined. The chaos around me reminded me of those large holding cells where I first arrived at MCC Miami or those in the federal courthouse.

Policeman were escorting recalcitrant prisoners around the lobbylike entrance to the jail as if they were wild beasts. It was a busy, dirty place. The jail, only a few years old and located in downtown Tacoma, held every type offender. People came in who had been arrested for driving while intoxicated, domestic abuse, robbery, murder, and all types of other crimes. After booking, all prisoners were mixed with one another and assigned to one of the various chaotic housing units.

As I approached the housing unit to which I had been assigned, I could feel the tension. I longed for the small city jail from where I had just been transferred. The confusion and clamor of the other large holding tanks where I waited for processing or court appearances was maddening, but prisoners were held in those environments for only hours at a time. In the Pierce County Jail, by contrast, prisoners lived in the midst of the tumult twenty-four hours each day for indeterminate lengths of time.

A guard led me through a series of sally ports to my wing of the jail. A "sally port," I learned, is a series of gates one must pass through when moving from one area of an institution to another. When one gate is locked behind the prisoner, the front gate opens for the prisoner to walk through to the next pod. It's like the series of gates Maxwell Smart used to walk through on the popular television series I watched as a child, *Get Smart*. Each wing of the jail held three living units. A single guard sat outside the units and monitored the men. The units held approximately one hundred and fifty prisoners, though. It was not realistic that a single jail guard could monitor all of the activities of nearly five hundred male offenders living in close and closed quarters. The units were wild.

When the guard locked the unit door behind me, I immediately recognized that my unit was an anarchic environment, filled with predators and prey. Survival in such an environment required assertiveness and strength, or at least the appearance of strength. The previous months I had spent in confinement hadn't prepared me for the atmosphere of living as a prisoner in this large county jail.

Here the living unit had about one hundred and twenty single-man rooms, but the jail was so overcrowded that another thirty to forty people slept on mattresses scattered on the floor in the common areas. Despite being a rather new jail, it was filthy, with air reeking of tobacco and dried urine. Two telephones hung on a wall from which the prisoners could place collect calls, but the line was always so long that unless one was affiliated with one of the gangs inside the jail, it was best to avoid them.

Both the Bloods and Crips, street gangs believed to have originated in California, had been fighting for control of the drug rackets in Tacoma. Several of the members populated the Pierce County Jail. I didn't know any of the gang bangers; I didn't even know the difference between a Blood and a Crip. On the streets they're identified by the color of their clothing, but in jail we all were wearing blue uniforms, and I couldn't identify one gang member from another. They flashed hand signs regularly, but I had no idea what all those twisted fingers meant. That trip to the Pierce County Jail was my first immersion into the urban street life, the first time I was around so many tattooed thugs with gold-capped teeth—or no teeth at all. It didn't take long for me to realize that the tension in the jail was gang related. A single television blasted rap videos, contributing to the constant ruckus. The BET station played a constant rotation of LL Kool Jay, Kool Moe Dee, Run DMC, and other rap stars of the mid-1980s. The loud, constant thumping began at 6:00 each morning and lasted until the 11:30 lockdown each evening.

Being new to the jail, I was given a floor mattress and some personal hygiene items. The guard told me to "find a place." With other mats scattered all over the red, ceramic tile floor, no single spot seemed preferable to another. It was a filthy environment, tough to breathe with all the smoke in the air, as different from the Kent City Jail as a coal mine is from a white-sanded Key Biscayne beach. I wondered whether my sudden transfer into that jail was a calculated move to make my time rougher. Either way, there was nothing I could do. I threw my mat down in a vacant corner and watched the hundred or so people walking in circles around the unit.

A few of the leaders in the unit introduced themselves, telling me they knew or had previous dealings with some of my codefendants. Several others tried to ingratiate themselves with me, hoping to find a new source of supply for cocaine upon their release. Being admitted to the facility with charges of being a cocaine kingpin gave me an unwarranted esteem within the jail. Indeed, my notoriety as being a leader among large-scale drug offenders spared me the "tests" all but the most visibly violent or well-connected new arrivals at the Pierce County Jail must endure.

As I passed time in the jail, I saw vultures immediately pounce upon other no-names who were assigned to the unit. Such a guy walked on eggshells, or didn't walk at all. He would set his mat on the floor and then wouldn't move, not even to shower. Food was brought to the unit, but instead of eating on one of the tables, the solitary guy would gather his food trays and eat while sitting on his mattress. As soon as he sat down, one of the other prisoners would come up to him, put his hand on the meal's main course, and then ask "You ain't eatin' dis is you?" But, the tone of the question made it sound more like an imperative statement. Seeing his food in the other prisoner's grubby hand, he generally responded, "No, go ahead." If he wanted to eat, he would have to fight. And with all the group connections, there was a strong hint that if the prey did choose to fight, there would be nothing fair about the predator's response.

I passed the next three months in Unit 4NA waiting for trial and watching prisoners use and abuse each other in their struggles to make it through another day. Fights broke out regularly, several times each day over what seemed to be the most trivial of issues—such as table games, space on the floor, or use of the bathroom or telephone.

The guards were stationed outside the unit. They could look in through the unit's windows, but if a fight broke out, they weren't quick to rush in. Instead, we'd hear an announcement over the loud speakers. "Code Red! Code Red!" Teams of guards would then come rushing in to stop the beating. A few people would be taken away in handcuffs. Watching it all gave me reason to associate with few, to avoid the drama.

There was always something more to the violence than the surface reason. The spark may have been something trivial, but the real issue was always respect, about creating a reputation for oneself. These guys were not like the part-time jailbirds at the Kent City Jail. Most were on their way to state prison, and if they could create a reputation for being aggressive while in the county jail, then their initiation into the prison would pass a little easier. They fashioned weapons out of regular products, like a mop ringer, or they melted the plastic of a toothbrush with a match to insert a razor blade. Such an instrument, I saw, sliced one's skin as effectively as a sharp chef's knife cuts through a tomato. The quickest way for one to create the aura of fearlessness within the unit was by demonstrating one's proclivity for violence and one's willingness to use it with deftness at the slightest perceived provocation.

Still, I learned something by watching the violence explode around me. Although rumors had spread around the unit that I was behind a ring of people who supplied cocaine, and that was enough to spare me some of the difficulties that others faced, I knew that if I were to serve a long term in prison, I wouldn't always have that peace. My skin wasn't covered with the gray-blue jailhouse ink designs of demons and skulls, and my diction was not the way of the streets. If prison became a part of my life, it was inevitable that times would come when I would have to respond to someone trying to bully me. To survive in the chaotic world that is jail, I knew there could be no talking, no attempt to reason. If someone put his hand on my food, or made an overt challenge to me, I would have to respond in the only manner prisoners respect. I wasn't looking forward to it, but I always kept my eye open for objects around me that I could use as a defense weapon. If a situation arose, I wanted to be ready.

CONCLUSION

Through this first chapter, I've tried to show readers the life upon entry into the criminal justice system. Most are granted bail and leave the system. They don't return to confinement unless they are convicted. If one is denied bail, however, he will serve his time in custody, as I did. Even though the person hasn't yet been convicted of any crime, and is said to be presumed innocent, he will live no differently from any other prisoner. He will be classified as a pretrial detainee, and his life will become a constant state of flux. Unlike the individual who already has been sentenced to prison, the pretrial detainee waits in a state of anticipation, wondering what will become of his case.

Pretrial prisoners lack access to long-term programs. Administrators can't devote resources to them because there is no telling how long they will remain in the facility. Instead, those in pretrial status spend each day waiting for time to pass and for the next stage of the criminal justice system to begin. Most plead guilty and are sentenced. This frequently results in the individual being transferred from the jail or holding-type facility to an actual prison. Once there, he can begin his adjustment. In my case, the next stage of the process was a criminal trial and the events that occur after conviction. I describe my own experiences in the next chapter.

2

After Conviction

In this chapter, I describe my federal trial proceedings, and life after my conviction—including my interview with the probation officer who prepared my presentence investigation report and the thoughts that passed through my mind as I waited for sentencing. Finally, I describe my sentencing and how I began to plan for the long term after I was sentenced to forty-five years.

THE TRIAL

In February 1988, my trial began. It had been six months since my arrest in Miami, and although I passed most of that time in county jails, I was bolstered by Henry and convinced that I would be free after the trial. Indeed, up until the time I was convicted, I felt no remorse for my actions. Of course, there were moments of weakness when I awoke in the night, looked around the filthy jail at all the raunchy smelling transients with whom I had been placed, and floundered in self-pity. Still, during those spurts of darkness, I didn't think of myself as a criminal. Rather, I was stuck in that superior attitude that had driven me all my life, feeling that somehow I was better than all the trash around me and that I didn't belong in custody with the sewage of society. Better things in life awaited me.

Unlike them, I wasn't depending on some court-appointed lawyer to represent me. With my proceeds from the drug racket, I had paid a mid-six-figure retainer to a top-flight Miami lawyer to come free me from this "setback" in my life. Somehow, I kept convincing myself that after the trial I'd return to my rightful place. The cavalier manner in which I approached the judicial system came back to haunt me at sentencing.

To get me to the court on time, the jailers unlocked my cell before dawn. I exchanged my blue jail uniform for the clothes my sister had left for me, and for the first time since my arrest I wasn't dressed as a prisoner. It was wonderful to rid myself of that jail outfit, which felt as if it were woven out of a fiberglass blend. It caused my skin to itch constantly. Knowing that I would appreciate the feel of well-made clothes, my sister brought a few pairs of silk-lined wool slacks and crisp white cotton shirts that were heavily starched and on hangers. She also brought me a few ties and two stylish designer sport jackets. I exchanged my rubber jail slippers for good socks and soft leather shoes. Once I dressed for court, I felt as if I were a man again, not a prisoner. I wanted others to see me dressed in clothes, to show the jailers and jailbirds alike that I didn't belong there. Somehow, the clothes alone distinguished me, and they would set me free. I looked forward to the trial's conclusion, expecting that my problems with the law were about to end. I was wrong.

Four other defendants went to trial with me. Alex and John, my original partners, were cooperating against me and didn't appear as defendants in the trial. Ronald was charged with being a courier who transported cocaine from Miami to Seattle. Jim, Dino, and Michael were charged with working as distributors of the cocaine. The five of us, each with our individual lawyers, crowded the defendant's side of the courtroom. We waited while all the attorneys, government and defense, began choosing the jury members from a panel of randomly selected citizens.

I wouldn't call Judge Jack Tanner's courtroom ornate, but it did have an air of formality. The ceiling was perhaps 20 feet from the floor, and several tall and narrow window columns that curved into an oval at the top brought *plein air* into the room. Judge Tanner presided over his courtroom from an elevated position. A dark, heavy hardwood paneled his podium, and it matched the section to his right, where the jury sat in comfortable, high-back chairs. An elegant rail, carved from a rich, dark wood separated the jury from the rest of the courtroom. Behind the tables that were reserved for the plaintiff and the defense was another elaborately carved rail that separated the front portion of the large courtroom from several pew-type benches for spectators behind us.

When I first saw the impaneled jury, I felt really confident about my chances for acquittal. All the members were white and looked as if they could have been my neighbors in Lake Forest Park. Most were middle-aged, but there were three young women, perhaps in their early twenties, who sat on the panel. Certainly, they wouldn't vote to convict me, I reasoned. I made eye contact with each on a few occasions and convinced myself that they wouldn't return a verdict that would send me to prison. In fact, the whole group looked friendly to me, and I couldn't conceive of this panel returning a guilty verdict. Not for me. After all, I had convinced myself that I wasn't a criminal; I didn't even look like a criminal.

Ken Bell, the prosecutor, presented the government's evidence. As the leader of this criminal enterprise, I was charged in sixteen counts of the indictment. The government didn't have voice recordings or photographs of me. And I was never found with any cocaine or money.

What the prosecution did have was approximately seventy people who testified that I was instrumental in organizing a chain of events that began with the purchase of cocaine in Miami and led to its distribution in Seattle. Several of the people who testified, including Alex and John, had direct knowledge of the events. They were my partners from the beginning, so of course they would know about every transaction, every effort we made to conceal our activities, and every effort I made to insulate myself from the actual cocaine. Prosecutors presented a massive chart, with my name at the head, to provide a graphic, hierarchical portrait of the organization I was accused of leading. But, neither that chart nor all the testimony presented by the witnesses shook my confidence that I would be acquitted. After all, each witness who testified was motivated to cast the blame on someone else to reduce his own exposure to prison, I kept telling myself.

After the government rested its case, my lawyer began presenting my defense. It was at that point that I really expected Henry to shine. But in reality, no evidence existed to contradict what the government witnesses had said. Regardless of their motivation, the witnesses had told the truth. Instead, we manufactured the defense through my own testimony. Henry had come to the jail to prep me for the planned perjury. We met in one of the private, tiny lawyer-client conference rooms. Henry asked me questions, then played the role of the prosecutor cross-examining me. Because I knew the government's case against me was based on testimony that others gave after they had been caught, I looked forward to sparring with the prosecutor. When the time came for me to testify, I felt invincible.

I approached the witness chair, pleased with the figure I cut, and a court officer swore me in to tell the truth. Henry began his direct examination. It was quite simple, really. He asked about my family background, about my father's business, about my move to Miami. Then, he asked about my relationship with the people who had provided testimony against me, saying that I had orchestrated the distribution of cocaine. I denied having any knowledge about cocaine sales. Although I knew several of the people who had testified, I swore that I had nothing to do with their cocaine distributions. After Henry had finished his questions, Ken Bell, the prosecutor stood up for his cross. Intoxicated with my own performance, and smelling freedom so close, I really felt I had swayed the jury. Each member, I felt, was on my side. During his cross, the prosecutor basically harped on the same theme, that many people had testified against me and that it was implausible for me to expect the jury— or anyone—to believe that they all were lying and that only I was telling the truth. I responded to Bell by saying that each of the witnesses had been caught with drugs and was trying to save himself by testifying against me. I was a fool to think such a simple story could exonerate me. Nevertheless, I believed my testimony would raise at least a reasonable doubt with the jury, and according to the law, that would have been enough for them to vote not guilty.

My testifying was an egregious mistake, showing not only my sense of self-importance but also my lack of contrition and utter contempt for the legal proceedings. My false testimony led to perjury charges on a subsequent indictment and likely contributed to my receiving a lengthy sentence. Consistent with my arrogance, I actually believed that my own perjurious testimony sufficiently countered what the government witnesses had to say. Once the jury was excused to deliberate over the charges, I reasoned, each member would recognize the motivations behind those who provided testimony and therefore discount it. Expecting to walk out of that courtroom as a free man, I didn't feel a scintilla of remorse for what I had done.

When the court began to read the jury's verdict, my confidence surged. The first two defendants, Michael and Dino, were found not guilty of all charges. According to the indictment and the testimony of Alex, John, and others, they were integral parts of the conspiracy, and those "not guilty" verdicts really encouraged me. But, Jim was called next. He received two not guilty verdicts on distribution counts, but then heard "guilty" verdicts on his later counts—drug offenses that the jury was convinced had actually occurred. Ronald was convicted on counts that charged he had driven cocaine from Miami to Seattle. Finally, the jury pronounced me guilty on all sixteen counts. All my charges were related to the distribution of cocaine, but the most important was count 1; I was convicted of being the kingpin of the criminal organization.

Only as I listened to the jury's verdict did the trouble I had created for myself finally become clear to me. Until that point, I never really accepted it as real. In my mind, I was passing through a temporary stage that Henry was about to reverse. With his encouragement, I had been deluding myself. After the jury's verdict, however, I realized that the carefree and easy life I had known was certainly a part of my past. I was not angry, not even sad. Just aware. And, I was no longer interested in anything Henry had to say.

My parents had flown up for the trial from Miami. I hadn't allowed them to visit me in the jail. I needed to believe that I soon would be free and that we could visit then. But they were present in the courtroom, and after listening to the jury's verdict, I turned my head around and saw their faces. Both of my parents were crying. Julie was there, too, clutching my mother for support while tears fell from her eyes. I saw their sadness and knew that I had caused it all. Instead of an easy retirement, they were going to have to live with a son in prison. I wasn't even thinking for how long at that point. All that was going through my mind was hope that somehow I could make things right with my family. Someday, somehow.

Henry tried to perk up my spirits, telling me not to be discouraged. "This is only the first phase of the judicial process," he said. "The judge made numerous reversible errors, and the appellate court won't allow this conviction to stand."

That was the same empty pabulum he had been feeding me from the start. I couldn't swallow it anymore. I then knew that I was not only returning to the jail, but that I'd soon be on my way to prison. I no longer wanted to lie to myself or to others. Each time the jury pronounced me guilty as charged, I realized that others from my community, people with whom I wanted to be associated, considered me a bad person. Ironically, that was a thought I hadn't considered before, and it was something I wanted to change. I told Henry that I no longer wanted him to represent me.

I had paid Henry over $200,000 in cash and signed over property to him that I owned in Spain with a market value of $300,000. The fee was high, but I expected that as a well-known drug attorney in Florida, Henry was charging me market rates. I did not shop for a second opinion because Henry had come highly recommended from Paco, a drug dealer whom I expected would recommend only exceptional attorneys. I had paid Henry virtually everything I had accumulated during my brief foray into the world of illicit cocaine distributions. So, I began my life as an indigent prisoner, and the government appointed Gil Levy to serve as my new counselor for sentencing and appellate purposes.

AFTER THE TRIAL

During the days immediately following my conviction, I began to realize how wrong I had been even to take my case to trial, to continue the foolish charade of proclaiming innocence. I was guilty and I knew that I was guilty. Although no one had ever caught me with cocaine or money, it was idiotic for me to think I could persuade the jury that all of those people who were testifying against me were lying. I was young and had no history of violence. Had I been wiser, I would have forfeited my assets to the government and accepted responsibility for my wrongdoing. Such a move would have saved the government resources and likely resulted in my being sentenced to a term of fewer than fifteen years. Instead, I had listened to Henry. For the purposes of what I only can presume to be securing the highest possible remuneration for his services, he didn't advise me to plead guilty. Instead, Henry misled me to believe that the best legal approach to my problems was to fight the government at every stage aggressively. In retrospect, the acceptance of responsibility would have been a far wiser strategy.

Although I wasn't willing to cooperate with the government in prosecuting others, I had told Henry I would plead guilty if doing so would be in my best interest. We have to fight, he had said. The government's case was weak, he had told me, lacking tangible evidence like wiretaps, cocaine, or money that could be linked to me.

The government's "weak" case resulted in my conviction on federal charges that exposed me to a minimum ten-year term of imprisonment or as much as life. There was no reason for me to whine or complain about what had happened, as it had become abundantly clear to me that I could blame no one but myself.

It was I who had agreed to participate actively in a scheme to distribute cocaine for profit. It was I who had foolishly assigned all decision-making authority to Henry and, like a petulant child, agreed to perjure myself in the courtroom and proclaim innocence. Finally, I was beginning to realize how not accepting responsibility for my actions had exacerbated the legal problems I had created.

And I was not the only one suffering. Despite the humiliation I had caused my parents, they willingly suffered the indignity of visiting me in a courtroom and listened as others provided testimony that their son orchestrated the distribution of cocaine. My sisters, too, regularly affirmed their support and made significant personal sacrifices on my behalf. Everyone wanted me to get through it all so I could resume my life as a family member. But, as I was facing the upcoming sentencing proceeding, I remember lying in my cell and questioning whether it made much sense to continue the struggle.

Thoughts of Suicide

A suicidal phase of my life had begun. I didn't share my thoughts with anyone else, but as the guard locked the heavy door of my cell each night—and as I paced the few steps forward, turned around and paced the few steps back in solitude—I would contemplate the days ahead and speculate about serving the rest of my life as a prisoner. In the darkness of my cell, I couldn't fathom the possibility.

Discussing my delusional thoughts with others was not a viable option. In jail, showing the slightest sign of weakness was an invitation for attack. Since my natural demeanor doesn't suggest latent violence, I couldn't risk discussing my contemplation with any of the prisoners around me.

I understood the only reason my time in the jail had passed without interference from jail predators was the common knowledge of my "respectable" charges and the large number of other jail inmates who either were direct codefendants of mine or defendants on related cases and indirectly related to me. In jail, strength typically comes in numbers. There were perhaps thirty defendants scattered on various floors of the Pierce County Jail with cocaine distribution charges related to my case. Some were codefendants in my trial, but most had pleaded guilty much sooner. All were responsible for selling multiple kilograms of cocaine, and the word had spread like a virus that the network I had been convicted of leading was the source of supply. Since I was the "mastermind" of many drug offenders, I had something like a "pass" within the housing unit. Discussing my thoughts, however, would have invited potential new problems I didn't want to confront.

I couldn't turn to staff members. By this time I had been incarcerated for over six months, and it had become clear to me that although guards called themselves "correctional officers," they did no correcting; they seemed to make it through the hours of their day by denying their common humanity with the prisoners. I don't write this to disparage those who choose corrections as a profession. The security-first structure that administrators have created results in a chasm between staff members and prisoners; consequently, they don't communicate on the same level. As I passed time in custody,

I realized that discussing any issue with a staff member couldn't help me in any way. Quite the contrary, doing so could come back to haunt me—especially if the matter was one of sensitivity.

Besides, I didn't want any reference of suicidal thoughts in a prison record. I knew every day I lived in confinement would become a part of some record. It couldn't help me to have records of such preoccupations in a file that future indifferent staff members would use to evaluate me. Also, despite the frequency of my thoughts, I knew they were delusions caused by my predicament. I wanted to breathe where there seemed to be no air; I looked for hope where there seemed to be no reason.

In spurts of clarity I realized that although I contemplated taking my own life to make things easier, actually doing so would be an indefensible expression of weakness and self-pity. It would be a selfish final act declaring I lacked the strength and the character to confront my own problems. I didn't want to disappoint my family further—to leave them with their last thoughts of me as a young man who created a world of problems and then took an easy way out to escape the consequences. Despite the stale taste of my life, I knew I had to swallow it.

The Presentence Investigation

Sometime within the first two weeks after my conviction, a guard called me from my cell and escorted me to one of the small conference rooms reserved for legal visits. Todd Sanders, a U.S. probation officer, was waiting for me. I now had been a prisoner for seven months. Still, I hadn't quite adjusted to the fact that as a prisoner, my status as a human being had changed.

It occurred to me that, while confined, I had been surrounded by only prisoners or jailers. The uniforms we wore defined our roles within this closed community, and we had no contact with outsiders. The probation officer was the first person with whom I had to interact, other than my attorney, who wasn't a regular in my environment. He wore normal clothing instead of a uniform, and I noticed he wasn't too much older than I. It felt awkward to observe the formality his position required.

When I walked into the small room, the probation officer was sitting behind a metal table with papers in front of him. He didn't rise to greet me or extend a hand for me to shake. I was a prisoner, ergo, inferior and not worthy of the initial greetings other adults extend to one another upon meeting. Instead, I was directed to sit.

Despite our similarity in age, the probation officer introduced himself as "Mr." Sanders and stated he had come to interview me for the presentence investigation. I was beginning to learn that within the criminal justice system, the use of first names isn't allowed. Everyone is "Mr." this or "Ms." that. Perhaps, this artificial respect or formality fosters the deference with which prisoners are expected to address all members of the criminal justice team.

The presentence investigation, governed by Rule 32 of the U.S. Rules of Criminal Procedure, culminates with a presentence investigation report (PSI) that is of crucial importance to every offender. The sentencing judge considers this PSI report when determining an appropriate sentence for the offender, but the report has implications that remain with the offender throughout his engagement with the criminal justice system.

Indeed, although volumes of transcripts and records will have been created during the pretrial and trial proceedings, after one is convicted, correctional personnel will rely upon the findings in the PSI to evaluate the offender and determine his or her classification within the system.

Mr. Sanders provided me with a document describing the details of my offense according to the prosecution. It described every count in the indictment and my exposure to penalties as a result of my conviction. Because of the Continuing Criminal Enterprise conviction, I was facing life imprisonment.

The probation officer showed me that in 1986, the administrative officer of the U.S. Courts reported that 133 defendants were convicted of this charge. One hundred percent of those defendants received sentences of imprisonment, and the average sentence imposed was 269 months. The average sentence was, therefore, over twenty-two years, a long time for a 24-year-old to contemplate.

After presenting this information, Mr. Sanders asked me whether I wanted to discuss my version of the events to provide the judge with more background about my particular case. Because several of my partners in the scheme to distribute cocaine cooperated with the government's prosecution of me, the government's version of the events chronologically detailed everything that happened. The cooperating witnesses told the prosecutors how we initiated and carried out the goals of the conspiracy.

I had refuted those charges during the trial by taking the witness stand in my defense, but I was no longer willing to proclaim myself wrongfully accused. Instead, I admitted to the probation officer that the government witnesses' version of the events was, in essence, true, only that they exaggerated my degree of control over the "enterprise." Acknowledging my culpability was the first step in putting this sordid part of my past behind me.

The probation officer continued by asking me about my family, my educational background, employment history, and other personal information that would help him prepare his report. Mr. Sanders said he would make an effort to talk with my family and others to verify what I had told him. After he had completed his report I would have an opportunity to review it with my attorney, he said.

Our meeting concluded and I was escorted back to my cell. Once the cell door was locked behind me, I lay on my bed and thought about my meeting with Mr. Sanders. Accepting responsibility for what I had done was like a purging. By acknowledging that I did orchestrate the sales of all that cocaine, that the witnesses had in fact told the truth, and that I was the one who was lying, I was taking a step toward washing the filth of my actions and the jail from my skin. Perhaps it was similar to the experience a junkie or an alcoholic passes through when he finally kicks his habit. There was a lot of work ahead of me, I realized, to complete the purging, but that meeting with the probation officer felt as if I had taken a first step. With that step, I resorted to my anxieties and contemplated the certainty of a prolonged prison term, which, as the probation officer had just told me, could last for the remainder of my life.

Sleep was the only escape from angst, but sleep didn't come easily. I spent a lot of time pacing within the confines of my cell, looking at the walls, and counting the tiles on the floor. I remember the pollution in my head and my conscious efforts to clear my thoughts.

I'd do push-ups until I was exhausted, masturbate for hours, run in place, then lie in my sweat, and wonder how long my sanity would last by living such a life. I'd look to the table, see a pencil, and wonder how effective it would be as a tool for suicide. "How about paper clips?" I thought, as I knew I had two in my legal papers. "Could one paper clip oneself to death?" This sounds funny now, but it wasn't then. Rational thoughts escaped me. My thoughts were mixed, moving from one extreme to the other.

Strength Through Philosophy

Although I knew I was drowning in self-pity, I couldn't escape the thoughts that life was losing its value to me. As a man in his early twenties, I saw no glory in serving multiple decades in prison. I had no children, and I recognized that even if I didn't receive a life sentence, I likely would be too old upon my release from prison to begin a family.

Once, when allowed outside of my cell, I looked through a box of books and found an anthology of essays by philosophers. I brought the book to my cell and began reading the works of Plato, Aristotle, Dostoyevsky, and Sartre. Those writings helped me realize I'm not the first person who has come to a crossroad in his life, and that my response to the complications I created would determine my future. I had a choice in how I could respond, and my choice, I realized, would be an indication of my character.

That initial exposure to philosophical writings strengthened me. It helped me realize that although I was certain to spend a significant portion of my life in prison, in time, perhaps, I could develop my mind and figure out ways to atone.

At that time, I was hardly prepared to understand the complicated and abstract writings in that philosophy book. But I made friends with a dictionary, and, after repeated readings of individual essays, sometimes passing entire afternoons dissecting single paragraphs, the meanings began to make sense to me. The more I understood, the more hope I began to develop that I could create some meaning in my life. At the very least I developed the strength to promise myself I wouldn't consider making any final decisions until I had received my sentence. Once I knew that, I reasoned, I could make a better assessment of how I would spend my life.

Getting Ready for Sentencing

I began drafting a letter to my sentencing judge. Writing didn't come easily to me, but after reading so many philosophical essays, I realized the importance of expressing how my convictions had caused me to reevaluate my life and the bad decisions I had made.

I wrote my letter with the understanding that anything I said would be received cynically. After all, during the trial, only weeks before, I had shamelessly taken the witness stand and arrogantly declared I had no knowledge of any drug trafficking, and that I certainly played no role in such an offense.

Because of my perjurious testimony, the sentencing judge likely would discount anything I had to say. He'd receive my proclamations of remorse as a transparent attempt to elicit sympathy and a shorter prison term. I had created a position for myself from which there seemed no escape.

Jail inmates aren't allowed access to pens, probably because some prisoners will find ways to use them as weapons. So, I used one of the 3-inch pencils available to write my letter to the judge, sharpening the point by scraping it against the cement floor.

I struggled to express my remorse for not only the contributions I made to America's problem with drugs but also for my tardiness in coming to accept responsibility. Further, I endeavored to convey the strength I was finding in the philosophical writings I had found, and that I was committed to spending my time in prison searching for ways to redeem myself. Knowing I could receive a sentence of life without parole, I asked the judge for mercy.

After writing my letter to the judge, I began writing letters to friends, asking them to attend my sentencing hearing and testify on my behalf as character references. The people to whom I wrote, neighbors from my childhood and friends of my parents, didn't know me as a young man responsible for the distribution of cocaine. They knew me as a normal adolescent, one who worked in his family's businesses and spent time with their own children. And indeed, several of the people to whom I wrote agreed to testify on my behalf at the sentencing hearing. For some peculiar reason, I believed their testimony would help persuade the judge that my sentence should be closer to the ten-year minimum than the life sentence maximum.

My codefendants and other defendants on related cases all were sentenced in the days preceding my own sentencing hearing. Those defendants were not assigned to the same housing unit as I, but the jail has an effective message delivery system. Inmates pass along information through the use of other inmate orderlies who have freedom to move around the jail to deliver food, fix plumbing problems, or perform special services. I frequently received messages about people whose cases were related to mine; the informal message system gave me an idea of the sentences others were receiving.

Most of the sentences I heard about ranged between ten and fifteen years. They didn't inspire hope, for the judge was not constrained by a mandatory minimum sentence in the cases of those other defendants. In other words, he had the discretion to sentence them to any term he thought appropriate. The defendants who pleaded guilty and cooperated with the government had received sentences of one to two years, so I expected the other defendants to receive sentences between three and five, maybe six years—which still seemed like an eternity to me.

Despite there being no violence in the case, none of the other defendants received short sentences. Ronald, the courier, received a ten-year sentence.

Jim received a fifteen-year term. This was a pretty good indication that as the convicted leader of the group, my own sentence would be substantially longer. It wouldn't be too long before I found out, as my sentencing day was approaching rapidly.

There may have been no violence in my case, but it found its way to me. A few days before my sentencing, four inmates brutally attacked another prisoner who had recently arrived in the jail. The victim had been watching television, seemingly minding his own business when the others came from behind and pummeled him with their fists. Everyone else in the unit, including me, stood by watching; no one considered helping or getting involved.

When the victim fell to the floor, the attackers began kicking him, stomping him with their feet as he curled into a ball, trying to protect his head. The assailants beat on him for several minutes, yelling, "This is what rats get in this unit." Finally ten, maybe twelve prison guards came in to stop the beating. The attackers and victim were led away. Normalcy, or what passed for normalcy in that environment, returned.

It was only one of several incidents of violence that regularly erupted during my stay in the jail, but it was the only one I saw where a group attacked a single inmate. Rumor had it that the person who was attacked cooperated against several defendants on another floor of the jail. I didn't know anyone involved, and I never saw any of the other prisoners again. But, seeing the victim's cheek lying on the cement floor and watching four other men kicking him mercilessly crystallized for me—more than any of the other fights I witnessed—the violent environment in which I lived. I wondered how long such volatility would surround my life.

A few days later, in the late spring of 1988, a guard came to my cell and escorted me to another holding cell. I changed from my uniform into the clothing my family had delivered to the Pierce County Jail for my court appearances. I was about to find out the length of time my judge deemed necessary for my imprisonment.

Since the other defendants in my case already had been sentenced, the marshal transported me from the jail alone. Once I got to the holding cell, and the marshals removed my traveling chains, I sat on the steel bench wondering about what was to come.

After a couple of hours in the cell, Gil, my attorney, came to see me. He brought a copy of the PSI report and told me to read through it, to see whether I noticed any discrepancies that needed to be changed. It was the only opportunity I had to review the probation officer's work, but I didn't have any objection to the report itself.

Basically, the PSI narrated what the government witnesses told the prosecutors and described the offenses for which the jury convicted me. The report went on to discuss my family and personal background, concluding with the probation officer's evaluation.

He made no particular sentence recommendation, but Mr. Sanders suggested the court give consideration "to the defendant's age at the time of the offense, while not minimizing his actions or the role he played in this conspiracy." The report could have been much worse.

Mr. Sanders' statement in the PSI gave me hope I wouldn't receive the life sentence that was possible. But, there was no telling what the judge would impose. With the probation officer suggesting the judge consider my age, though, I breathed a little easier. Either way, I knew that within a matter of hours, closure would come to this part of my legal proceedings. I prayed that I then could begin working toward a specific release date, one that I could measure from here to there.

While waiting for the judge to impose my sentence, I hoped that in some peculiar way, hearing the punishment would erase a portion of my anxiety. Since my arrest, the real punishment had been the unknown. I didn't know the conditions under which I'd be living once I got to prison or the length of time I'd be confined. There seemed to be no end, and that uncertainty was the torture. This question mark, I hoped, would be replaced with an answer soon enough. I still might not fully comprehend the conditions of prison I would face, but at least I would know—assuming the sentence wasn't life— when the sentence would end.

THE SENTENCING

After waiting in the holding cell for several hours, marshals returned to the holding tank, put me in chains, and then led me to the courtroom. Every time I was transported to the courthouse, the marshals led me through a back basement entrance, so I never saw the building's exterior.

During the trial, however, I had become familiar with the inside of Judge Tanner's courtroom. Judge Tanner sat godlike upon a podium overlooking the entire room. The witness stand was adjacent to him on his right, and further over, against the courtroom's wall, was the jury box. Directly in front of Judge Tanner's perch were the prosecutors' and defendants' tables. And behind us was a banister that separated the courtroom participants from several rows of seating for courthouse spectators.

While waiting for the judge to enter, I remember looking over at all the attorneys and wishing I had made decisions similar to theirs. Instead of sitting at the defense table in a criminal court, I should have exercised discipline, attended school, and become a productive member of society. Instead, I had become someone my community wanted locked away. Wishes were not going to save me from the punishment about to be bestowed.

Looking majestic in his black robe, Judge Tanner finally entered from his chambers and everyone in the courtroom rose.

"Be seated," he said, and the bailiff made his announcement.

"Now comes the matter of the *United States of America v. Michael G. Santos.*"

Realizing this would be my last court appearance unless I won something on an appeal, I felt some relief in knowing I was moving forward toward finality—whatever that meant. Still, I'm sure I felt the urge to pee when I saw the judge.

The judge indicated that he had received and digested the presentence investigation report and, unless there were some objections regarding the PSI, he was prepared to listen to counsel on the matter of sentencing. When there were no objections, the hearing proceeded.

The U.S. Attorney spoke first, detailing the arrogance of my behavior and reminding the judge of the contempt I showed the court by taking the witness stand and proclaiming innocence. Despite my arrest, he said, I failed to stop the enterprise from continuing. Arguing passionately that my actions demonstrated a total disregard for the law, the prosecutor asked for a severe sentence to ensure the protection of society.

While listening to the prosecutor, I looked up at the judge. He seemed absorbed in every word. After perhaps fifteen minutes, the prosecutor concluded his opening remarks and sat down. Still not knowing what sentence the judge would impose, I felt certain it would be longer than the twenty-four years I had been alive.

Gil came on board soon after I relieved Henry of his responsibilities as my attorney. And I liked Gil. He was local and struck me as being honest, straightforward. Gil never sugarcoated the fact that my conviction was of extreme significance. His candor helped me prepare mentally for the likelihood of a long prison term.

Gil began his statement by emphasizing my age as a redeeming factor. In his attempt to minimize my culpability, he stressed the fact that no violence was attributed to me and that my youthful indiscretions shouldn't be used to put a premature end to my life. Gil argued eloquently, but as I watched the judge's expression, I had the feeling my sentence had been decided before the perfunctory hearing began.

Gil had arranged for several of the people kind enough to provide letters of support to appear at my sentencing hearing and testify about their long-term relationship with my family and me. These character references couldn't diminish the gravity of my offense, but my attorney and I hoped their testimony would persuade the judge that life imprisonment was not an appropriate sanction for me. The witnesses all told the court that although they had no knowledge about my involvement in the distribution of cocaine, they had known me for several years; they said they didn't believe a prolonged sentence was necessary.

The judge sat indifferently through these proceedings. As I watched him, I tried to put myself in his place. Every day he listened to advocates argue different sides of the same issue. Prosecutors would insist that defendants are evil and that their behavior warrants severe sanctions; defense attorneys, many of whom were former prosecutors themselves, would urge in opposition that the defendant's actions were an aberration and not indicative of a need for extreme punishment. Knowing that attorneys are professional advocates, equally capable of contesting either side of an issue, judges most likely dismiss—I reasoned—a large portion of what they say during the sentencing hearing. After all, by the time of the hearing, the judge has already sat through a trial and developed an intimacy with the case. For the most part, the sentencing hearing provides the participants a staged forum to express themselves. Judge Tanner, I believed, already had made up his mind about what sentence he would impose.

Still, I felt compelled to address the court directly, and, when the judge asked me whether I had anything to say, I eagerly stood and accepted his offer to speak. My newfound passion for finding meaning in my life during my sentence compensated for my total lack of oratory skills. I apologized to the court for the arrogance I displayed during the trial and expressed remorse for making the wrong decisions of participating in a scheme to distribute cocaine for profit. Also, I told the judge that despite the bad character traits I had displayed so far, I was committed to using the time I would spend in confinement in a consistent effort to redeem myself.

The judge listened to my plea for mercy, asked me a few questions, and then told me that despite my proclamations about efforts to redeem myself, he had the responsibility of sanctioning me for the serious crimes I had committed. He seemed cynical to me then, and, in retrospect, I feel no differently now.

The prosecutor asked to speak again. He told Judge Tanner that he didn't accept or believe my apology. "This man is not sorry for the harm he delivered to our community," the prosecutor said. "He is sorry for getting caught." On behalf of the government, Mr. Bell renewed his urge for the sentencing judge to impose a sentence that would send a message to others that selling cocaine is unacceptable behavior. I believed him.

My facial expressions didn't reveal the anguish I felt while listening to Mr. Bell's words. As he spoke, I looked around the courtroom. I saw my parents and sisters weeping behind me. I felt so embarrassed for them, having to sit through this proceeding and listen to a federal prosecutor declare my wickedness, saying that I am utterly incapable of remorse. There was nothing I could say; the prosecutor's comments suggested that anything I said would be a transparent attempt to have my sentence reduced. I felt totally humiliated for the shame I had caused my family.

Finally, the judge announced he was ready to pronounce my sentence. I had been convicted on sixteen counts, and he was responsible for imposing a sentence on each count. By the time he had moved through every count, the judge had sentenced me to a total of 214 years imprisonment, plus 37 years of special supervision. He also imposed a $500,000 interest-bearing criminal fine, and $1,100 in mandatory penalty-assessment fees.

The sentence sounded far worse than it actually was because the judge structured most of the individual sentences I received to run concurrently with each other. His sentencing structure left me with a total aggregate term of forty-five years imprisonment, a four-year term of supervised release after the completion of my imprisonment, plus the $501,100 in monetary penalties. Assuming I received the maximum amount of available "good-time" allowances, I would remain in prison until 2013, serving a total of just under twenty-seven years. The judge concluded the sentencing hearing by saying "You will be an old man by the time you leave prison. But you've earned it."

AFTER SENTENCING

After the judge imposed my sentence, the marshals led me back to the holding cell and eventually back to the Pierce County Jail. The other prisoners assigned to my housing unit—many of whom I'd been sharing the same close quarters with for the past several months—came to me, eager to know the sentence I'd received.

Although I was grateful not to have life, the forty-five-year term seemed like an eternity. After all, I was only 24. If nothing changed, I had more time in prison ahead of me than I had life behind me. Thinking of the sentence in such terms gave me a rather clear measure of the severity of my sanction. Still, I now had a date toward which I could work and plan.

Battling Depression

I spent the next couple of weeks in the jail in a near manic-depressive state. My moods would swing from one extreme to the other as I thought about the future. For nearly the next three decades, I'd be working to prepare myself for release. Not knowing what prison was about, I thought I'd be living my life in a shell secluded from the world beyond prison gates until my release. But, my environment would be much larger and more complex than I could imagine at that point in time.

Some days I'd sleep too much, missing the regularly scheduled meals. Other days, I wouldn't be able to sleep at all. My dreams started to change. I no longer dreamed from the world I knew outside, rendering me helpless to escape the prison environment even during sleep. Sometimes I'd awake in my now familiar bed, in the confines of my locked cell, unable to fill the vacuum in my head. I couldn't focus on anything other than the sound of the guards' clanking keys outside my cell, the overwhelming stench of tobacco, and the constant announcements over institutional loudspeakers.

During those times, I'd fold my hands behind my head, stare around the room, and return to my mental debates over the merits of suicide. I'd read the Bible and pray for strength to move me through another day. Still, I questioned the sense of allowing myself to pass what amounts to another lifetime inside a prison cell.

When I wasn't wallowing in self-pity, I contemplated steps I could take during my incarceration to distinguish myself. I hoped prison would offer me an opportunity to educate myself formally, to work myself into great physical shape, to develop a high degree of discipline and introspection.

These thoughts about the possibility of accomplishing some personal goals during my term allowed me to put my suicidal thoughts in abeyance. Once I saw the world in which I would be living for the next several years, I could make a better determination of what I could expect in the future. I made the commitment to control my thoughts at least until I made it to prison.

I started to fantasize about the best possible outcome of my sentence. Assuming I would choose to move forward once I arrived in prison, what goals should I strive to accomplish before my term expired? That was the question I needed to answer.

With twenty-seven years of imprisonment ahead of me, however, it seemed to me that asking myself that question was akin to asking a newborn baby what career he or she expected to pursue after completing graduate school.

Planning for the Long Term

A twenty-seven-year plan seemed overwhelming, so I decided to break the sentence down and focus on the first decade. During that time I hoped to earn a university degree. If college studies were not going to be available to me, I committed myself to developing an independent study program designed to help me become a better writer. I knew that unless I could learn to communicate through writing, I wouldn't be able to connect with anyone on the other side of prison fences. As time passed, I feared, my relationships would be limited to the other prisoners with whom I was serving time. I didn't want that to be the case.

I wanted to develop skills that would ensure I could lead a satisfying life upon my release. The alternative was completing my sentence at near fifty and then being forced to begin my life without any assets, any work experience, and few years remaining to prepare for retirement. It scared me. On the other hand, if I developed skills during my first decade, I could apply those skills during my second decade and open opportunities for me to pursue upon release.

This practical, goal-setting approach to my sentence helped lessen the pains of confinement. Instead of dwelling on what had happened to poor ol' me, I began to develop a degree of hope, an ambition against which I could measure my own efficacy. Despite the chains around me, I'd work toward developing a career for myself.

To complete my many dreams about finding ways to bring meaning to my life, I imagined whether there would be opportunities to open relationships with women during my incarceration. I couldn't stand the dreadful possibility of living without romance. When I waited in that cell and thought about passing the next twenty-seven years in celibacy, or even without a woman to love, everything else seemed to lose all value.

To stop these concerns from sending me into another hellish vortex of suicidal contemplation, I convinced myself that I would create opportunities to develop a relationship with a female staff member. To endure the initial stages of my confinement, I needed to believe I could develop opportunities for intimacy. I hoped I could create a pseudolife to replace the life I had forfeited.

I wondered about children. Now that I knew I'd likely remain in prison until I was nearly fifty, I doubted whether I would ever have the opportunity to father a child. Perhaps, I would have the biological capacity, but what kind of guidance could a man who served nearly three decades in prison provide for a child?

Again, unless something changed, I expected to leave prison without any assets and only a short time available to prepare for retirement. I would have no home, no car, no work experience, and probably not even a woman in my life. So, it didn't seem realistic that I would have time during this life to enjoy the miracle of parenthood. The punishment for the bad decisions I made during my early twenties, I was beginning to realize, was much more pervasive than the forty-five year sentence imposed. It would impact every aspect of my future.

My two sisters, Julie and Christina, both would marry soon. They would begin families, and I hoped to live vicariously through them. Still, I knew that participating in important family events wouldn't be an option for me. I wouldn't have the privilege of attending their weddings or of comforting them when they needed me. We were a close family, but jail restrictions prevented me from coming any closer to them than during our inevitably degrading visits separated by a glass wall.

While waiting for my transfer to prison, I contemplated the reason for my punishment. What was it that prompted legislators to create laws urging multiple-decade sentences for offenders with no histories of violence? The question hit me particularly hard when I compared my term of confinement with the terms violent offenders around me were receiving. I remember reading of one prisoner in the local paper who had been convicted of molesting seventeen boys on the basketball team he coached; he received a sentence of five years. The paper told of another prisoner who was convicted of armed robbery and home invasion; he received four years. Did my sentence length imply that society perceived me as being nine times more dangerous than a sexual molester of seventeen boys? Am I ten times worse than an armed robber? What was the meaning or the intent of my sentence? What would it accomplish?

These questions contributed to the confusion I encountered whenever I tried to create a mental map, a personal plan that would lead me out of the labyrinth in which my conviction and sentence placed me. After allowing my trial counsel to make all my previous decisions regarding my defense, I became convinced it would be wiser to use common sense in figuring the way to move forward.

My guilt had been established, and my sentence had been imposed. I realized it was time to move ahead. I needed a compass to guide me, but until I understood what would be expected of me I couldn't be certain of which direction to travel. If I could determine the objectives of the criminal justice system, I reasoned, then perhaps I could establish a course for myself that would ensure I reached those goals in the shortest possible time. Through reason and conscience, I hoped to work toward something besides the passage of time.

By understanding the mission of the system I hoped I'd be able to establish and follow a trajectory to lead me out of my punishment. I needed to believe a real pattern existed: man comes in contact with the criminal justice system; man rejects crime and criminal values; man purifies himself through conscious choices; man is forgiven and returns to society as a contributing citizen. By identifying the goals of the "system," I hoped to work my way through it.

Legal proceedings continued. My attorney was preparing an appeal to seek redress for perceived errors that occurred during the trial. I wasn't particularly interested in the appeal, or, for that matter, in any further legal proceedings.

As my ten-year plan for coping with confinement began to take shape, my thoughts about suicide began to subside. They didn't disappear, for I regularly told myself that I'd reevaluate everything once I made it to prison. Building the rough framework of a plan and setting measurable goals was helpful in my initial adjustment. By thinking about how I would approach the time, what I would accomplish, and how I would compensate for aspects of life that would be missing, I hoped to perceive both meaning and an end to my tribulation. The trials were over but not the tribulation.

CONCLUSION

In this chapter, I showed the impact the jury's verdict had on my life. The obvious result was the lengthy sentence that followed my conviction. Not so obvious was the change it had on my thinking.

With the jury's verdict of guilty on every count, I finally came to realize the seriousness of the trouble I had brought upon myself. That verdict caused me to examine the decisions I had made with my life up until that point, and it convinced me that I had been wrong. I was wrong in engaging in the distribution of drugs and wrong in refusing to acknowledge my criminal behavior.

That revelation influenced my behavior as a long-term federal prisoner. Because the jury's verdict convinced me that my community condemned my actions, I realized that I needed to make every effort to redeem myself and to compensate society for my criminal actions. As we proceed with the story, it is important for readers to distinguish between the prototypical experiences that all prisoners encounter and the sometimes atypical responses that followed my own conviction.

3

From the Pierce County Jail to the United States Penitentiary in Atlanta

This chapter describes my transformation from a pretrial jail inmate to a long-term prisoner en route to federal prison. I use the terms "prisoners" and "guards" rather than "inmates" and "correctional officers"—as the system would refer to us—because I am telling this story from the perspectives and experiences of actual prisoners. I also use vignettes and dialogue to help readers appreciate the subculture of prison, which differs substantially from the world beyond prison fences.

After my sentencing, no one told me where I would serve my time. In 1987, when I came into the criminal justice system, the Bureau of Prisons (BOP) held fewer than forty thousand people scattered across the country. But the system was growing rapidly, and I had learned already it was overcrowded.

I also knew the BOP employed a classification system designed to separate offenders according to their offense levels and the length of their sentences. Some prisoners serve their terms in camps with a high degree of freedom; others serve their terms in high-security penitentiaries.

Most prisoners, I had heard, are incarcerated in low- and medium-security prisons known as Federal Correctional Institutions (FCIs). Despite my lack of a criminal history, I had a serious conviction and a lengthy sentence. I had no hope of serving my term in a prison camp, at least not at the beginning.

Although I didn't expect to serve my term in minimum-security, neither did I expect to serve it in a maximum-security penitentiary. I had no history of violence, and I had heard that federal penitentiaries held only murderers, armed robbers, rapists, and other serious offenders prone to use violence as their favored means of persuasion.

As a jail inmate for nearly a year, I'd heard others describe the various institutions and hoped the BOP would send me to one where I could accomplish the goals I was setting for myself. Still, I had no expectations. I just waited to find out where I'd be sent. Once I arrived, I reasoned, I'd look for ways to refine my plan and begin the journey that I hoped would lead me home.

THE TRANSFER

On Saturday morning, August 1, 1988, nearly a year after my initial arrest, a guard came to my Pierce County cell and woke me. Ever since my sentencing I had been anticipating my transfer. I didn't know how long it would take, but I didn't expect the transfer to begin on a weekend. In fact, I'd been expecting a visit that day from my parents and sisters. But when the guard unlocked my door and said "Santos, roll up!" I knew he meant for me to gather the few belongings I had and follow him. I was about to leave the county jail.

During my time in jail, I had made friends with a few guys in my unit. Because I was being transferred so early in the morning, before the other prisoners were released from their cells, I didn't have an opportunity to say good-bye to anyone. I slipped a note under a friend's door, gave him my father's phone number, and asked him to call and pass the news not to visit me because I was being transferred. By then I had grown accustomed to being treated like a piece of furniture, and the sudden transfer didn't surprise me. I was ready to move.

Another guard escorted me downstairs, put me in a holding cell, and instructed me to place all my belongings in a box. I didn't have too much. I left the commissary items and books I had accumulated in my cell for the other prisoners. All I brought with me were photographs and legal papers. I put them in the box and left it for the guards to mail home.

Then the familiar strip search and an exchange of jail clothing for the large jumpsuit I was issued for traveling. On a Saturday morning the jail was short-staffed and the guard who issued the clothing wasn't able to locate a pair of socks or shoes. Instead, he told me to wear a pair of the shower-type rubber sandals. "It's summer anyway," he said.

The guard led me to another holding cell. A few other prisoners were there, and more trickled in over the next hour. Finally, a trio of U.S. marshals came and began fastening the steel chains around us.

This time the cuffs around my ankles were bothersome because I didn't have shoes or socks. The manacles are heavy and the steel felt sharp and cold against my skin. Without shoes the steel constantly rests upon the top of the foot; without socks, the restraints dig into the ankles.

To lessen my discomfort I tried to weave the pant legs of my oversized jumpsuit between my skin and the steel. It wasn't an easy task because my wrists were cuffed, too, and they were fastened to a steel chain wrapped around my waist. Besides that, the holding cell was crowded. It wasn't easy to maneuver. Still, I was determined, and my persistence paid off, as once I separated the steel from my skin, movement was less painful.

About an hour after I was secured in the steel restraints, the marshals escorted about ten of us to a waiting van. There, I learned I had been designated to FCI Ashland, in Kentucky, a medium-security prison. I was relieved to learn the BOP hadn't classified me as a high-security prisoner. I didn't want to be confined in a penitentiary, notorious for their gangs and racial problems. Although I knew nothing about Ashland, and I didn't know anyone in Kentucky, I was eager to get there and begin to assess my new environment and refine my plan for my first decade behind bars.

Riding south on Interstate 5, I expected to be taken to the Seattle-Tacoma Airport where we would board the marshal's plane. But, when I saw the airport exit pass, I figured we were moving on to Portland, Oregon, where I'd departed the plane the last time I made the cross-country journey courtesy of the government.

I didn't know for sure, though, because other than telling us our final destinations, the marshals didn't speak to us. As far as they were concerned, they just as easily could have been transporting boxes of hammers. They secured us and drove the van. Talking with us or answering our questions was not part of their job descriptions. Finally, we arrived at the Portland Airport. The van pulled into an isolated area and parked. For the next hour or so we waited in the van.

Since I had traveled this route a year before, I explained to the other men that we likely were waiting for the airplane to arrive, at which time we'd exchange places with other prisoners who would depart the arriving plane. The prisoners on the van with me were being sent to different prisons in the western states. I was the only one being transferred cross-country. I wondered how long it would take me to arrive at my destination.

Flying the Friendly Skies

The plane finally arrived and taxied its way next to the van. Once it stopped, our three marshals joined several others who had been waiting in other cars.

All the marshals wore navy blue clothing and caps, and each carried a large rifle that resembled a machine gun. Rather quickly the plane was surrounded by at least a dozen federal agents, the rear of the fuselage was opened, and soon prisoners in chains were hobbling down the stairs where they met a team of marshals who directed them where to stand. The prisoners passed through the gauntlet of agents, allowing one to check the wrist restraints and another to check the leg restraints; another, apparently, ordered the prisoners to open their mouths so he could look inside.

After all of the prisoners getting off the plane in Portland had disembarked and been inspected, the marshals aligned them in an area away from our van. The other prisoners and I were then ordered out. We went through the same inspection ritual. When the guard inspected my leg irons, he tugged up the pant legs I had used to protect my skin.

After everyone was checked, we ascended the plane's stairs. When we made it into the plane we were met by a marshal who held some paperwork pertaining to each prisoner. He asked some identifying information, then directed us to our seats. The marshal asked me my prison number—which I didn't know. He then asked my birth date and I told him. Passing his test, he told me my number was "one-six-three-seven-seven-zero-zero-four" and that I'd better remember it. I then moved forward into the capacity-filled plane.

Once airborne, the marshals passed out paper bags containing the usual— two slices of white bread, some baloney, an apple, and a can of soda with a straw. With our wrists cuffed and fastened to the chain around our waists, eating was work. Being hungry, though, I was able to push the food into my mouth and consume it.

The plane stopped once in Los Angeles for a prisoner exchange before we landed at the Oklahoma City Airport where all prisoners departed. I didn't have a watch, but I could tell it was early evening when I walked off the plane.

We were searched again and directed onto several buses that were waiting to deliver us to a holding facility. I knew I would be going to El Reno, the same place I had stopped after leaving Miami a year before. Oddly enough, the year seemed to have passed quickly. I still had a vivid recollection of my arrest, but then all events seemed to speed up to where I was at that moment. The time just evaporated, like the early-morning mist of a spring day. Although I hoped all of my time in prison would pass quickly, I couldn't allow it to vanish. I wanted something to show for it, as I expected my time in prison to consume a significant portion of my life.

After I clambered off the plane, and before I was directed onto the bus, I watched as every other prisoner disembarked. After all the men (who must have filled the back 80 percent or so of the aircraft) disembarked, I saw dozens of women prisoners who must have been seated in the very front of the plane begin to make their exit. It was a sight for which I was unprepared because I hadn't noticed them during our flight.

Seeing any human being in chains—the symbol of slavery—is anger generating and even horrific, but when the prisoners are female, the barbarism appears so much more severe and offensive. Some women, apparently those who had been arrested recently, wore street clothing—dresses, slacks, blouses, high-heeled shoes. Others wore the degrading, identity-stripping prisoner clothing. All had the same steel chains and cuffs fastened around their bodies, restricting the movements of their limbs.

These female prisoners, between thirty and forty in all, varied in age. Some appeared as young as their late teens, while others might have been grandmothers. Perhaps, it was my own longing to see the beauty of women after having been confined with so many unkempt male prisoners for the past year, but I felt the taste of vomit when I saw the look of horror on their faces— when I saw their tears falling as indifferent federal agents commanded them down the plane's stairs.

As I watched, I wondered what these women could have done. Then it struck me that not only were they going through this degradation, they also endure everything else I'd lived through the past year: the processing, the dehumanization, worst of all, the strip search.

I envisioned ungallant prison guards demanding these women to strip and open their genitals. I imagined the crude language the guards would use when issuing their commands. These women likely had passed through such an experience only hours before, and I sympathized in knowing they'd be encountering it again in the next few hours as the marshals delivered them to their places of confinement.

On the Bus to El Reno

When the plane was cleared, and all the prisoners had gone through the ceremonial reinspection process, we boarded our respective buses and headed to prison. My bus was of the long, school-type variety, but it had been modified for prisoner transport. Steel bars covered the windows, and a steel cage separated the prisoners from the driver. In the rear of the bus, a tobacco-chewing guard sat in a phone booth-sized cage, rifle in hand, watching over the prisoners.

I had a window seat and took in the midwestern scenery as we drove. It had been a long time since I had seen so many free people. It was early on a Saturday evening and people were obviously beginning a pleasant few hours. I tried to imagine the conversations, tried to remember when my life was so pleasant, and wondered when tranquility would return—if it would return.

When the road signs changed, I could tell we were getting close to the prison. As we drove along a narrow highway, I began to see signs warning drivers that they were near a prison and not to pick up hitchhikers. These signs were spaced every few miles or so and more frequently as the bus moved closer to the prison. Finally, the roar of the bus slowed as it made its turn off the highway and onto the winding road that led to the prison.

Then it appeared, large, old, and imposing, completely enclosed with high shining fences and the endless coils of glistening razor wire.

FCI EL RENO

The bus stopped in front of one high-steel gate. Some marshals got out. The gate slid open, the bus drove inside, and then stopped again as the gate closed behind it. I watched outside the window as the guards then removed firearms from the bus and placed them in a storage unit. There were some transfers of boxes and paperwork, then greetings between the prison guards and marshals who made careers of handling human cargo. A second gate in front of the bus then opened to swallow us into the prison's compound.

By then the moon had replaced the sun, and the night's natural darkness covered Oklahoma but not FCI El Reno. Prison surroundings are never dark, as countless lights keep the fences gleaming and bright.

Finally, we stopped in front of the R&D Building: not "Research and Development" but "Receiving and Discharge". Unfortunately, the other prisoners and I were not being discharged. We were being received.

After unloading some other boxes from the bus, a guard stepped on and began barking orders. "When I call your last name, step to the front and give me your prison number or your birthday."

Somewhere near the middle of the group, the guard called my name. Not remembering my number, I recited my birth date. It was good enough as the guard told me to move on.

As I stepped off the bus, a few other guards were present and directed me to follow the others into the R&D building. Several buses had arrived, carrying most of the prisoners from the filled airplane on which we'd been traveling. So within minutes, the holding tanks into which we were led were packed to squeezing room only.

When no more prisoners could be crammed into the tank, the steel bars were slammed shut and the other prisoners were forced into another tank. By the time all the buses were unloaded, we were crammed into three large tanks. There were perhaps four hundred men in that building. Many were screaming. All were hungry, tired, and in chains. Still, the prisoners were animated, knowing the day's travels were about over.

"Gi' me a smoke."

"Get off my neck!"

"Who goin' to Lewisburg?"

"Noodles, dat you?"

"Where da fuck you been?"

"Yo what up play'r?"

Hollering all around me, it was impossible to think. There was so much noise, I could have screamed whatever I chose with all the force I could muster and no one would have noticed a thing. We spent a long time, perhaps forty minutes standing in this madness—almost cheek to cheek we were so close—before the guards began emptying the tanks in groups of ten or so to unfasten the steel around our bodies.

I noticed some of the men wore the black boxes around their handcuffs. They were like the ones I saw Carlos wearing when I made my first flight as a federal prisoner. I knew the black box indicated they were considered problem prisoners or were serving life sentences. No release date. It made me grateful that I had a date, even though it loomed multiple decades in the future. For many of those black-boxed prisoners, I realized, prison was the last stop.

Once we were liberated from the chains, the guards started processing. The processing was the same everywhere I went. First the chains came off, then the forms, the photographs, the fingerprints, and the questions. By then I was a veteran of the booking procedures and completely used to it. What else would I get used to as time passed? I wondered. The tanks finally began to empty, but everything was moving slowly.

Finally, the guards passed out brown bags containing the expected stale white bread, slice of baloney, apple, and a carton of milk. My taste buds obviously had changed because I devoured the bland, stingy ration as if it were prepared in the warmth of my mother's kitchen. I was famished and grateful when the prisoner next to me offered his meal. Obviously, he was new in the system, I thought.

"Want this?" the prisoner asked.

"Sure," I said. "No appetite huh?"

"No. Just come in."

"Where you from?"

"Chicago. On my way back."

"Are you just starting?" I asked.

"They busted me last week in L.A. Hit me with a conspiracy indictment and I'm on my way back," he said.

"Yeah? I've been in about a year," I said. "I'm just starting my sentence. On my way to Ashland, some FCI in Kentucky. Ever heard of it?"

"Yeah, I have. I did some Fed time a few years ago. It ain't a bad joint. At least it din't use to be. Good food I heard. How much you got?"

"Forty-five years," I answered.

"Holy fuck! What the fuck you do?" he asked.

"Cocaine. I'm 848," I responded with my statute number.

"That's fucked up man. You must've went to trial." He guessed, recognizing that those defendants who exercise their right to trial usually receive much longer sentences than those who plead guilty.

"Yup. I took the stand, too. Even got time for perjury."

"Been in before?" He asked.

"No. First time. No violence either. Not even a weapon in the case."

"Shit. How much they catch ya with?" he wanted to know.

"Nothing. Just a lot of testimony."

"Motherfucking rats. I hate them bastards. This system is full of them cocksuckers. You'll find out."

Such was an example of the typical conversations I had with other prisoners. We didn't know each other, likely would never see each other again. I wasn't really looking for dialogue. I was just happy to have the food. We didn't ask each other's names. We were just talking while standing there with the others and watching as guards emptied prisoners from our tanks in groups of thirty or so for further processing. I was tired. I wanted to be released from the madness of the holding tanks and assigned to a bed.

"Santos," the guard yelled.

I stepped forward, pushing my way through the crowd to the front of the tank and joined the other prisoners whose names were called.

We walked to another room and were ordered to strip. The guards did their inspection thing, a process which now was familiar. I was given the "holdover" clothing, which included a pair of blue slippers I was glad to receive. I even was issued socks, mismatched though they were. Still, it was a comfort to have my feet covered once again.

After dressing, I was led to another holding tank where I waited to have my fingerprints stamped and photograph taken. It's not the type of photo where one smiles. Just like in prison films or on television programs, I was holding the miniature bulletin board with white letters identifying my name, number, and the name of the prison. It's a mug shot, preserved for eternity to accompany my fingerprint files.

Once the guards recorded my entry, I was sent to another room for screening. I moved to the back of the line and waited for my turn. Finally, I made it to the front, where I caught a glimpse of the guard's watch. It was 9:40 P.M.

"Name and number," the guard demanded.

"Santos, Michael. I don't know my number. I was born on January fifteenth, nineteen sixty-four," I answered.

He looked through his stack of red paper files, finally pulling one out and reading. Without looking at me he asks, "Have you ever worked for law enforcement?"

"No," I responded.

"Ever testify against someone else in a court of law?" "No," I replied, wondering what other type of court existed.

"Any reason you can't be held in general population?"

"No," again.

"Take these papers with you and a pencil, fill them out, then stand in the next line." Our interview was over. It was almost exactly like the one I went through at MCC Miami when I was transferring from the Special Housing Unit to the general compound. The monotony and routines of living in prison were becoming clear to me.

The papers were all forms requesting information about medical histories, people to contact in case of death, educational background, sentence length, and so on. There were too many questions on the government forms to believe anyone would ever evaluate them. I had to list my height, my weight, eye color, religion, whether I drank alcohol, smoked marijuana, used drugs, had a cold, coughed blood, and on and on. The forms seemed like paper filler to give the bureaucrats who would manage my life something to file. I dutifully filled them out.

Once the forms were completed, I moved on to the next line, where eventually I was questioned by someone in a white coat. The guard's questions confirmed my guess that he was a representative from health services.

"Are you on any medication?" he asked as he collected the papers I had completed.

"No."

"Do you have any health issues?"

"No."

"Move on."

It's like talking to robots.

I followed the crowd into the next tank where space was still available on the floor. I sat down, rested my back against the wall, supported my head by placing my elbows on my bent knees, and used my fingers to plug my ears. To block the stench of the room, I pulled the neck of my T-shirt up over my nose. The room quickly filled, and I eagerly waited for the next event, which my memory suggested would be the issuing of bedrolls and assigning of quarters.

I was correct. After another half hour or so, a cadre of permanent prisoners from El Reno wheeled some carts in and began passing out bedrolls to us as the guards called our names. "Finally," I thought, "sleep is within reach."

When my name was called, I collected my bedroll and marched in line with the others. Walking was so much easier after I exchanged the rubber sandals I'd been wearing all day, not to mention the removal of the steel restraints. It was after 11:00 P.M. when the guard led me to the third tier of the Oklahoma unit and locked me inside the cell. It was the same steel hole I remembered from my last trip through.

Oklahoma Unit

The prison at El Reno, Oklahoma, is one of the BOP's medium-security facilities. It has several different housing units, but as a holdover prisoner—someone who is just passing through en route to another destination—the only housing unit I was authorized to enter was the Oklahoma Unit, where I had been assigned.

The Oklahoma Unit is a large shell-like structure shaped in rectangular form. About 15 feet inside the shell, a six-story steel island stands as the unit's guts. Each floor of the island is called a tier, holding a long, rectangular row of small old-fashioned jail cells.

The front wall of the tier is a steel-mesh screen used to block inmates from throwing each other (or staff) off the tiers. The other side of the pathway is an extended line of round steel bars, evenly spaced about one fist apart, that enclose each tiny cell.

The interior of each cell is identical. One can stand in the center of the cell, stretch out both arms, and simultaneously touch each plate of steel that serves as a side wall. A steel-framed bunk bed attached to one of the walls stretches from the front bars to the cement wall in the rear of the cell. And inches from the other side of the bed, a stainless-steel toilet/sink combination touches the rear wall.

The fluorescent light in the cell was turned off, but I could see another prisoner was sleeping in the lower bunk. Exhausted, I threw my bedroll over the thin mat on the top bunk and tried to sleep.

It was a late summer night in Oklahoma, about 90° F outside. The shell of Oklahoma Unit, however had an ovenlike quality with triple-digit temperatures. No air conditioning was available in this elderly facility. Instead, large fans, perhaps 3 feet in diameter, roared from each end of the tier. The air in the cell was so hot it felt like the air blowing out of a dryer's exhaust vent. Despite my body's fatigue, I lay on that mat and sweated instead of slept.

Someone had wedged a paperback Bible between the mattress and wall, and since I couldn't sleep, I used the light coming through the bars to read. I'd read the Bible through, a couple of times, while I was in the Pierce County Jail, so I knew right where I wanted to go: The Book of Job. When things seemed rough, I found strength in reading about Job's fortitude in the face of adversity.

As I watched the finger-sized cockroaches crawling along the ceiling, and swatted a few that strayed to my chest, I prayed for equanimity. Then, all of a sudden, the bed's frame began to shake vertically and horizontally in increasing rhythm. Either the earth was quaking from side to side, or the prisoner who I thought was sleeping below had awakened.

"Hey, bud, you're shakin' the whole bed," I said.

"Oh. Sorry. I didn't know you'd come in."

There was no more conversation and no sleep for me. "What kind of nuts am I going to live with," I wondered. I just folded my hands behind my head, read the graffiti on the walls and ceiling, and thought about passing the next few decades.

A few hours later a guard came by and flashed a light in the cell.

"Reynolds," he yelled.

"Yeah," came the voice from below.

"Roll up. You're leaving. You got five minutes." Feigning sleep, I watched through slightly opened eyes as the guy gathered his things together. He looked to be about my age.

Just before the guard came by to pick him up, Reynolds asked, "You 'wake?"

"What?" I answered.

"I'm leaving a pair of sneaks under the bed. They're tens. Use 'em if you want, otherwise someone'll take 'em."

"Thanks," I said.

"Yeah. Good luck," he said, as the guard unlocked the bars and slid them open for my cellmate to leave.

It was before dawn on a Sunday morning, and I was surprised to see transfer activity. The BOP is a busy system—a machine that never stops. Welcoming the solitude, and relieved not to have to go through an awkward meeting with Reynolds in the morning, I finally dozed off.

The rest was brief, however, because the sun soon began beaming through the unit's long glass windows, and the guards, with their heavy, clanking key chains, were walking along the tiers sliding each cell's steel-bar doors open. The noise felt loud enough to vibrate the building. It certainly woke me. Anyway, I wanted to have a look around.

I got off the bed and splashed water all over me. Moisture must have been in the air because despite not having used it, the towel in my bedroll was damp. After drying off my body, I hung the towel over the side of the bed's frame. I got dressed, putting on the hi-top sneakers Reynolds had left me. A bit beat up, but they fit perfectly and were far better than the government-issue blue slippers that had been assigned. I walked down stairs and saw the guard's office. I asked for a toothbrush, toothpaste, and some soap.

"Didn't you get any when you came in?" he barked.

"No. I just got in last night. It was late and all I received was a bedroll."

"They should have given it to you when you come in. Can't be givin' out all my supplies. Here's a roll a toilet paper. It's all I'm handin' out this morning. See me later."

Not knowing what else to say, I took the toilet paper and walked back to my cell. On the way up the stairs I grabbed a small broom I saw in a corner so I could sweep some of the filth out of my cell. Then I headed back downstairs and followed the crowd. Everyone was heading to early-morning chow.

A Breakfast Conversation

The dining room was huge, much bigger than the one I remembered from MCC Miami. But then again, for the past year I'd been eating lukewarm food delivered on trays to the units at the Pierce County Jail. Perhaps I'd forgotten. Anyway, it was a large cafeteria, holding maybe five hundred people. It was less than half full, though, and its emptiness may have caused it to look bigger.

I walked through the line and was issued a choice of either a greasy doughnut or half of a grapefruit. I took the fruit and two of the miniature boxes of Frosted Flakes I used to eat as a child. I picked up a plastic spoon, a bowl, and a plastic cup and filled the cup and bowl with milk from an unregulated stainless-steel dispenser. Then, I sat at an empty table to eat.

"Como 'ta usted?" a stranger sitting at the table beside me greeted in Spanish. "Esta nuevo?"

"Sorry. I don't speak Spanish," I said to the friendly face.

"Oh. You look Spanish."

"Well, my father's Spanish, but I never learned how to speak it. There aren't too many Spanish speakers where I'm from."

"I was saying good morning," he said.

"Good morning," I replied.

"Just get in?"

"Yeah. Late last night," I said.

"I'm Tony."

"Michael." We shook hands.

"Where you from?" Tony asked.

"Seattle."

"No kidding. My roommate's from Seattle. He's still sleeping. I'm from L.A."

"Been here long?" I asked.

"This is my second week. Hopefully my last. I'm on my way to T.I."

"What's that?"

"Terminal Island. I been in Big Springs for the past six years. They're finally moving me closer to home," he answered.

"Where's Big Springs?" I asked.

"Texas. It's a good joint, just too far from home. Where you goin'?"

"Ashland, Kentucky," I answered.

"Ashland? What's up with that! You on disciplinary?"

"What's disciplinary?"

"Oh, you're just starting," he observed.

"Well, I've been in for a year, but I've been going through trial and I'm just now on my way to prison. They told me I was designated to Ashland. Know anything about it?"

"I've never been on that side of the country. You can find out, though. There's people here from everywhere. El Reno is like a transfer station and people in Oklahoma Unit are passing through from every prison. How much they give you?"

"Forty-five," I answered.

"That's not too bad. I know it sounds tough now that you're just getting started, but it'll pass soon enough. Been in before?" he asked.

"No, first time," I said.

"Usually, they send guys like you straight to camp. Ashland's a medium," he said.

"I thought camps only take people who are about to get out."

"Well, in here, forty-five months isn't that long. There are guys in here serving twenty years and more," he answered. "If you're ten-years short, you can get to camp."

"I wish I had forty-five months. I've got forty-five years," I corrected him.

"Motherfucker! For a first offense! How many did'ya kill?"

I laughed. "No one. There was no violence in my case. Just cocaine."

"A tanker full, I'll bet. How old are you?" he asked.

"Twenty-four. How old are you?"

"Thirty-one. I was 24 when I came in, too," he answered.

"Six years already, huh. Are you almost done?" I asked.

"Well, compared to you I am," he said. "I get paroled in two years. I had a fifteen-year bid."

"I can't get parole. I'm an 848," I said. "No parole."

"Man, that sucks. None of the new law guys get parole. Whad'ya do, 'bout thirty?" he asked.

"I don't know. I heard 27, but I'm not even thinking about it. I'll figure something out," I said.

"Yeah. Like hitting the fence. You'll find a way out."

Bright lights in my head. Upon his allusion to escape, I immediately remembered my conversations with Terry, the jailhouse lawyer I met in Miami, his warnings about most of the people in transit looking for information on other prisoners. They want to feed it to the government in exchange for sentence reductions, Terry said. Here I meet this guy, unsolicited, and he's talking about escape. I stopped chatting.

"Well, look. If you need anything, come see me," he said as he began gathering his things to leave.

"Actually, I do," I replied, figuring I'd be the seeker of information. "I don't have a toothbrush or anything. Can you help me?"

"Oh, sure. The guards are pretty tight-assed about giving up supplies. They're either taking 'em home or giving 'em to the orderlies. Let's go back to the unit. I'll introduce you to my cellie and give you some things to get you through."

"I'll meet you there," I said. "I'm getting in line for another grapefruit."

"Okay. What cell you in?"

"I'm in 318. Oklahoma Unit," I answered.

"Oh, we're neighbors. I'm in 323. See ya in a bit."

"Bye."

He seemed like a friendly guy. His statement about hitting the fence just threw me off. I didn't need to be hearing such talk from a stranger. I really wanted to make my own decisions about prison, and I didn't want my thoughts clouded with more advice from others. Besides, after just having received my sentence, I sure didn't want to talk about breaking any more laws.

I finished my food and carried my tray to the dishwashing entrance. I could use the morning to walk around the compound. The last time I was in El Reno, it was just for overnight. There was no telling when they'd wake me again to resume my journey to Ashland. I walked out to check it out.

Eager to see the law books again, I walked over to the library. Being able to walk around was a huge treat after being confined in the county jail for so long. When I was in Pierce County, I was confined to my cell or to my unit. Federal prisons, on the other hand, were like huge communities with fences or walls around them. Within those fences I had opportunities to walk from building to building, sometimes relatively freely.

After I left the chow hall and entered the library, I found some encouragement from something posted on a bulletin board. It featured the schedule of several college courses and indicated it was time to sign up for the next quarter's courses.

Like a kid encountering Disneyland for the first time, "Wow!" I thought. "They have college here." I started to wonder whether they'd let me stay in El Reno instead of going on to Ashland. I would ask someone when I had a chance. "Maybe Tony could help me," I hoped.

I gravitated to the library and felt like I was back at MCC Miami. Scores of prisoners were huddled around the desks reading law books and engaging in discussions I didn't understand. I wanted to participate, but their knowledge about law and the system intimidated me. As the cliché holds, better to remain silent and thought a fool than open one's mouth and remove all doubt. I just looked around.

"What do I need to see a law book?" I asked the clerk who stood behind the counter.

In Miami, the law books were on bookshelves and all inmates could freely grab the books they wanted and read or browse through them as long as they remained in the library. El Reno was different. All the law books were in a separate section within the library, and a clerk issued them over a counter. When I first saw the clerk, I wasn't sure whether he was a prisoner or a staff member.

"Which one you want?" he asked.

"It doesn't matter. I just want to read something."

"You want case law, rules, procedure, the U.S. Code? I'm not a mind reader. What d'ya want?"

"What do you have on 848?" I asked.

"You new?" the clerk asked, but seemingly already knowing the answer.

"Yeah. Just came in."

"Holdovers can't check out law books."

"C'mon. I'm just gonna sit right there and read it," I said.

"You got an 848?" he asked.

"Yes."

"How much time you get?"

"Forty-five years. I'm just starting."

He whistled. "Yeah, you need a law book. You need a lot of law books, more than we've got here. Got a lawyer?" he asked.

"Of course. But I'm not into lawyers right now. I just want to read."

He gave me a few books and asked me to stay in front of him because he wasn't supposed to hand the books out to holdovers.

I took the books to a nearby workstation and happily began to read. It felt good to see the sophisticated indexing system in each law book, and I liked trying to figure out what all of the symbols meant. It was like working my way through a puzzle. Reading the text was interesting, too.

I passed a couple of hours with those books before the clerk came by to collect them. He said it was recall and I had to return to my unit in order to be released for chow. "Can I stay here?" I asked.

"Only clerks can stay. If you get caught you'll get a shot."

"What's a shot?"

"Just go back to the unit. My name's Brett Kimberlin. Come back after chow and see me. I want to talk with you about something."

I returned the books, told him my name, shook his hand, thanked him for helping, and then returned to my unit.

On my way back to the unit an officer stopped me. "Turn around," he said as I approached him.

"What's up?" I asked.

"Pat search. Lift your arms."

The guard started frisking me right there in the middle of the compound. The other prisoners walked passed me not paying attention. I guess this stop-and-frisk thing was something new I'd have to get used to.

"Get a move on! It's recall," he said.

I continued the walk back to my unit and returned to the third tier. I went by Tony's room.

"Where ya been?" he asked.

"I went by the library and got caught up in some law books," I said.

"This is Jimmy," he said. "He thinks he knows you."

"Oh yeah, sure," I said as we shook hands. "I saw you in Pierce County. I'm Michael Santos."

"Jimmy Feets," he said. "I was in the unit across from yours, Four-South, with Pat, your codefendant."

"Yeah, sure. Pat's a good guy. Is he here?"

"No. He was. They shipped him out last Thursday. Went to Phoenix. Where you going?"

"Ashland, Kentucky. How 'bout you?" I asked.

"La Tuna, Texas. I heard you got an assload of time. I figured you'd be going to the pen."

"Glad I'm not. I heard they're the worst. Actually, I'd like to stay here."

"It just seems that way now. You'll see. They're all about the same," he said.

"Were you on trial in Seattle?" I asked.

"No. I went back to court. I've been at La Tuna since 1985. They brought me up for the grand jury, but I wouldn't testify. Now they're sending me back."

We spent a bit more time discussing the activities available at La Tuna, and Tony gave me a toothbrush, toothpaste, a comb, a razor, and some soap. He also gave me some shower shoes, which were in pretty good shape, considering they'd been passed around to so many prisoners. I welcomed the donation, and after telling them both that I'd see them after the noon meal, I left to shower.

After my shower, I walked around the unit looking for a telephone. I wanted to call my parents, to let them know where I was and where I was going. More than twenty people were waiting in the phone line, though, so I just passed by and went outside, took a walk around the compound, and waited for the library to open again.

When it finally did open, I went back in and saw Brett. We started talking about my case and it became clear to me that he was quite knowledgeable in the law—at least it sounded like he was to me. He kept pressing upon me the importance of hiring an appellate attorney who specialized in preparing appeals for those who've been convicted of §848. Brett urged me to call his friend, a Chicago attorney whom he said had the best record in overcoming these convictions.

At that stage in my sentence, the first tentative steps of a marathon, I didn't want to hear about attorneys who were going to change my life. I considered myself completely responsible for the situation I was in, and I didn't expect anyone "to save the day" for me. I had to go through it, figure out how to cope with the time myself, and determine whether the commitment necessary to succeed would be worth the trouble. If I decided that it wasn't, then I always had my backup plan of ending the game. But I wasn't going to give control of my life, or my hopes, to an attorney. I declined to accept Brett's friend's phone number. Besides, it smelled like Brett was looking for a commission.

I read the Code of Federal Regulations (CFR) section that pertains to the BOP; I wanted to develop a better understanding of this organization holding me. Through my readings, I learned some things about the custody and classification process. For one thing, I found that although I had been designated to serve my sentence in FCI Ashland, after eighteen months I could request a transfer to another prison, perhaps one that was closer to my home.

One thing that became clear after reading the CFR, however, was that I wouldn't be able to persuade the BOP to leave me in El Reno. In the BOP, prisoners were designated to serve their terms in prisons by bureaucrats who worked in centralized offices across the country. I knew that I wouldn't have access to them and that I wouldn't be able to make any type of case that would persuade them to leave me in a particular spot. So, I dropped that idea and just tried to make the best of my time while I was there. All indications were that the stop would be relatively brief—about two to three weeks.

Work Call

The next day, at 4:00 A.M., the guards came by my cell and shined the flashlight inside. Despite the sweltering heat, the roaches, and the light pouring through the unit's windows, I had been sleeping soundly, exhausted from my previous travels and the processing.

"Santos," the guard yelled.

"What?" I answered, hoping he would tell me to "roll up" for my transfer to Ashland.

Instead, the guard said, "Get up. Report to the chow hall for kitchen duty."

"Great," I thought. "I'm in prison for one day and I've already been assigned to a job beginning at 4:00 A.M." I hadn't been in Miami long enough after my initial arrest to be assigned a job, and no federal prisoners worked in the county jail. This was going to be my first work experience as a prisoner.

"Be downstairs in five minutes," he ordered as he unlocked the cell door.

I reported to the food services building, as required, with about thirty other holdover prisoners who had been randomly assigned to this work detail. Besides us, there must have been another fifty "designated" prisoners, people who were serving their sentences at El Reno reporting for work. All together, some eighty of us were working in the kitchen that morning.

The designated prisoners were responsible for preparing the food; the holdovers performed the grunt work—sweeping, mopping, and handling the significant amount of garbage generated by a cafeteria serving 2,000 prisoners three meals each day.

After the noon meal I was free to leave the kitchen, and I returned to the unit. I wanted to make a phone call, but the line was still too long. With so many people in the unit, I was surprised so few phones were available for inmate use. Instead of waiting, I wrote a letter home, letting my family know where I was and that I was on my way to Ashland, Kentucky.

I remained in El Reno for about two weeks and my routine was pretty much the same. I was required to work in the kitchen in the mornings, but I was free to roam the compound during the afternoons and evenings. Other than the ability to walk around and my assignment to a work detail, though, confinement as a holdover was not too much different from life in the county jail.

As holdovers, all relationships were transient. Hundreds of prisoners were coming and going each day. One never knew when the guard would order him to "roll up and prepare for transfer," so each night there was a lot of hoping. Everyone wanted to move on to his final destination, a place where he could settle in and build a routine. The irony was not lost on me that we "wanted to get to prison."

Holdovers kept no personal property, didn't receive mail, didn't have address books or stamps, and thus found it difficult to communicate with the outside. As a holdover, the prisoner lives as a homeless person, unable to make any plans and not knowing what to expect. Worse, because of his inability to communicate with the outside world and establish a routine, he lacks the solace—minor though it may be—available to designated prisoners.

The one thing I was able to accomplish as a holdover was to gather information about what I could expect as a prisoner in the BOP. I was cutting into a network of myriad experiences; everyone in my unit was in transit from one prison to another. Some men had been in prison for as long as a decade, and they had lived in many different institutions.

Although I heard few positive remarks about what one could accomplish while incarcerated, I did learn about the programs available in various prisons. Most prisons, I learned, offered college courses. Some prisoners even earned college degrees during their terms.

This was a huge source of hope for me, giving me the strength I needed to keep moving forward. To cope with my sentence, I had to believe I would have opportunities to make my life useful. If I could educate myself, I reasoned, I would find ways to contribute to the world, to be a part of it, to bring meaning to my life.

Although I was alone, new in the system, and consumed with anxieties about what was to come, this hope of being able to create a life emancipated me from the self-pity, negativity, and despair surrounding me. Instead of living for the day, I began to live for the ten-year plan, eager to initiate and work toward it.

NEXT STOP: FCI TALLADEGA

Finally, after more than two weeks of kitchen duty, the guard flashed his light in my room earlier than the usual 4:00 A.M.

"Santos," he said.

"Yes."

"Roll up. Be downstairs in five minutes."

I didn't have anything to bring, just the sheets from my bed which went to the laundry. I left the shoes and hygiene items I had accumulated for the next holdover. I walked downstairs, eager to be chained again and move closer to my destination. "Perhaps I'd even get there today," I hoped.

Actually, though, I expected to move through Talladega, Alabama, the next stop on the circuitous prisoner-transport route. From the other holdovers I'd learned that although some direct trips to Ashland exist, the standard route is an airplane ride to Talladega and then a bus ride to Ashland, Kentucky.

Once I joined the other prisoners downstairs, we were identified, counted, and then moved to the R&D unit. The same thing again. A brown-bag breakfast. The noise of a stadium rock concert just minutes before the band takes the stage. The stench of hundreds of unwashed men in close quarters. The strip search and clothing exchange. Hundreds of men walking around in a stupor as guards confine them with steel cuffs and chains. The waiting. And the final march to the bus.

The bus drove us to the Oklahoma City airport where we boarded the marshal's plane. This time the plane flew to New Orleans, Miami, Atlanta, and Orlando for prisoner exchanges. Finally, we landed in Alabama, where we boarded the bus that drove us to FCI Talladega.

It was late in the evening when we arrived, but the lights around the prison verified Talladega's design is much more similar to MCC Miami than to the old prison at El Reno. The same type of high, doublewide fences, sprawling and covered with the rolls upon rolls of glistening concertina wire, encapsulated the entire facility. Yet the prison was modern, featuring rounded, low-rise buildings that looked like islands connected by concrete walkways in an ocean of manicured green lawns. FCI Talladega, a medium-security prison, models a college-campus design with which the Bureau of Prisons is becoming identified.

The guards unlocked our chains, and in time we were fed, strip-searched, issued new clothing, fingerprinted, photographed, and, by about 11:00 that evening, admitted into the Alpha unit, which was reserved for holdover housing. By that time, the other inmates were locked in their rooms. Once I was assigned to a cell, the door was locked behind me.

My degree of hope and optimism took a leap forward upon entering the housing unit. The prison shone like it was brand new. The conspicuously missing steel bars, highly polished white tile floors, and stained oak doors and trim throughout the unit were a welcome change. With its freshly painted walls, the living conditions looked more comfortable than anywhere I'd been confined before. All the men were locked in their cells for the evening, so the unit felt peaceful, like a sanitized hospital ward—attractive nurses in pressed white uniforms would have completed the scene nicely.

When the guard locked the door behind me, I had entered a room with a wooden-frame bunk bed, a wooden desk and storage area, a porcelain sink, and a porcelain toilet—not connected, but of the standard type found in an inexpensive apartment.

Indeed, after having been confined in a filthy, noisy county jail for the past year, and a decrepit old prison for the past few weeks, the room to which I was assigned at FCI Talladega felt like I was in my own condominium. Even though it was the size of a small bathroom, the room felt private. Since I was alone, I made up the lower bunk and lay down to sleep, praying I'd find the same hospitable conditions at FCI Ashland.

The New Roommate

Later that night, long after I'd fallen asleep, I heard my door being unlocked. The guard opened it, turned on the light, and assigned another prisoner to the room.

"Take the top bunk," the guard said, then locked the door behind him.

By that time, I'd been confined for over a year, but I don't think one ever grows used to being awakened in the middle of the night and having a complete stranger installed in one's bathroom-sized locked cell. The idyllic euphoria quickly vanished with this reminder that I was just a prisoner and must not be fooled by any illusions of privacy.

I was still tired from the previous day's travels and processing, so I didn't rise to "welcome" the new guy to what I considered "my" cell. Instead, I feigned sleep and allowed him to fend for himself.

He was pretty charged up from his own transfer, though, and clearly wanted to talk.

"You wake?" he asked soon after the guard locked the door.

"Yeah."

"Sorry 'bout dis. We just got in from Ashland," he said.

"No kidding," my interest immediately picked up. "How'd you get here? Bus?"

"Yeah, 'bout a ten-hour drive. I been on da road all muthafuckin' day," he answered.

"I'm on my way to Ashland," I said.

"I been der for three muthafuckin' years. Couldn't wait to git out dat bitch! I'm goin' Terry Haute," he said.

"Where's that?" I asked.

"Indiana. What, you new?"

"Yeah. I've been in a year, but I've been going through trial and in transit," I answered.

"I gotta shit," he said.

We hadn't even exchanged names. I was lying under the sheets, a pillow blocking the light from my eyes while we talked. Without any sense of modesty, the guy dropped his pants and started grunting 8 feet away from my head while he continued his dialogue.

"How much you get?" he asked.

"Forty-five years, no parole."

"Muthafucka! You'll have more time up der dan anyone else, dat's for sure. Least day'll know you ain't no rat. Better watch yo self. Place be full dem muthafuckas. Snitches be ev'ywhere. Dat's what fucked me up," he said, between farts and flushes.

"What'd they do to you?" I asked.

"My cellie," he answered. "I copped some smoke off a dude and was hiding it in my mattress. My cellie found it, and the muthafucka ratted me out. Caught me a hun'red series and raised my level. Been in the hole for sixty days. Now I'm goin' to the pen."

"What's a hundred-series?" I asked.

"Shot. Incident report. It stays on my record for ten muthafuckin' years," he explained as he wiped himself and dressed again. "I ain't give a fuck, though," he continued. "Don't give a damn 'bout no FCI. Full a rat muthafuckas anyway."

When I was in El Reno and I read through the Code of Federal Regulations in the law library, I learned all about the BOP's disciplinary system.

Incident reports, the citations issued for violating prison rules, I now learned, were called shots in the federal system. When I was held in the Pierce County Jail, where most of the people around me were from the state of Washington prison system, disciplinary infractions were called tickets.

In the federal system, the BOP divides disciplinary infractions according to four different severity levels. Incident reports (shots) in the 100-series group are of the greatest severity and have the highest sanctions; the BOP considers 200-series shots high-severity violations. Prisoners who receive 100- or 200-series incident reports must appear before a special Disciplinary Hearing Officer (DHO) who is responsible for imposing the sanctions. Prisoners who receive 300- and 400-series incident reports, moderate-severity infractions, may have unit counselors or case managers determine their sanctions.

The CFR explains the various ways that BOP disciplinary infractions work against a prisoner. When classifying a prisoner for his security designation, BOP administrators use the sophisticated Custody and Classifications Manual to attach a score to each inmate. The objective system considers the inmate's criminal history and sentence length—over which the inmate no longer has control. It also considers the individual's institutional behavior, though, and inmates who receive disciplinary infractions receive higher points against them and are thus classified as needing higher security. Most disciplinary infractions count against a prisoner's classification for one year, but prisoners who receive 100-series disciplinary infractions, like my new cellmate, are penalized on the custody and classification-scoring matrix for ten years.

"What's your name?" I asked.

"My name's Clevis, but day calls me Booka, ah-ight."

"Cool. My name's Michael. Let's talk more tomorrow, Booker, I'm beat."

"True, true," he said.

I didn't sleep as easily after hearing his brief description about Ashland. I told myself the guy was serving his sentence differently than I would serve mine, but I still was uneasy. I slept, but Booker gave me some heavy news I didn't need to hear that night.

I woke the next morning when the guard unlocked my door for breakfast. I was too tired to go and Booker didn't move. Still, I couldn't get back to sleep after I heard the door open, so I just lay in my bed and stared at the springs above me curving down like a hammock; I thought about what Booker had said the previous evening.

I didn't like the idea of being assigned to a cell where my cellmate could bring drugs into the room. Drugs weren't an issue in the county jail where I'd been held, but I'd heard the prison system was infested with them. Still, I knew that if prison guards came into the cell and found drugs, anyone assigned to the cell would have a problem. I didn't have a cellmate in Pierce County. From now on it appeared I would.

I wondered about the appropriate way to respond to this problem. What would I do as a long-term prisoner if another man assigned to my cell started doing something illegal—something that could implicate me? I knew that going to the guards was not an option. Did this mean that as a prisoner I'd be subject to not only my own actions but also the actions of everyone else around me? Here was another dilemma for me to contemplate.

I got up, took a shower, and walked around the unit. In Talledaga, holdover prisoners were confined to Alpha unit and couldn't walk outside unless a staff member escorted them. A telephone was available so I called my parents to let them know I was okay and on my second stop. I didn't know when I'd get to my destination. But I told them everything was fine and they shouldn't worry about me.

A television room was available inside the unit. There were several tables in the common area and a small shelf of books. Prisoners were returning from the breakfast meal, and I saw a few familiar faces from El Reno, even a guy or two who had been in MCC Miami with me the year before. So I had some people with whom I could talk, other sources who could tell me more about what I could expect.

One of the guys told me there were a lot of men in the unit who had been designated to Ashland originally, but that the counselor in Talledaga recently told them they'd been redesignated to USP Atlanta. Apparently, there was a food strike in Atlanta and a hundred guys or so were being transferred out. People who previously had been designated to Ashland now were going to Atlanta. He suggested I check with the counselor when he came in.

I received the information calmly, but it wasn't what I wanted to hear. I'd set my mind on serving my sentence in an FCI, a medium-security facility which I understood to be much less volatile than a penitentiary.

I'd heard that college programs were available in the FCIs, and I was determined to educate myself while I was in prison. If I was sent to USP Atlanta, a maximum-security penitentiary, I wondered whether college programs would be an option. I returned to my room, where I found Booker just getting up.

"G'mornin bud," I said.

"What up?" he answered.

"Just hangin' 'round downstairs. I was talking with a guy I knew from El Reno. He said a lot of the guys who were going to Ashland had been redesignated to Atlanta."

"Yeah," he said. "Could be. I heard der been a lotta action in A'lanta since dat riot last year. Place wide open. You be better off goin' A'lanta. Weatha's better than Kentucky. Won't be so many Johnny Blazes runnin' round either."

"Johnny Blaze?" I inquired.

"Yeah. Johnny Blaze. Rat muthafuckas. They be hot as a firecracka . . . blazen," he explained.

"We'll see. I'll ask the counselor whether I'm going there when I see him."

"You play spades?" Booker asked me.

"Not really. I played a few times in the county jail," I answered.

"I'm a spadeologist," he said. "Let's go find us some victims."

With nothing else to do, I joined Booker and passed part of that first morning playing cards. But not being much of a card player, I soon left someone else to play with Booker while I went to talk with some of the other guys I'd met during the few games I did play.

One of them, Carlos, also had been sentenced to a forty-year term for a CCE conviction. He kept insisting that 848s have eligibility for parole after ten years. I told him I read the U.S. Code book myself and was certain it said people convicted of this statute were not eligible for parole. We argued over the issue, but by that time I was so cynical about the law and judicial opportunities for relief that I didn't even like talking about it. I just wanted to get to where I was going, and despite what Booker told me, I was hoping I'd still be going to Ashland.

When I first encountered other prisoners, their initial expectation was that I must be serving a relatively brief sentence. My temperament must suggest as much. When they heard I was serving a forty-five-year term, their immediate reaction usually was one of disbelief, then an initial assumption that I must understand and accept the "prisoner mentality."

The *prisoner mentality*, I was beginning to realize, concerns itself with which prisoners are *solid*. Little else. Solid men never provide information to law enforcement and are prepared to respond to all problems with lethal force. "You've got to take a position," solid prisoners will say. Education, work histories, leadership, community participation and such—all irrelevant. Just don't rat, and handle all problems *like a man*. Those are the understood values of the prison community. And anyone who questions them or does not abide by them is *suspect*.

"If it ain't rough it ain't right," as the prison saying goes. But as one who was and is trying to climb his way out of prison, I was hoping to serve my term in the least volatile environment possible. Of one thing I was certain: USP Atlanta would not be less volatile than a medium-security prison. I went to wait in line to see the counselor so I could find out.

USP ATLANTA

Sure enough, when my turn came up to see him, he told me I'd been redesignated to Atlanta. He said that most likely I'd be leaving by bus in a day or two, as the unit was pretty much filled with people on their way there.

So now I knew. I'd begin serving my term in a U.S. penitentiary. And according to the counselor, I'd be leaving within a few days. Thinking hope an elixir for my anxieties, I began convincing myself of the good points.

For one thing, I'd be confined in a major city, thereby making it easier to receive visits. True, I'd still be at least 1,000 miles away from anyone I knew, but at least people who wanted to visit could take a direct flight to Atlanta. Had I gone to Ashland, Kentucky, receiving visits would not have been impossible but certainly much more difficult.

Also, being in Atlanta, I thought, might make it easier for me to connect with the world outside. I was thinking in terms of Atlanta being a vibrant, growing city with several nearby universities and cultural activities. These types of institutions, I convinced myself, attract sophisticated, well-educated people who might prove willing to open relationships with people in prison.

I would need help educating myself, and the more well-educated people I could bring into my life, the more opportunities I would have to find mentors—advisers, or learning partners crucial to my goal of advancing during my incarceration. Indeed, I thought Atlanta might prove easier for finding mentors than a relatively small Kentucky town.

Still, the penitentiary myth concerned me. Atlanta was a maximum-security penitentiary, and these facilities are notorious for excessive incidents of violence. I wanted to avoid problems while serving my sentence. My objective was to leave prison at the earliest possible time—and not in a horizontal position.

Each day since leaving the Pierce County Jail, I'd become more immersed in my idea of designing a program that would help me earn freedom. My mind was becoming stronger, my thoughts clearer. Somehow, I told myself, I would survive the penitentiary experience—and I convinced myself I could achieve my goals without interference from the perils around me.

"Survive it," I told myself. "Focus on your goals and get through it. No matter what, get through it." I had to keep sending myself these messages to overcome the fear I had of living in an environment where I expected I would need to keep weapons around me and be willing to use them. No matter how frequently I tried, I could not see myself plunging a steel shank into another man's flesh—yet I knew that was the expected course of action in a maximum-security prison. Bloody.

Soon after the counselor told me of my new destination, the final transfer of my initial journey began. BOP personnel put us in chains, led us to a bus, and drove from FCI Talledaga to USP Atlanta in a few hours.

CONCLUSION

My experience of being transferred from the county jail system into the federal prison system is fairly typical. Some of the prisoners who begin serving their sentences in minimum-security camps can avoid the transfer system and self-surrender to their institutions. Most of the men, however, must go through the transfer procedures. It's a treadmill routine that may require booking into several different facilities, plane rides, and bus rides. The uncertainty is always present, but as one converses with other prisoners, he gathers information about what to expect as the journey continues.

4

USP Atlanta: First Encounters

My first months in the prison were not spent in the volatile environment I had expected. Actually, they were a reprieve, a time to settle myself in and build some alliances. I learned that I shouldn't look to staff members for guidance and that not knowing the prison rules—written and unwritten—could aggravate my problems. Things changed after my first year; the routine violence and junglelike environment I had expected returned to USP Atlanta. By then, I was well entrenched in the institution and protected because of my relationships. Others, however, weren't as fortunate and faced constant dilemmas. Through the use of vignettes, I describe their adjustment.

ARRIVAL AT USP ATLANTA

As the BOP vehicle turned off McDonough Boulevard and into USP Atlanta's long circular drive, I sat on the bus looking at the fortress through the bars covering my window. Intimidated, I saw a huge structure that struck me as the looming archetype of everyone's nightmare or Hollywood prison.

The bus stopped in front of the mile-wide steps leading up to the imposing granite edifice. Adding to the dramatic effect, a concrete wall, 40-feet in height, surrounded the entire facility. A doublewide chain-link fence, complete with coils of razor wire woven through it, then enclosed the wall itself, as if to reemphasize that evil needed to be contained within. It was a magnificent piece of architecture, but I would have preferred to limit my knowledge of it to an outside view.

Several guards, all carrying their automatic rifles prominently across their bodies, surrounded the bus and looked alert as a lieutenant stepped on board to address the prisoners. After the lieutenant called our names, we each stepped forward, answered his identifying question, then wobbled off the bus, and began ascending the stairs leading to the prison.

A massive riot, one of the longest running in the history of U.S. prisons, had rocked USP Atlanta only a few months before I arrived. The prison had been holding thousands of Cuban prisoners whom the government had threatened to return to Cuba. The Cubans, deciding that life in American prisons was better than being returned to Castro's prisons, seized control of the institution. They destroyed several of the institution's buildings and held nearly one hundred BOP staff members hostage. No one was killed, but many of the rioters spoke about abusing the hostages. The bus on which I arrived was one of the first admitted into the facility after the administration regained control of the prison.

Opened around 1903, USP Atlanta is the second oldest federal prison in the United States. Unlike the campuslike settings of the newer federal prisons, it's designed along the pattern of a telephone pole. The main corridor represents the long stem of the pole, while the four cellhouses branch off either side like crossbars. Each unit has a capacity of about six hundred men. The entrance gates of the prison are at one end of the main corridor, and about a football field in length away, the chow hall stands at the other.

Once inside the prison, the guards locked us between two gates, the sally port. Once we were inside, the guards unlocked our chains and then led us downstairs into a dungeonlike cavern replete with a series of dank holding cells. As I sat in my holding tank together with the forty or so other prisoners who had ridden the bus with me from FCI Talladega, I looked around the decrepit basement—with its nicotine-stained walls and echoes of slamming steel doors—for more signs that I had been admitted into hell. Perhaps the inscription above the gates to Dante's inferno would have been appropriate: "Abandon all hope, ye who enter here."

Essentially, we went through the same admission procedures I'd come to expect. Since my initial arrest, I had been processed through at least six different penal facilities, some more than once. The only difference in Atlanta was, as a prisoner designated to serve my time there, the guards issued me a complete set of prison garb, an ID card, and a few extra forms to complete. After the three- to-four hour process, the guards led me to A-cellhouse, telling me that I'd been assigned to room 519.

A-CELLHOUSE

A-cellhouse felt like the prototype for the Oklahoma Unit in El Reno. It, too, was a large, rectangular shell with the island of steel cages in the center that lifted up six tiers. The guard unlocked the heavy steel door separating A-cellhouse from the prison's main corridor, and I looked up at all the cages—the rows upon rows of steel bars. I accepted the environment as one in which I would have to learn to live for the next ten years.

It was just before 4:00 P.M. The other five hundred or so prisoners who were assigned to the housing unit were locked in their cells waiting for the count to begin. The Officer in Charge (OIC) issued me a bedroll, then ordered me to climb the stairs leading to the fifth tier. He told me to report to room 519, bed 7.

Anxieties

I experienced a lot of tension as I entered the cellhouse and made the way to my room. After all, this was a maximum-security penitentiary, and I had no idea what to expect. I'd heard rumors of the chaos that reigned behind these walls, but other than living as a "pretrial" and "holdover" prisoner for the past year, I had no experience of living in prison.

The prisoners in USP Atlanta, I'd heard, all were serving lengthy sentences. Some had been locked up for decades and never expected to be released. "How were these prisoners different from what I had known?" I thought to myself as I walked toward my cell.

I was determined to walk into the room with a tough-looking face and introduce myself in a no-nonsense way. But this stance was contrary to my nature. I stand just under 5'10", am of a medium build, and weigh approximately 170. With an easy, almost reflexive smile, I doubt I strike much fear in people.

Besides, I wasn't likely to intimidate anyone while I was quivering with fear myself. As I walked up those ominous stairs, I played scenes in my mind of what I would do if someone approached me the wrong way. By then, I had a year of imprisonment behind me. Those walls outside, and the feel of USP Atlanta, however, were different from any of the other places where I had been held before. People committed desperate offenses behind Atlanta's walls. They killed. They raped. And I knew that I was going to have to live around such madness for years to come. Much of how I lived, I reasoned, would be determined during these first days I served inside.

People in prison lived by their reputations. I was well known in the jails where I was held during my trial, but in Atlanta I wouldn't know anyone. The prison had a capacity of two thousand, and, from what I had heard, its population frequently swelled to nearly three thousand. I knew that it was underpopulated then, because it was being rebuilt after the riot. But that didn't assuage my fear as I walked up those stairs, carrying my bedroll and tormented by my thoughts. I thought of mop ringers, metal garbage cans, locks in socks, folding chairs, and every other object that I had seen turned into a weapon over the past year. If pressed, I convinced myself that I was prepared to use whatever was within reach to strike if anyone tried to prey upon me. I knew that I was young. I expected my appearance and deportment would invite attempts from the predators with whom I was sentenced to share the next quarter century of my life. If they came, I told myself, I would respond in the only manner prisoners understood. Although I had no history of violence, I convinced myself that I could and would employ it to defend myself.

I had heard the prison system is divided along ethnic lines: whites, blacks, and Hispanics. Those groups, I understood through the conversations I had during my first year in confinement, were further divided into subgroups that made up various cliques.

For example, within the group of white prisoners, Italian Americans would generally form one of the more cohesive groups. As long as one wasn't a government informant, an Italian American would be embraced by the group—at least upon his initial arrival.

Other subgroups of white prisoners might be formed along geographic lines, with prisoners from like regions sticking together. Bikers form another subgroup within the white prisoners.

Blacks, I had heard, gravitate toward other blacks who are from their own parts of the country, while foreign blacks—those from the West Indies or Africa especially—usually stick around with their own countrymen.

Prisoners who identify themselves as Hispanics, with Puerto Ricans, Mexicans, Cubans, and Colombians making up the largest groups, also stick together among themselves. I'd heard that one encounters relatively few Asian people in prison.

Besides the racial and ethnic breakdowns, I'd also heard that several prison gangs exist within the penitentiary walls. Generally, these gangs are formed to support the common needs of the gang members. Some of the gangs have ties to criminal organizations on the street, while others exist to form a pseudo-family within the prison system. Each member of the prison gang must follow the gang's code and agree to do whatever is necessary to maintain the gang's "honor," "integrity," or commitment to the gang's values.

Never living as a part of any real group, I was determined to live independently throughout my sentence. I didn't know what this commitment meant or what ramifications would follow it. I just knew that I had goals I wanted to achieve, and that if I obligated myself to follow patterns of behavior inconsistent with my own, I'd be a prisoner forever.

I knew my background of living in an affluent suburb contrasted with those that most of my fellow prisoners had endured; still, I had convinced myself that I'd survive the challenges I was expecting.

Although I have a Spanish surname, my mother is American, and I was raised in a business household with little Hispanic influence. I intended to learn to speak Spanish during my incarceration, but when I began my term I couldn't converse in that language. Instead of trying to learn it right away, I looked to spend my time around others who seemed to come from backgrounds similar to that of the predominantly WASP suburb of Seattle from which I came and identified. Having heard about the volatile race relations in maximum-security prison, I was quite nervous as I walked to my room, and I didn't want to align myself with a group I didn't really understand.

Red, My First Cellmate

When I got to my room, I saw that five other men were already there. All the rooms in the unit were identical: rectangular cement capsules with the front wall of round steel bars separating them from the long tier. Each room held four steel military-style bunk beds. There were eight small, waist-high wall lockers in which prisoners were required to keep all their belongings. An open stainless-steel toilet stood against the back wall.

Red, the only Caucasian, was assigned to the lower bunk below my bed. He was to be my "bunkie." I entered the room, saw the clearly marked bed to which I was assigned, placed my bedroll on it, and introduced myself.

"My name's Michael," I said. "I've been assigned to this bed."

Standing up to greet me, "Red," he said, and shook my hand.

Meeting Red did a lot to ease my anxieties. He was like many of the people with whom I was reared.

Red was about forty, of my same height and build. He completely disarmed me with his easygoing, friendly manner. It was as if we were meeting at a tennis club or social event instead of behind the ominous walls of USP Atlanta. He was a pharmacist, I learned; he had graduated from Columbia University and was in his second year of a five-year sentence for his conviction related to the improper distribution of pharmaceutical drugs. He was hardly the type of prisoner I expected to encounter in a maximum-security prison, a penitentiary.

"Why aren't you in a prison camp?" I asked.

"I was in a camp," Red answered, "but I caught a *shot* (disciplinary infraction) during my second month there for asking a guard to bring me in a pair of tennis shoes. Then, I got shipped to the low in Tallahassee. When I heard about the program here, I volunteered to come. My family lives in Atlanta," he concluded.

"What program?" I asked.

"Didn't you know?"

"No. I just got designated here," I said.

"We're here as a work cadre to keep the prison going while they finish the construction to repair the damage from the riot. To keep the prison running, the BOP shipped out all the high-security guys and brought in volunteers from lows and mediums to work while the prison is being rebuilt. Sometime next year, when the prison brings back the penitentiary guys, we can transfer wherever we want. I'm going to the camp outside the walls," Red said.

"So no one here is high-security?" I asked.

"Not that I know of. We all transferred here in the last couple of months. We expect to leave in about six to ten more."

"I wonder if I'm in that program," I said. "I was designated to Ashland at first, but a couple of days ago, when I was in Talladega, the counselor told me I'd been redesignated here. He didn't say anything about a volunteer program, though."

"How much time do you have?" he asked.

"Forty-five years," I answered.

"Oh my God! That's terrible. No one here, at least I haven't heard of anyone, has that much time. Are you appealing?" he asked.

"I guess. My attorney is working on it, but I'm not really paying much attention. I'm just trying to settle in and get myself together," I said.

"Well you oughta start thinking about your appeal. Your sentence is too long to just let it go."

Red completely relaxed me. Hearing that every other prisoner in Atlanta had come from a low or medium essentially meant there was no danger, no volatility. "Perhaps I'd be able to accomplish my goals after all," I thought. His news that I would have an opportunity to pick the prison I wanted after the work-cadre program expired put me at ease. I was thinking I'd like to return to Talladega. After the bars opened, Red and I left the room and he walked with me around the prison.

Red and I walked to the chow hall, a huge room that looked even bigger than it was because so few prisoners then were confined there. Indeed, prior to the riot, USP Atlanta had held nearly three thousand prisoners; when I arrived, fewer than five hundred men were on the compound. The prison felt open and free. From the chow hall, Red and I walked to the education building, which offered very little because most of the books had been destroyed during the riot. No classes were available.

We went outside to the recreation area, which was huge. It had everything that's available in a large American high school, including a full-length football-soccer field, three baseball diamonds, two weight sites, six tennis courts, and a half-mile running track.

The early September climate was ideal. Indeed, my first day as a prisoner in USP Atlanta couldn't have gone better. Instead of encountering the chaotic atmosphere I anticipated, I found an easy environment in which I was confident I could achieve significant personal goals.

The First Days

As a newly arrived prisoner, I was relatively free to do what I wanted for the first few days. It was such a huge place, like an entire city behind a wall. That first year when I was enclosed in the county jail was nothing like this. With all the freedom to walk around, living in prison was not at all like living in jail. I didn't have a job assignment, so I spent most of my time in the library. Five or six typewriters were available, and I wanted to acclimate myself to the keyboard. So, I began typing letters to people I knew—and to some people I didn't.

When I read a newspaper article expressing views I thought sympathetic with my predicament, I'd type a letter to the author. My hopes were to draw attention to my situation, to let taxpayers know about the lives that would be wasted if these long sentences for nonviolent offenders stood. My problem was that writing didn't come easily to me. I knew I needed to educate myself further. I had the time, but how was I going to accomplish this goal in a prison with no library, much less a school?

Admissions and Orientation (A&O)

The following week I had to proceed through admissions and orientation (A&O). A&O is supposed to help explain the prison's operations to incoming prisoners. A staff representative comes in from each department to describe its function and answer questions. Each staff member speaks for no more than ten minutes, most actually for fewer than five. And the prisoners, especially green ones like myself, ask question upon question, believing the bureaucrats can provide sound advice about how to enhance one's quality of life behind the walls.

During those initial days of my imprisonment I didn't pick up on the prevailing atmosphere of indifference. I wanted to know what I needed to accomplish to demonstrate my commitment to personal growth—to show I'd been "corrected." By then, I had read hundreds of pages of BOP literature and several publications in the law library that detailed BOP rules. Nothing I read, however, defined an exceptionally well-adjusted prisoner. I wanted a model to follow, something to which I could aspire during the years I had to serve. No matter where I looked, I found no guidance.

The other newly arriving prisoners who sat through the A&O procedure with me, many of whom had been confined before at other prisons, were much more cynical. They understood that no answers would come through A&O; staff members participated because policy required it. The guards who spoke would much rather have been sitting behind desks and "supervising" than standing before a group of prisoners rattling off platitudes.

Naively convinced this question–answer session would provide me with guidance, I persisted, totally oblivious to the other prisoners' goals of letting the bureaucrats babble so the meeting would end as quickly as possible.

Employment

When the A&O meeting finally concluded, I continued with the routine I was setting for myself. Wanting to spend as much time as possible in the library, inadequate though it was, I asked one of the supervisors for a job. During A&O I learned that all prisoners were required to be assigned to a work detail with the exception of those who were medically unable to. Prisoners who couldn't find a job on their own would be assigned to job details at random, with most going to food services. After my experience of working in food services at El Reno, I knew I didn't want to get stuck there. So I asked Mr. Buhner, the "educational technician," for a job.

"Submit a cop-out," he said.

A *cop-out* is the informal name staff and prisoners in the federal system give to a one-page form prisoners are supposed to use when requesting staff to do anything. I was learning that virtually every action within the federal prison system requires a form, so I submitted the cop-out as requested. Mr. Buhner signed it, and a few days later I noticed my name on the *callout*, indicating that I'd been assigned to the education work detail.

I was required to show up for work each day at 12:30 P.M. and remain until the 3:30 recall, at which time I was required to return to my assigned room for count. After count was dinner, and at 6:00 I was supposed to return to the education building for my evening shift, which lasted until 8:30.

I had been spending most of my time in the education department during that first week anyway, so I didn't really expect anything to change by my being assigned to work there. It didn't. Mr. Buhner said I could sit behind a desk with a typewriter and pass out books as people requested them. Since there were only two shelves of books in the library, the job didn't task me.

On weekends, the prisoners looked forward to movies shown in the prison's big-screen theater above the chow hall. *Good Morning Vietnam*, with Robin Williams, played on my first Friday evening. Not thinking it mattered where I was in the prison, after the evening meal I went to the theater to watch the movie. After the movie ended, about 8:00 P.M., I walked to the library and received my first reprimand in prison.

"Where were you?" Mr. Buhner asked.

"I went to watch the movie," I answered.

"You were supposed to report to the library for work after dinner," he countered.

"What work? I just sit at the desk and type letters. No one actually comes here. There're no books," I said.

"That doesn't matter. You're on my detail, and I have to know where you are at all times. I'm supposed to write an incident report, but since you're new I'll let it slide. This time. Don't be absent again or I'll write a shot," he warned.

I didn't realize the guards took these jobs so seriously. Mistakenly, I thought that as long as we were within the walls everything was fine. Apparently not. Prisoners had to be at their required spots during the required times. If prisoners were caught out of bounds, as I had been when I watched the movie, they could be cited for violating a prison rule and disciplined. I realized I needed to avoid these incident reports and resolved to learn more about the prison rules and what was expected of me.

Over the next week or so I went about my activities without any complications. I met several other prisoners, all of whom were incarcerated in some other prison prior to their transfer to Atlanta. Everyone seemed to have transferred on a volunteer basis to participate in the work-cadre program Red had told me about. I felt little or no tension in the prison and really grew hopeful I'd find a way to reach my goals. I began writing to schools I'd read about in a guide to correspondence study programs.

Ohio University offered a correspondence program that could lead to a bachelor's degree. Eagerly, I wrote the university a letter and felt motivated when I received a catalog in the mail. I contacted my family, and everyone agreed to support my efforts to educate myself. After I spoke with the supervisor of education, Mr. Thomas, who gave me the authorization I needed to enroll, I sent off for my materials. Finally, a year after my arrest, I was beginning to move forward toward a productive goal. I hoped to earn a college degree within four years.

Team Meeting

During the month, I was called for my initial *team meeting*. Each federal prison uses a unit management system, with each housing unit keeping a mini-administration that controls the activities and prisoners within that unit. As a department head, the unit manager leads the unit team.

Although the prison's warden, the chief executive officer of the prison, sets the overall policy, in an effort to decentralize control and delegate authority, he allows unit managers to implement policies with some degree of discretion. The unit manager also oversees the work of case managers, counselors, and the unit secretary.

BOP policy requires the unit team to schedule an individual team meeting or initial classification with a prisoner within the first four weeks of his arriving at a prison. The unit manager, case manager, counselor, and a representative from both education and psychology attend. During the team meeting, the case manager is supposed to brief the other team members on the prisoner's history and help coordinate a program for him to follow during his period of incarceration.

When I read about the unit management system in Title 28, section 500 of the Code of Federal Regulations, which governs activities of the Bureau of Prisons, I began to anticipate my first team meeting like a child who waits for a report card on which he's confident to receive perfect grades.

After talking with Red and a few other guys, and learning that they would be given a choice of where to go after a year, I felt I would be considered for redesignation, too. By switching me from Ashland to Atlanta, BOP administrators must have recognized me as being worthy of this privileged opportunity to participate in this program, despite the long sentence I received. Or so I thought.

Surely, the team would be impressed with my enrolling in an undergraduate program through correspondence. Perhaps, when my year was up and the prison reverted to holding high-level offenders, the unit team would approve my transfer to FCI Talladega or some other modern prison where I could continue my efforts to earn freedom.

When I appeared before the team, however, I learned that, to say the least, my enthusiasm was premature. The case manager began by reciting information from my presentence investigation report to the other members of the unit team.

"This is inmate Santos, one-six-three-seven-seven-double-zero-four," my case manager, Mr. Terry, began. "He was the leader of a major cocaine distribution network in Seattle. Inmate Santos received a forty-five year sentence, and he is not eligible for parole. His projected release date is October 2013. As the leader of a sophisticated criminal enterprise, I am recommending inmate Santos for special monitoring in both our Central Inmate Monitoring system and our Sophisticated Criminal Activity system. We'll keep a watch on him."

He continued, "Santos graduated high school and there is no record of psychological problems. I'm placing two public safety factors on him: one for sentence length, another for being convicted of a greatest-severity offense," he concluded.

After reciting his summary, and without yet acknowledging me, Mr. Terry asked the other team members whether they had any questions. When no one expressed an interest, I asked permission to speak.

"You speak only when spoken to, Mr. Santos," the unit manager cut me off. "Does this inmate have a financial obligation?" he asked.

"Yes," the case manager answered as if I weren't in the room. "He has a $500,000 fine, and $1,100 in criminal assessment fees. I will enroll him in the inmate financial responsibility program."

Then, for the first time, the case manager addressed me.

"Sign this form. It authorizes us to take $25 each month from your account to apply toward your financial obligations," he says. "If you refuse to sign, the unit team will place you on refusal status and discontinue your privilege of telephone use, commissary, and visiting. Do you agree to participate in the financial responsibility program?" he finally asked.

"Yes." I answered.

"Sign this form."

I did.

"Are there any more questions?" the case manager asked the other members of the unit team.

When no one responded, he turned to me a second time. "Now, Mr. Santos, do you have any concerns or questions for your unit team?"

"Yes. First of all, please call me Michael. I'm only 24, and when I hear Mr. Santos I look around for my father."

"Don't get cute with us," the unit manager broke in. "I don't know where you think you are, but you are an inmate at USP Atlanta. In my unit you will address my staff as Mr. or Ms. followed by the staff member's name. There will be no first names used, and don't get smart," he added.

"I wasn't getting smart, I just ..." he cut me off again.

"Do you have any questions for the unit team at this juncture?"

"Yes. Some of the other inmates told me we are here on a volunteer work cadre program and that when the prison reverts to holding high-security inmates, we will have the opportunity to choose the prison where we would like to transfer. Where can I get more information on the choices available?" I asked.

"Mr. Santos," the unit manager began. "You must be a little slow. A federal judge sentenced you to forty-five years imprisonment. Although it may not be apparent to you, it is obvious to me and the other professional members of this unit team that you need the high-security of USP Atlanta; you're the kind of man this prison was built to hold. You have been appropriately designated and will remain within these walls until we determine a transfer is warranted. In your case, Mr. Santos, I can assure you it will be longer than one year. Now, since you have no further questions, we will adjourn this meeting. The unit team will see you again in six months."

After that initial team meeting, I began to realize two things. First, it became patently clear to me that my unit team didn't place me in the same category as the other prisoners. They were volunteers in a work-cadre program and were waiting for transfer to other locations. I was a long-term prisoner who "needed" to be held behind the 40-foot walls. I also learned the unit team didn't exist to help me plan my future. I would have to move forward. Alone. "Fortunately," I thought, "the supervisor of education had already granted me permission to begin through correspondence." That program, I hoped, would bring me some freedom, even if it was mental rather than physical.

My life during those first months in prison revolved around my job. It gave me a reason to wake up in the morning and helped my time pass. I wouldn't have known what to do with my time without it. Staying in the unit and getting hooked on soap operas and card games didn't feel like a realistic option. I had begun an exercise routine and wanted to develop my physique, but that was an evening routine. At 7:30 each morning, I enjoyed going to the library, reading, and figuring out some way to make my day productive as I waited for my schoolwork to arrive. I wrote a lot of letters to my sisters, my parents, and friends I had known prior to the time I joined Alex in the scheme to sell cocaine. I described my environment to them, but mostly, I was eager to tell anyone of my commitment to grow during my confinement.

The materials and instructions for my first courses arrived, and over the next several months I kept to myself and served relatively easy time, content to work through my correspondence courses.

Most of the prisoners with whom I was originally in USP Atlanta were like Red. They were docile guys who, for the most part, didn't bother anyone. Many had come from prison camps, and if it were not for their khaki uniforms, one wouldn't even know they were federal prisoners. Their mannerisms didn't differ much from people outside of prison. Clearly, prison was a temporary stop for these men who had come as volunteers on the work cadre. They weren't doing anything behind prison walls to aggravate their problems. Indeed, with most of the other prisoners trying to move on to new destinations, there was little tension behind the walls of USP Atlanta. I was fortunate to arrive when I did.

Although I didn't know it when I first got there, USP Atlanta was designated as an administrative facility when I arrived, which meant it was authorized to hold prisoners from all security levels. Since most of the prisoners were there on a work cadre to keep the prison running while construction was being completed, the administration managed the prison as if it were a lower-security institution. By early 1989, however, several changes were being made. After I'd been in the prison for about six months, the prison began reverting to penitentiary status, meaning only high-security prisoners could be held there.

Changes

Six to ten months after the Atlanta gates closed behind me, buses began arriving daily. They deposited prisoners from other federal penitentiaries and removed the work-cadre prisoners. By 1989, most of the 500 prisoners who were with me originally had transferred out. Eventually, the prisoner population swelled to over twenty-seven hundred, most of whom were brought in from Marion, Lewisburg, Terre Haute, and Leavenworth—all maximum-security penitentiaries. The population and everything else about the prison changed dramatically.

The first changes started when the administration began installing numerous fences around the compound and stretching cables across the tops of the walls to tighten security. Then, it implemented a controlled-movement system, limiting the prisoners' ability to move from place to place within the institution.

Whereas I used to walk directly to the yard from my unit when I wanted to exercise, the new rules required prisoners to request a written pass from the unit officer before going anywhere. Passes were issued during a ten-minute span, beginning five minutes before the top of the hour and concluding five minutes after the top of the hour.

Besides having to request a pass, prisoners had to wait for guards to unlock all the doors and gates that block access from one area to another. To get to the yard from my housing unit, prisoners had to wait for the guard to open the unit door. Then we'd have to wait for the corridor officer to unlock the door opening into the main corridor. If visitors were walking through the corridor, the guard would delay these ten-minute prisoner moves.

Once prisoners made it through the main corridor, we'd have to wait in line to pass through a metal detector. If the metal detector went off, the offending prisoner would be required to remove any metal he was carrying. If the metal detector continued to beep while the prisoner walked through it, the guard would require the prisoner to strip naked for an inspection before he'd allow him to pass. Because scores of prisoners from both directions would be trying to move through the metal detector during designated hourly moves, delays regularly occurred. After passing through the metal detector, prisoners going to the yard would have to pass through two additional guarded gates before making it to the yard or gym. The security became tighter after the newer prisoners arrived, a stern indication of their presence.

By the time the prisoner population changed, construction had been completed on two of the other housing units, B- and D-cellhouses. I was transferred to B-cellhouse, room 616. The new cellhouses were much more accommodating, with two-man rooms and individual showers. When I was housed in my initial room in A-cellhouse, it was like living in a high-school locker room. And most of the guys, serving short sentences and eager to move on, weren't too much different from the people with whom I grew up. Many of the new prisoners coming in to USP Atlanta, on the other hand, had been living in prison for several years or decades already, some never expecting to go home. It was a different group entirely.

B-CELLHOUSE

The new two-man rooms and single showers offered at least a semblance of privacy. One could close the door. My new cellmate, Mike, was a decent 40-year-old guy who'd just arrived after having received a twenty-year sentence. He was convicted of smuggling 500 kilograms of cocaine through the Windward Passage in the Caribbean Sea. We called him Windward.

After Windward and I moved into B-cellhouse, and the buses began delivering new long-term prisoners, Paul and Dan, two Italian-American brothers from St. Louis moved into the cell next to mine. Paul and Dan were much older than I, both in their forties or early fifties. They were pretty well acclimated to the prison environment.

Accused of being leaders of an organized criminal organization, they were serving long sentences and were well respected by other prisoners. Indeed, many of those who arrived—whether they knew Paul and Dan personally or by reputation—came to say hello in an obvious attempt to ingratiate themselves.

Paul and Dan became good friends of mine. In fact, although I had passed two years in prison by the time I met them, they became the first good friends I made in confinement. I introduced myself when they first arrived, and we got along well from the beginning. Before long, we were eating dinner together every night and spent hours talking about different life experiences. My naïveté about the world in which my actions had put me—totally incongruous with the sentence I was serving—amused them. It also freed them to open up with me.

Just as the notoriety I received from media attention and rumor had shielded me from conflict while I was in the Pierce County Jail, I am certain my friendship with Paul and Dan shielded me from problems other green prisoners had to endure at USP Atlanta. Although we were from different generations, it was easy to like both Paul and Dan. Whereas I felt humiliated at being a prisoner, neither of them saw anything wrong with their status in life and expressed no regret for where their choices had brought them. Besides that, they had absolutely no fear and were completely at home in the penitentiary. I admired their courage and hoped that, in time, I, too, could develop the same level of comfort with living in that abnormal, caged environment where I was destined to spend so much of my life. Dan and Paul became role models for me.

As the prison population began to transform from low to high security, the level of problems within the institution began to escalate. Instead of prisoners like Red and the others who were held in the penitentiary when I arrived, many of these newly arriving prisoners accepted their place in the prison and seemed perfectly content to make it their world; instead of thinking about "moving on" or "getting out," career prisoners, I was learning, choose to live inside the walls and express virtually no interest in matters outside.

This isn't to say the prisoners around me didn't complain about the long terms they were serving. They did. Constantly. It's just that after having served so many years, and having so many more years before release would come—if it ever would come—these men chose to live day by day with what goes on around them.

Rather than committing to what seemed like a futile struggle to advance their release dates, the prisoners looked for ways to re-create the world they knew outside within the walls of the penitentiary.

The Other Prisoners

Generally, the people designated to serve their sentences at USP Atlanta have been convicted of violent crimes or large-scale drug trafficking offenses; have long criminal histories; or have been found guilty of violating too many disciplinary infractions at lower-security prisons. The prison monotony bores a lot of them, so they look for ways to bring some excitement into their lives.

Unlike the world beyond prison walls, inside the penitentiary a person doesn't distinguish himself by achieving a high level of academic or professional success. Instead, an individual advances within the social hierarchy by establishing a reputation as a *stand-up guy*.

Honor and respect are not virtues given to the family man or the individual who works through traditional channels to achieve personal goals. In prison, such people are *legitimate suckers* or *square johns*. An *honorable guy*, or a good guy, is one who can be counted upon to keep his mouth shut when confronted by law enforcement; a man who will back his friends regardless of the consequences; a man who has no compunction about splitting another man's head open, smashing him with a pipe, or stabbing him with a prison-made knife if there is the slightest perception of "disrespect."

The penitentiary is civilized society turned upside down. It's a place where cheers are loudest when movies show the cop getting shot or the rat getting killed. Violence is the order of the day, and if one wants "respect" in the penitentiary, one must let the other convicts know, in no uncertain terms, that they'll pay a heavy price for conveying disrespect.

Living in the Jungle

Because I was familiar with USP Atlanta before the other high-security prisoners began to arrive, I noticed new faces before they noticed me. The predators of the prison generally wouldn't begin looking for trouble, "drama," until they had settled in. They'd need to spot their marks, their easy prey.

There's no doubt in my mind that had I not been considered a close friend of Paul and Dan, I would have been "tried" by any number of predators. And as a long-term prisoner at USP Atlanta, the only long-term solution would be to respond violently. Seeking protection from staff or other prisoners isn't a credible solution. Rather, it's an invitation for even greater problems.

There were countless flatterers, sycophants, and wannabe gangsters trying to impress or win favor with Paul and Dan, and everyone in the prison knew it. Both were well known among prisoners from St. Louis, Chicago, and

Florida as being fearless, capable, and ready to respond to any threat to their reputations. Whereas others glorified their criminal exploits to Dan and Paul, trying to enhance their reputations by appearing as supercriminals or well connected to other criminal groups, I made it clear that, although I was serving a lengthy sentence, I was a nobody in crime. They laughed when I described myself as a square john. "Square Johns don't get forty-five years on their first offense," Paul said. As I told them of my so-called criminal organization, and that seventy people testified against me at trial, I made no secret that I had never carried a weapon and that no one on the planet had reason to be afraid of me. They accepted me as a friend, I think, because I didn't disguise myself or try to affect the aura of someone I wasn't.

Because prisoners never escape the thousands of eyes and constant gossip within the penitentiary, it was well known that Paul, Dan, and I ate dinner together and walked around the yard in the early evenings. Since we spent a lot of free time together, any attempt to "try" me would simultaneously be construed as being disrespectful to them. We were friends. And in prison, what is done to one is done to everyone within a group. Our friendship spared me conflicts I otherwise would have encountered.

When we became friends, I didn't realize how important our relationship would be to my own ability to focus on my goals. Dan and Paul came on one of the first buses of new prisoners, and when they moved into the cell next to mine the prison was still relatively peaceful. Within a few months later, however, the complete atmosphere of the penitentiary had changed. All of the prisoners like Red and his ilk had been moved out to minimum-security camps. Whereas they had minded their own business, the new fellas were committed to the penitentiary way of life. There was a lot of open drunkenness. Extortion artists banned together. Strong-arm robberies of prisoners leaving the commissary were a weekly happening. It was a different world. Without Dan and Paul's protection, instead of working toward my goals and keeping a clean disciplinary record, I would have had to focus on defending myself against becoming a target of the psychopathic personalities that the penitentiary breeds.

I was working on my schoolwork nearly all the time. When not working directly on school assignments, I was struggling to improve my writing skills by interviewing other prisoners and writing stories or op-ed pieces that described the prison environment to taxpayers who had no concept of the length of time people were serving behind the penitentiary's walls.

Perhaps people didn't care about what went on behind the walls because they didn't know, I thought. So if I were between assignments or classes, I'd interview other prisoners about their experiences within the penitentiary and attempt to describe the questionable justice by which the courts had sentenced them.

Other prisoners who weren't perceived as being well connected within the walls—at least the ones who were unfamiliar with the code of penitentiary behavior or were unwilling to plunge steel into another man's skin—paid a heavy price.

PREDATORS IN THE PENITENTIARY

The interviews I conducted within the prison helped me understand the traumatic experiences some other prisoners endured. Many of them hadn't been confined before and didn't know a soul when they arrived. Worse, they began serving their time with the same hopes that I had: they would mind their own business, stay out of trouble, and do what they could to get out of the environment.

The difference between us was their lack of powerful friends—and they weren't given time to find allies. From the moment they walked into the unit, with bedrolls under their arms and nervousness in their step, eyes were watching. Then comments and questions circulated.

"Did you see the new guy?"

"What's he about?"

"He's got sugar in his tank, walks like a bitch."

"Scared of his shadow."

"Is he a snitch?"

"Did he go to the store yet? I want his commissary."

"Who's he with?"

With so many predators watching the newly arriving prisoner's every move, the mark has no avenues of escape. It's an immediate test, and his response to the environment will establish "what kind of guy he is." If it becomes known that he seeks protection from the guards, the mark begins an unshakable reputation as being a rat and worthy of everything bad that comes to him.

Gangs and Crews

Predators from the different gangs might offer a target protection—for a heavy price. Or the mark might be tried by a "crew." Although both can be predatory, gangs and crews differ in their structure.

Gangs are pseudofamilies within the prison, with members referring to each other as brothers. They have a hierarchical structure, and when one joins the gang, he becomes a member for life, beholden to the leadership and expected to carry out the gang's business. Even if it means killing, stabbing, or slashing, a loyal gang member will perform the order without hesitating or concern for the consequences. Indeed, many are proud of their evil deeds, happy to demonstrate their honor in carrying out the orders they receive that result in bloodshed or death.

Gang members make themselves easily known. Many black gang members flash signs by contorting their fingers and flashing hand movements, or they wear their clothing in a particular manner. White gang members cover themselves in tattoos, many of which have identifying meanings. The gang members associate with each other, pass their time together. They are involved in different rackets within the penitentiary, and when someone wants to join the gang, they have to subject themselves to some type of initiation rights. They may have to perform acts of violence, for example, or they may have to make themselves vulnerable to a particularly risky activity—like smuggling heroin into the penitentiary. People join gangs to bolster their reputation among those whom they admire in the penitentiary society. It's as if they have no further interest in participating in the society outside of prison again. I'll always remember one gang member bragging about how he "just got out of the hole in Lewisburg after having left C-low's guts falling out his stomach."

With few exceptions, the members of predatory groups are of the same race, and frequently they come from the same geographical areas. Sometimes the group members pledged allegiance to their gangs while on the street. Most, however, join the gangs during their terms of confinement.

Crews are different. A crew represents a group of guys who may participate in activities together or spend time shoulder to shoulder. But unlike a gang, there is no formal alliance, established leadership, or pledges to do each other's bidding. Predatory crews may form alliances with other gangs or operate independently. Either way, they're not part of the brotherhood and have no obligations to each other.

In an effort to find some protection within the predatory walls of USP Atlanta, many young prisoners stand in line looking for opportunities to prove themselves worthy of membership with gangs, or they may seek to form their own crews. They recognize that in the penitentiary, strength comes through alliances; the more people with whom one is connected, the less vulnerable he will be to predation.

Ron's Predatory Crew I spoke with Ron, a guy who ran with a predatory crew for the first few years of his term. Since then, Ron says he's tried to get his life together and quit living in a way that could bring him more problems.

Ron, who stands about 6'4" and weighs well over two hundred, says he participated in the schemes because he was bored in the prison and had nothing to do. He'd made friends with some of the other guys in the crew, and he began standing with them on their money-raising ventures as a kind of enforcer. Ron's look intimidates.

"We'd see a young white guy come in who didn't seem to know anyone in the joint," Ron explained. "We'd keep asking around what the guy's about, questioning others about whether the guy's a rat.

"By asking enough guys if the mark's a rat," Ron continued, "someone is bound to say they heard that he was. And once a guy's got the snitch jacket, he's pretty much open and no one's going to step up for him or care if he's taken out.

"Anyway," Ron went on, "we'd usually just wait for the guy to get his money and go to the store to buy shoes, sweats, and other commissary. Then, once he'd put his stuff away, maybe climbed on his bunk to rest, five or six of us would roll in his cell; one or two guys would stand outside the cell to watch for the cops.

"While one of the guys opened the locker and started taking the goods he'd just bought from the commissary," Ron said, "another would tell the dude he had two choices: he could stand up and get his ass whipped, or he could just keep lying there and say nothing.

"Most of the time, Ron concluded, "the guy wouldn't do nothing. And before we left, we told the guy he oughta just check into protective custody. Or, if he chose to stay on the 'pound, he'd better just forget our faces. Otherwise he'd have a problem with all of us, and others he didn't know."

"Nine times out of ten," Ron estimated, "the guy *checks in* (seeks protective custody) and we never see him again. It's easy when you know the mark doesn't know anyone. Especially once he has the rat label."

When I asked Ron whether it bothered him at all to participate in these vulturelike moves, preying on the weak, he told me he didn't even think about it when he was doing it. He was just bored in the prison; he didn't have anything to do, had nothing to look forward to, and wanted to make a reputation in prison. He did it for kicks and proudly became known as a crazy white boy.

SEXUAL PREDATORS

Another form of pressure, or *press game*, is sexual in nature. Prisoners will attempt to *turn out* a guy, to convert a nonhomosexual into a prison prostitute who will then be used to generate money for a gang or crew. A variation on the turn-out approach is a "softer approach" that feigns friendship. How a prisoner responds when approached may well dictate how well he will spend his time in prison: some yield, some ask for protective custody, and some fight with varying results.

The Turn-Out Game

Some prison crews were notorious for this power-tripping game, convinced that the more men they turned out, the more they enhanced their own status as men. Sometimes they did it for their own sexual gratification; ironically, such prisoners didn't consider themselves homosexuals. "I ain't no fag just 'cause he be sucking me off. He da bitch," these predators reasoned. Most of the times, though, the turn-out crews were about power and creating prostitutes whom they considered as their own property. Just another exploitative move in the abnormal world behind prison walls.

One strategy the turn-out crews use is to spot the newly arriving prisoner who seems to be lost. They loan the mark whatever he needs to settle into the prison. After the debt grows large enough to the point where they know the guy would have a problem repaying it, the predator asks the mark for some type of favor that's beyond the mark's reach. For example, they might ask him to procure an unattainable knife from the kitchen or steal one of the radios the guards use to communicate. Neither is a realistic option.

"What, you motherfucker," the predator will scream, after being denied by the target. "I've been looking out for you all this time, and you can't even do this favor for me when I need it! Fuck you then. Give me my shit."

The predator then demands payment of $500, perhaps $1,000, knowing the mark can't pay it. When he doesn't, the predator forces his target to perform sexual acts and uses him as a prostitute to pay off the debt.

A Softer Approach

There's a softer approach to the turn-out game, too. A predator befriends a target when he comes into the prison. He invites the mark to eat with him or to work out. As they get to know each other, the predator starts joking in a sexual way. He says something like, "Yo, I'm working on the vascularity of my love muscle. Check it out and see how it's coming." If the target just laughs it off, the predator continues, each time becoming more graphic and personal.

If the mark just keeps laughing it off, thinking the dialogue a joke, his problems escalate. Quickly. The jokes actually are a violation of the target's manhood and a test of his character. Clearly, no one would insult a *solid* guy with such jokes. If the target doesn't respond assertively to the test, the jokes soon may turn into pressure to perform a homosexual act.

Rick's Experience Rick was sent to the prison in 1993. A rock musician on the street, he had shoulder-length blond hair and a slim build. Fear was written all over him. His look, coupled with the fright on his face, rendered Rick a target of every type of predator in the penitentiary.

Upon his arrival on the tier, two physically intimidating convicts stepped to Rick with a commissary list. They told Rick he was living on "their" tier, and if he wanted to live without problems, he would have to pay. Rick told them he didn't have much, but he would pay what he could. Rick's meek response to the predators was his big mistake. By failing to stand his ground assertively, he became a mark. Once Rick showed his weakness, the predators began exploiting him in every way they could.

At first, the predators ordered Rick to shop for them. Rather than confront them, Rick figured he would avoid a potential problem by buying the predators what he could. When they began submitting commissary lists for more than he could afford, they began demanding that he perform other "services" for them.

They gave Rick a choice. Either he could work for them as a prostitute in the prison, or, since he was from the Atlanta area and frequently received visits, he could smuggle drugs into the prison for the predators.

Rick was serving a twenty-five year sentence for distribution of cocaine and possession of a firearm. With so much time ahead of him to serve, Rick was lost and saw no way out of his problem. Instead of responding to the extortion in the only way that predators understand, and refusing to expose himself to further stiff penalties for convictions of drug crimes, Rick—who was not a homosexual prior to his incarceration—chose the lesser felony of sodomy for pay. He was allowed to split part of the fee with his predators.

Before long, Rick was walking around with shaved legs and using colored pencils for eyeliner and lipstick.

Protective Custody (PC) A prisoner who can't cope with the pressure from other prisoners may seek protection from the administration. To seek protective custody, he must approach a staff member, usually a guard, or a lieutenant, and tell him that his life is in danger and he needs to get off the compound. After some questioning of the prisoner, the guards will escort him to segregation, where he will be confined in a small cell and denied access to the relative freedom others, including the predators, enjoy on the prison's compound.

Many in the general population despise prisoners who check into protective custody. Instead of feeling sympathy for another human being who is living in fear for his life, long-term prisoners view checking into PC as a cowardly act and suspect all who move to PC as being rats or government informants. They firmly believe that lieutenants allow the victim to hide out in PC until he provides them information about various people on the compound.

After a period of time, the individual who checks into PC may transfer to another institution. Wherever he goes, though, his record will remain tainted as a prisoner who sought protection from others through staff members. It's a reputation that likely will subject him to victimization by the thousands of other prisoners with whom he lives. For that reason, many prisoners who can't make it on their own choose to join a gang to seek protection; some, like Rick, succumb to the pressures of the predators.

Jim's Response Jim, a twenty-year-old prisoner, came to prison with a life sentence. Slim, white, and fair-haired, he looked like the type of guy the predators could victimize. As with Rick, two guys stepped to Jim and told him he was living on their tier and that he'd have to pay. Jim shook his head and said fine. He told the extortionists that he'd be going to the commissary the following day, and that they ought to give him their list.

The next day, before going to the store, Jim put one of the large mop buckets and ringers in the back of his cell. After Jim returned from the store with his bag, the predators came calling. Jim stood with his back to them and appeared to be mopping his cell.

"Yo. Got my shit?" the predator asked.

"Sure," Jim said. "It's in the bag in the locker."

The guy stepped in the cell to get it. When he did, Jim reached for the metal mop ringer, which he had strategically placed in front of him, smashing it down on the predator's head, knocking him down to the ground, and causing him to bleed profusely from the wound. The predator's partner took off running.

Jim stood over the predator-turned-prey and said, "I'm already serving one life sentence. You'd better stay the fuck away from me before I catch another."

I asked Jim why he used a mop ringer instead of a *shank* (prison-made knife), a pipe, or one of the other more popular prison weapons.

"I don't like shanks or other weapons. If the cops find 'em, they not only take 'em, but they also might give me a charge. Really, I don't like weapons at all, and I'm not looking for problems. But if someone brings 'em to me, I'll give 'em all the trouble they want. And I'll do it without weapons that can put me in a pinch. I like the mop ringer because it's heavy and can do a lot of damage. But I could just as easily use one of the steel-folding chairs, or I could put these two locks in a sock and stop somebody in a hurry. And don't underestimate the use of these steel-toed shoes," he said with a grin.

Jim fit the profile of a stand-up con. A problem came to him, and he handled it without "runnin' to the man"—and without becoming a victim.

Rico's Story Rico came into the prison as a young man, in his early twenties, with a five-year sentence. Upon his arrival, a well-known sexual predator eyed Rico, and he was convinced the predator was scoping him out as a target.

At the time, Rico was trying to ingratiate himself with one of the prison gangs. He told the leader of the gang, Henry, about his problem, and Henry told him how to solve it.

"Look, Homes, if you're willing to solve this problem yourself, we'll back you. But we can't solve it for you," Henry said.

"No," Rico answered. "I can handle him."

The predator hadn't actually done anything to Rico. He was just following him around, and, Rico said, looking at him as if he were a woman. Such glances are disrespectful in prison, and Rico intended to resolve it.

"Who's the dude," Henry asked.

"Tyrell," Rico answered.

"That muthafucker up to his same ol' shit? He's a big bastard though. We can catch him on the weight pile."

Rico says that in addition to being a well-known sexual predator, Tyrell also was a body builder. He spent all day on the bench press with over three hundred pounds on the bar.

"This afternoon," Henry said, "when he's working out you be down in the yard. I'll bring some of my brothers. We'll be around, but no one'll know we're with you. When you see him with a lot of weight on the bar, close to his max and only pushing three or four, and after he's pressed it enough times that he needs a spot, be ready," Henry instructed.

Then, Henry issued his instructions. "I want you to grab one of the curl bars. One of them z-shaped muthafuckers. When Tyrell's racking the weight, smash the bar down on his head. When you do, my brothers and me will let anyone in the gym know that you're with us. No one else'll get involved."

"Cool," Rico said. "I'm down."

"Okay. So I'll see you in the gym after lunch," Henry assured him.

After lunch that day, Rico said he did exactly as Henry told him. Tyrell was pressing close to his max, and just after he racked the weight, Rico slammed the bar down on Tyrell's head, killing him with the blow.

Rico believed Tyrell had disrespected him, and that was enough, in his mind, to warrant lethal force. It was not enough for the U.S. Attorney, though, as Rico was charged with first-degree murder and given a life sentence to run consecutive to his five-year term.

"Anyone can be a tough guy in prison," Rico said. "You've just got to be willing to pay the price." Rico was willing to pay the price.

CONCLUSION

Through the use of re-created conversations and vignettes, in this chapter I described my first encounters as a prisoner inside USP Atlanta. My experiences differed significantly from those who enter the penitentiary without strong ties to the criminal world because when I initially arrived, there were no high-security prisoners on the compound. There was no one to threaten or challenge me. By the time the higher-security prisoners began arriving, I already had made close alliances with leaders in the prison population. Those alliances shielded me from the life-threatening problems others encountered. In the next chapter, I continue the use of vignettes and dialogue to provide a closer glimpse into the prison subculture.

5

Prison Society

The society behind prison walls is at odds with the society outside because the people have such different values. In this chapter (and those that follow), I will try to explain prison society and its values. Prisoners advance themselves in the social hierarchy in ways that are totally incongruous with the outside society. Concepts like integrity, honor, and respect take on entirely new meanings behind prison walls. I will look at the norms of the prison subculture, and then, through the continuing use of dialogues and vignettes, explore the individual aspects of it.

PRISON SUBCULTURE

Administrators at USP Atlanta may attribute the significant amount of violence that occurs behind its walls to the violent cultures from which the prisoners come. Many of the men confined have long histories of violence, and their ways don't change upon entry into the penitentiary. Outside, these men surrounded themselves with weapons, and, if they felt others had abused or disrespected them in any way, the code of the streets and their peculiar concepts of masculinity required them to respond with violence—lethal violence. One morning I heard Mongo, a prisoner outside my cell, describing his competence as a man to another prisoner.

Mongo said, "What'cha talkin' bout? When I was on the street I was 'bout my business, and I'm 'bout my muthafuckin' business in here. You wanna see my paperwork? I'll show you!"

It was understood that Mongo's "business" wasn't a local Texaco station that he managed, and his "paperwork" wasn't his résumé. Rather, Mongo was talking about his legal documents from court, which likely would have identified the many occasions when Mongo had been charged with crimes of violence.

In addition to their backgrounds, however, the deprivation that all prisoners endure contributes to the violence as well. Being cut off from legitimate opportunities to meet their needs, and recognizing weak incentives to abide by the rules, many long-term prisoners espouse and support an underground society that differs significantly from the one found outside of the walls. Since prisoners have little or no access to opportunities for earning meaningful incomes, they engage in illicit money-raising ventures; since they have little or no access to female companionship, they pressure weaker male prisoners into sexual submission; since they have little or no control over their choice of entertainment, they invite "drama" to enliven their days and nights.

This lack—coupled with long, nonparoleable sentences—encouraged the nearly three thousand high-security prisoners in the USP Atlanta penitentiary to develop their own rules and values, many of which diametrically opposed the rules and values that bind legitimate society.

THE VALUES OF THE PRISON SUBCULTURE

The subculture of prison, spawned by violent histories and the deprivation environment, may contribute to the high recidivism rates from which long-term prisoners suffer. Because the "expected" behavior of individuals in the prison subculture contrasts so significantly with the "expected" behavior of people in a nonpenal community, it follows that the more one accepts and immerses oneself in the prison subculture, the less capable he becomes of functioning in the world beyond prison walls. It turns out that the "system" is not correctional in nature at all.

Activities leading to respect and advancement among one's peers outside of prison include educating oneself, distinguishing oneself in one's chosen career, contributing to one's community, building a strong family, and helping others. Outside, people generally respect laws and live their lives within the boundaries those laws establish. While locked up, on the other hand, one demonstrates his allegiance to the values of the penitentiary by cheering in a crowded television room whenever the villain triumphs over a victim—and especially whenever a law enforcement representative is killed. In the brotherhood of felons, an antisociety mentality prevails.

In the "society of captives," as one celebrated criminologist refers to penal institutions, the men reject these values. No long-term prisoner will advance his position in this abnormal society through educational accomplishments. Despite the multidecade sentences these men serve, few give serious thought to developing meaningful careers to be entered into upon release.

Further, contributing to the community implies that one is in harmony with the administration. This is anathema to most prisoners. It can lead to excommunication or worse. Even helping a victim or showing compassion represents a sign of weakness. In prison, cooperating with the law or administrative rules represents the surest way to create enmity and invite open hostility from other prisoners. Success in prison is based on becoming known as a stand-up guy and developing a reputation others must respect.

Stand-up Guys

When a man commits to the subculture of prison, definitions of honor, respect, integrity, and character take on entirely new meanings that are completely at odds with the world of noncriminals. To a *stand-up guy*, perhaps the pinnacle of the social pecking order, robbers, racketeers, extortionists, drug dealers, and even killers are good guys. They're *honorable men* as long as they never rat.

Indeed, when men of character in the prison subculture talk about a man's honor or integrity, they refer to a man's commitment to the criminal code. The core of that code involves taking care of one's own problems and never cooperating with the law. Becoming a man of character and respect means one has advanced in the criminal world, mastering deception so as to elude detection of law enforcement.

Law-abiding citizens believe that integrity and good character imply a life of no secrets, a model life where one feels pride in his actions, leaving them open for the world to examine. *Transparency* has become a favored term in the discussion of personal lives, corporate behavior, and political action. Not so in the subculture of prison.

Integrity and good character to stand-up guys in the prison imply the opposite: that one can keep his mouth shut and mind his own business. Indeed, prisoners frequently express pride in their commitment to this code of behavior.

When one long-term prisoner says, "We have to check his pedigree, find out what kind of guy he is," he actually wants to determine how committed the individual is to the criminal way of life. "We're criminals," stand-up guys will say. "Our code of conduct doesn't allow us to live like legitimate suckers. We've got reputations, a pedigree to maintain."

Prison Reputations and the Social Hierarchy

As a person serves time in prison, he develops a reputation among his fellow prisoners. Because he lives in a closed, circulating society, a prisoner's reputation (usually formed and typed early on) follows him around for the duration of his term.

The men keep their eyes on each other at all times, wanting to know who is involved in which racket and how each individual copes with the stress of the inevitable challenges that present themselves inside the walls. Whereas I structured my time to avoid interactions, participating in classes, holding a full-time job in the prison factory's business office, and spending a lot of time alone, reading, writing, or exercising, others lived in the penitentiary as if they were on their own turf. I purposely lived as a stranger inside the walls, hoping to move through the time unnoticed, while others were conspicuous, hostile, reckless, and oblivious to the volcanic volatility around them.

Every day I calculated the steps I could take to avoid conflict, yet I knew I was living in a community where others felt comfortable or at ease with Armageddon and looked to altercations as a welcome break to the daily monotony of penitentiary structure. Rather than avoiding conflict, some (whom I will describe in this and subsequent chapters) actually courted it, knowing that battle and calloused defiance would bolster their reputations and distinguish them within the twisted value system of the penitentiary just as top-tier educational credentials distinguish job applicants in the broader American society. I present vignettes of such prisoners, frequently using their own words.

Smoke Smoke, for example, enjoys a fierce reputation in Atlanta. Prisoners know he won't hesitate to kill if provoked. When I was there he already had served over twenty years of a life sentence.

In the 1970s Smoke entered the state of Maryland prison system with a charge for inciting a riot. He was twenty and faced a twelve-month sentence. He's never gotten out since that initial arrest.

"I'd just come in da pen," Smoke said. "I was carryin' my bedroll as I was walkin' down da tier towar' my cell. Some muthafucka slid his hand through the bars and grabbed my ass. 'Yo. You mine, bitch nigga tells me. I took a good look at dat nigga's face, knowin' I'd have to handle im.''

"Later dat afternoon, when da bars open, da muthafucka comes to see me. He starts talkin' out 'is ass 'bout how I's 'is bitch. Dat he gonna pass me 'round to a few a 'is homies, but says mostly he'd be havin' me suck niggas off for a carton a smokes and shit. He tells me to let 'em know if I get any money sent and he'll tell me what to buy.

"Man, looky here. I stood der listenin' to this G runnin' 'is press game on me 'cause I want'd ta see what he's 'bout. Nigga wadn't shit. Da muthafucka din't know I had my shit wit me. When I heard 'nough, I drove my steel right square in dat bitch's heart, looked him in da eye and tol' dat nigga if he want'd me to suck 'is dick he'd have to wait for me in hell. Nigga done picked da wrong nigga ta fuck wit."

That was Smoke's first killing in prison. Since then he said he's been convicted of killing six other people, including two Maryland prison guards. When an appeals court converted Smoke's death sentence into life without parole in the early eighties, the state of Maryland deemed him too violent to hold in its system and transferred him into the Federal Bureau of Prisons.

Smoke identifies himself as the leader of a large religious group that many prison officials deem a front for his gang. He freely states that people give him his respect because they know he won't hesitate to "peel their skull" if they don't.

"The truth is," Smoke says, "I'm a peaceful man. Just don't fuck with me or my peoples." His reputation in the prison is intact.

Gene Gene's another prisoner who has a solid reputation in USP Atlanta. He had recently transferred to Atlanta from the penitentiary in Lompoc, California. Gene, a white guy in his mid-forties, had kept in top physical shape by working out with weights and hitting the heavy punching bag. He had come on the tier and was next in line for a particular room. As he was going to see the guard about being assigned to the room, however, Snake, a weight lifter from the CRIPS (Common Revolution in Process) street gang, was standing by the guard's door and yelled over to Gene, "Yo, old man. You go in there and tell dat cop you ain't want dat room. I might let you have da next one."

Gene, who was standing with his buddy Gypsy, walked over to Snake and said, "What'd you call me?"

"I din't stutter," Snake said. "Ol' man."

Pow! Gene hit Snake square in his jaw, knocking him to the floor and sending his glasses in the other direction.

"I ain't gotta take dis shit," Snake said as he was getting up.

"No, you don't," Gene said. "We can walk down to the end of the tier and handle this ourselves."

They did. Gene proceeded to knock Snake down four more times. Finally, Gene stood over Snake and said, "Now look, I can hurt you real bad with these," as he showed him his clenched fists, "or we can take this to the wall. Where you tryin' to go?"

Snake looked up, shook his head to gain his composure, then extended his hand, "Man, I can take an ass wuppin'. I 'pologize. Take da muthafuckin' cell."

And Gene's reputation was preserved. Snake, on the other hand, took some ribbing from his homies for challenging Gene, who is well known throughout the penitentiary system for his boxing skills.

Transfers of Prisoners and Information

Every day, thousands of prisoners are transferred among the institutions of the Bureau of Prisons. The men begin serving their sentences in one institution, then, for whatever reason, like Smoke and Gene, find themselves being transferred to another. Prisoners may transfer for any number of reasons. One frequent reason for transfer is that a prisoner requests to move to a prison closer to home. Another reason may be that the prisoner's security level has changed, and, according to his classification scoring, he needs to transfer to a more appropriate facility.

As the men transfer from one prison to another, they bring news about prisoners they know or deliver messages about "what kind a man a guy is." In a world cut off from family and lasting relationships, many consume their thoughts with what's going on in other prisons and with other prisoners. Reputations stick with a guy throughout his sentence. For example, no one doubts what kind of guy Smoke is. He's a killer, a "good guy." Gene is solid, too, for he handles his own problems and doesn't tolerate any form of disrespect. Gene and Smoke's reputations place them high on the penitentiary social hierarchy. Bad reputations travel just as quickly. One who is known as a "rat" or someone who has "checked in" can never live it down. More than in most places, a prisoner is known by the company he keeps. And one who talks to a "rat," the subterranean part of the social totem pole, is just as bad as the rat himself.

This who's-a-rat syndrome dominates a substantial portion of the conversations within the prison. Everyone wants to know what the next "guy's about," or "who he hangs with." This is more than a casual matter. Sometimes, prisoners in USP Atlanta held presentence investigation (PSI) nights in the television room, requiring anyone whom they didn't know to bring their PSI reports to the room if they wanted to watch television. The PSI indicated whether the guy "stood up" by not giving information to law enforcement. Those not willing to show "their papers" weren't allowed in the television room and usually were coerced into "checking in" to protective custody. "No one wants a rat on the compound." The prisoner mentality holds that the person who doesn't rat, regardless of the circumstances of his crime or life choices, always holds higher rank and reputation than someone who does. Once one acquired the rat label at USP Atlanta, the reputation spread faster than a gasoline fire, and the individual had extreme difficulty surviving the hostilities, abuse, and violence that converged on him.

Those who are believed to have cooperated with the government or provided damaging information about other prisoners to staff members spend significant portions of their sentences in protective custody. They remain locked in a cell twenty-three hours each day waiting for transfers to other facilities. Once they transfer, they may walk the compound until other prisoners hear about their reputations and hold them accountable in absentia on behalf of their accusers.

These problems become less intense as the individual moves to lower-security prisons, where the number of government informants escalates. Generally, those offenders who cooperated in the prosecution of others, or who worked for law enforcement as informants, receive lower sentences or sentence reductions. Those lower sentences and individual circumstances usually result in administrators placing the prisoner in lower-security prisons. While they're held in high security, however, those with the "snitch jacket" are shunned by other prisoners.

More than sixty percent of prisoners in USP Atlanta are black or Hispanic. The next largest group are white prisoners who are not of Hispanic origin. Asian prisoners represent the smallest racial group. Although prisoners generally socialize with others of the same ethnic background and creed, all are unified in their scorn of prison rats and understanding of what constitutes being a good guy. Good guys openly express their solidarity by shaking hands whenever they meet, regardless of how frequently they meet each day.

Despite the sixteen years I've already served, I've never gotten used to the frequent handshaking. We shake hands at breakfast, after lunch, at the beginning of the evening, and before going into the unit. Too much, and completely out of sync with the world I remember outside of prison walls. It becomes awkward because not offering or accepting a handshake may be perceived as a slight.

The Rest of the Social Hierarchy The top of the social hierarchy, the men who receive the most respect are the perceived leaders of large criminal enterprises or organizations. Surrounded by yes-men and sycophants, these criminal leaders generally stay among themselves, eat together, and limit their associations with others.

The vast majority of prisoners who go about their day-to-day business without bothering or interfering in the lives of others might occupy the penultimate level, with the prison entrepreneurs who keep the underground economy humming standing just beneath them. (Explanations of each follow later.)

THE PRISON ECONOMY

As in most prisons, prisoners in Atlanta are not authorized to handle money. Instead, money is sent via a U.S. Postal money order. When staff members screen a prisoner's mail—and all mail is screened before a prisoner receives it—they remove any money orders and deposit them into the prisoner's commissary debit account.

The Cost of Living

The government provides food, clothing, shelter, and medical treatment for all prisoners. It also offers a commissary from which federal prisoners can purchase various items to supplement the government-issued supplies. An underground economy also exists to supply goods and services to prisoners; its currency is commissary items. Prisoners with outside resources can use them to make life inside easier. Others sell skilled services to make their money.

At USP Atlanta, the commissary sells canned foods, chips, packaged cakes, soups, fruit, and cigarettes. It also sells sneakers, some athletic apparel, Walkman-type radios, and watches. Prisoners also can purchase items for special hobby craft projects, stamps, and debit credits they use to make prepaid telephone calls. Theoretically, prisoners could live without spending anything in prison. If prisoners want to communicate with the world outside, however, they at least will need to purchase telephone credits, stamps, and envelopes.

Around 1992, the Bureau of Prisons stopped supplying aspirin, cold medicines, and other nonprescription medical products to prisoners. Instead, federal prison administrators now require prisoners to purchase personal care and hygiene products from the commissary. No reason was provided for this change; prisoners are required to comply with policy changes, not participate in them. Consequently, almost every prisoner uses the commissary at least occasionally.

Federal prisoners are allowed to shop on one designated evening each week. When I began serving my sentence in Atlanta, prisoners were given a purchasing limit of $120 per month; when I left, in 1994, the monthly purchasing limit had been raised to nearly $200.

Not counting stamps or telephone expenses, most prisoners spend at least $20 each month at the commissary. At the other extreme, prisoners with

outside support and resources may spend upwards of $1,000 per month—
more if they make frequent long-distance calls.

Prisoners also can earn a small income through prison employment. The
Bureau of Prisons requires all prisoners who are physically and mentally capable to hold a prison job. Some of these prison jobs, like my original job as a
clerk in the library, pay as little as $5 per month; other jobs, like a senior
worker in UNICOR—the federal prison factory—pay in excess of $700 per
month for prisoners who work a significant amount of overtime. An extremely conservative estimate, based on my sixteen years experience of living
in prison, suggests that between wages and outside support, each prisoner
averages over $40 per month in income.

Between the institutional pay prisoners receive from their prison jobs and
the substantial amounts of money sent into the prison for prisoner support, I
would estimate, the administration deposits well over $100,000 per month
into prisoners' accounts. These prisoners' earnings, together with the money
prisoners receive from outside sources, provide fodder for prison entrepreneurs and predators alike.

The Underground Economy

In every society or community, people work to enhance their quality of life.
Prisoners confined in the abnormal world of concrete and steel are no different. They must break prison rules, however, to overcome the deprivations
imposed by administrators. In USP Atlanta, this need fosters a thriving underground economy through which entrepreneurs look for ways to supply goods
or services—for a fee—to other prisoners.

Since prisoners do not have access to money, they use commissary items
as a currency to conduct a significant amount of business. Years ago, when
the prison population was made up of older prisoners, cigarettes were known
as the prison currency. Today's younger prisoner population prefers receiving
payment in $1 cans of mackerel or tuna for their prison debts. When accounts
are regular, or involve large sums of money, prisoners may use their family or
friends to send money out to an address the supplier provides, or they send
money into the supplier's prison account.

One prison business that constantly thrives involves food service. Prisoners
who work in the kitchen have access to onions, tomatoes, and other vegetables they can bring to the unit and sell to others. Since there is such a huge
demand for tomatoes and onions on the compound, and it is sometimes difficult to obtain them from the kitchen, those who procure these vegetables
charge a premium price: two tomatoes or one onion for $1. A good vegetable
hustler can earn up to $20 each day. Some of the prison literature refers to
these vegetable hustlers as *swaggers*, but I've never heard this term during my
sixteen years as a federal prisoner. In here they're known as *hustlers*.

Besides procuring vegetables, kitchen workers also may prepare sand-
wiches or special meals to supplement their incomes. As kitchen workers, few
earn enough to meet their prison expenses. An average kitchen worker earns

about $30 per month, hardly enough to purchase personal hygiene items, stamps, and telephone credits. If the kitchen worker wants to purchase other items from the commissary, or use the services of other prison contractors, and if he doesn't have financial support from outside, he might supplement his income by *relocating* vegetables and other edible items from the kitchen to the housing units and selling them to others.

Other prison service businesses that don't attract too many problems from staff include cleaning rooms, doing laundry work, or providing cooking services for a fee. Prisoners who are assigned to orderly details in the housing units usually monopolize these contractual services because they are in the units all day and have access to cleaning supplies. These janitorial and domestic services cost anywhere from $5 to $30 per month, depending on the work involved. Ironing costs $1 per item; room cleaning services cost $1 per day.

As with all prison businesses, commissary items are the usual currency, but sometimes prisoners barter. A prisoner with writing skills, for example, may write letters for an illiterate prisoner in exchange for having his room cleaned and clothes ironed. Like everywhere else, supply and demand dictate the value of services rendered.

During my first decade of confinement, I never participated in an activity that would have resulted in my earning an income from other prisoners. For several years I held a clerical position that paid me enough to meet my expenses, and I was fortunate to have financial support from family and friends. Although I didn't earn money from others, I did participate daily in the underground economy by purchasing goods and services from other hustlers.

Prison administrators recognize all activities in the underground economy as a threat to the security of the institution. Those businesses remove a significant degree of control from staff and place that control in the hands of prisoners. Further, the prisoner businesses encourage other problems in the institution, such as loan sharking and extortion. Predators will attack any individual whom they perceive as being weak or an easy mark. Predators also are attracted to underground entrepreneurs when they believe they can take over the business or the profits the business generates.

Accordingly, successful entrepreneurs need to ensure they have backup to protect their interests. These competing interests fighting to control their share of the underground economy encourage gangs to become larger and more powerful; they also contribute to the cycle of violence within the institution.

Despite staff attempts to quell the underground economy, they can't stop it. With over $100,000 in prisoner earnings being added to the substantial receipts prisoners receive each month from family and friends, there is too much of an incentive to find ways around the rules. Stopping an underground economy from spawning in an environment of deprivation has about as much chance of succeeding as the U.S. government had in its efforts to stop the flow of alcohol during the years of Prohibition. The prisoners want it.

However, those needs change for each individual as he passes through the cycle of his sentence. In fact, administrators rely upon the nearly three thousand prisoners confined in USP Atlanta to help them operate the prison. When the prisoner is thinking about release and trying to stay out of trouble to ensure his release date won't be suspended, the chances are better that he will abstain from participating in the underground economy.

Since parole was abolished by the federal system in 1987, however, most prisoners in USP Atlanta see nothing to look forward to besides release dates that linger decades away. Their interests lie in the present, in overcoming the deprivations wrought by confinement. Accordingly, this new, ostensibly tough atmosphere actually encourages the underground economy that provides the goods and services prisoners believe will lessen the pains of their incarceration. And that economy promotes violence. Penal policies are infamous for generating unexpected outcomes.

Big-Money Prisoners

Prisoners who have outside resources and regularly receive "yellow slips," indicating money has been deposited into their commissary accounts, can use their disposable income to break up the monotony of prison life. Outside income also provides an opportunity for others to earn an income within the prison walls. All expenses considered, some prisoners spend as much as $1,000 per month to lessen the hassles of institutional living. The relatively few prisoners who have access to this level of income serve significantly easier sentences than others. They never eat in the chow hall. They avoid the frustration of using laundry services, long waits in the commissary lines, and haggling over cleaning supplies. Instead, they spend their time reading, playing cards, exercising, or participating in activities they enjoy.

Instead of waiting in constant lines, and always being around crowds, prisoners of substance can pay others to eliminate many hassles of institutional living. Affluent prisoners can arrange for family members or friends to send money to the account of an indigent prisoner, who will make purchases for him. If the commissary spending limit is $200, he may arrange to send the indigent the $200 with the understanding that the indigent will purchase and store $180 worth of commissary items for him. The indigent prisoner, then, earns $20 for waiting in the approximately two-hour line to shop; the prisoner of substance avoids the hassle of the line and the exposure to the hundreds of other prisoners whom he would otherwise have to stand around.

After all, many of the frustrations and problems in prison occur because the thousands of deprived men who are forced to live in proximity never have a moment's privacy. There's no place a prisoner can go where he knows he will be completely alone. Never. He always will be within 10 to 15 feet of another man. And if he closes a door, he does so with the knowledge that at any time, without notice, a guard may appear. Prisoners who have resources sometimes use them to lessen their exposure to crowds. To them, hell can be equated with other prisoners.

Some prisoners avoid eating in the dining room completely by having money sent to several prisoners to maintain full supplies of food from the commissary and to have hundreds of cans of mackerel available to purchase vegetables and special food items from kitchen workers.

Paying for services by arranging to send money into other prisoners' accounts can present problems. In an effort to maintain security and control in institutions, BOP administrators created a code of disciplinary infractions that includes prohibitions like "running a business" from prison, or giving anything of value to another prisoner. Staff members who suspect that a prisoner is running a prison business or sending money to others to pay for services may intercept mail and monitor phone calls in an effort to catch the unauthorized activities. Prisoners can avoid these inconveniences by using third parties to transmit messages or providing instructions during visits.

Skilled Services

Prisoners with long sentences may look for projects that will help them pass time. The recreation department at USP Atlanta offers a few hobbies prisoners can participate in. Over the years, they may master these crafts and eventually use them to support themselves in prison.

For example, Al, a long-term prisoner, enrolled in a drawing class when he began serving his sentence. When I met Al, sixteen years had passed since his first class. He said he draws or paints every day of his term and became widely known as one of the premier artists in the penitentiary. Al specializes in drawing portraits of other prisoners or their families but also paints still life and abstracts.

Other prisoners purchase Al's work for their family or friends, and in the early 1990s, Al estimated he was averaging no less than $300 per month for his work, or nearly $4,000 per year. Since he has no family outside of prison, he uses the money inside.

"I charge $30 for a graphite portrait," Al says, "and up to $300 for an oil painting. Since people are so far away from their families, they're happy to receive my drawings. And I can draw from photographs or paint in oil or acrylic. Three to four people come to me each week looking for me to draw a portrait for them or their families, and I always have a couple of paintings I'm working on. It helps me pass the time, calms me," Al concluded.

Besides being therapeutic, Al's painting has helped keep money circulating in the prison. It's not only used for purchasing Al's commissary needs, but he also uses it to purchase services from other prisoners. He has people shop for him, do his laundry, and prepare his special meals. Instead of subjecting himself to the rituals of prison, allowing administrators to determine when and what he eats, Al's talent has given him a piece of independence. Every day, from early in the morning until late in the evening, Al mentally escapes the prison and his life sentence by drawing or painting in his little corner of the hobby shop.

Although earnings of $4,000 per year may seem high for a prisoner, skilled artists are not the highest paid of the prison contractors. That distinction belongs to the *jailhouse lawyer*, whose special skills always are highly demanded among USP Atlanta's high percentage of illiterate and semiliterate prisoners.

None of the jailhouse lawyers I met at USP Atlanta had legal experience prior to their incarceration. Instead, all were long-term prisoners who had spent their terms prowling through legal texts and developing writing skills. Some have established relationships with postconviction law firms or paralegal workers in the Atlanta community, but most work independently inside the prison itself.

As construction progressed over the years in USP Atlanta, the authorities opened a new education building complete with a large, adequately equipped prisoner law library. Federal law requires all BOP prisons to maintain a current set of books that report published case law in the various federal courts. The libraries also include several legal digests, journals, reports or changes in decisions on criminal law, and cross-referencing resources. There are no computer databases, of course, and one former lawyer told me that on a scale of 1 to 10, law libraries in prison are at about a 2 when compared with law libraries in the broader community. Nevertheless, prisoners who have learned to use these books can pass years refining their skills and supporting themselves in the process.

Prisoners constantly are searching for hope, and as long as they have a legal argument in court, many dream that some break will come their way. Failing to appreciate the extraordinarily slim odds of obtaining relief after one has been convicted, prisoners regularly pursue jailhouse lawyers with requests for them to review their papers. "Just find something," they say.

Jailhouse lawyers, too, understand that the odds for obtaining relief are low, but occasionally their work does result in a "client" being called back to court. Sometimes, an individual even receives a time cut. When one person finds relief, it perks up everyone's spirits, thereby generating more work for the jailhouse lawyers.

Essentially, jailhouse lawyers create pseudocareers for themselves. Some pay typists $1 for each page they type, and some create partnerships with writers and researchers so they can turn out more, or even better, quality work.

Experienced jailhouse lawyers charge anywhere from $200 to $2,000 per client for their work. They are available in the law library for counseling every day. Many prisoners are willing to pay for this legal therapy, as it gives them hope that relief might come. It is not uncommon for competent, hardworking jailhouse lawyers to earn over $20,000 per year—a princely, tax-free sum for a prisoner.

Besides preparing legal briefs and motions, jailhouse lawyers also may help prisoners with disciplinary infractions or those seeking relief through administrative remedy. Living in an almost perfect bureaucracy, prisoners are well aware of the importance of paperwork. Since the majority of the incarcerated are poorly educated and have difficulty expressing themselves in writing, many rely on jailhouse lawyers or other prison writers to help them resolve problems with administrators.

Many prisoners serving long terms welcome the intellectual challenge of educating themselves in the law. They put two-to-five-year plans together with the ambition of reaching a level of competence as skillful jailhouse lawyers. As their writing skills improve and they become more comfortable in framing legal arguments, they may join experienced jailhouse lawyers to work in apprentice capacities. Soon the apprentices begin acquiring clients of their own. There's no shortage of people who need legal assistance in the penitentiary.

In addition to preparing legal work, experienced writers can supplement their incomes by writing letters for less literate prisoners. Hundreds of the men in USP Atlanta can't read or write. Still, they sometimes need to communicate with family members or others. If they don't have a friend who will help them, they always can go to the library and retain the services of a writer for two or three cans of mackerel per page. It's all part of the underground economy.

Staff members intermittently work to obstruct these various prisoner businesses, but after years of living behind the fences, prison entrepreneurs become skillful in evading problems with staff. Although I didn't perform work for other prisoners, I did facilitate my schoolwork by inappropriately using the access my clerical position provided me to word processors. To camouflage my work, I would compose the documents I was writing in the middle of a longer, authorized report that was stored in the computer's hard drive. That way, if a staff member came snooping around to see what I was working on, I could immediately scroll to another page of the document. And when I was ready to print, my work would be disguised as part of the sanctioned government report. This was one technique I used effectively to accomplish my own goals, and prison hustlers devised their own quasi systems to help them avoid detection. Besides, in USP Atlanta, staff members have more serious problems to address than a guy hustling onions or writing futile motions for court.

PROBLEM ACTIVITIES IN
THE PENITENTIARY

There is an age-old understanding among prisoners that anyone can avoid problems in the penitentiary by simply staying away from gambling, homosexuals, and drugs. While one always must be on the alert for predators and thieves, there is some truth in this adage. These three are prohibited—but ever-present—activities in USP Atlanta. Other problems include alcohol, or "hooch," theft, and the absence of women.

Gambling

Prisoners look for ways to escape from their time, finding activities that keep their minds busy. Many spend their time exercising, attending educational programs, or participating in some type of productive project. Others, though, court excitement and vice. Some of these gamble to enliven their time. One always can find a few prisoners who work as bookies in the prison or others who run poker games from their rooms.

A bookie takes bets on sporting events in several different ways. He may offer prisoners an opportunity to bet games straight; he may offer a ticket through which bettors must pick at least four winning teams for a high payout; or he may offer opportunities for gamblers to place wagers in other creative ways. Gambling helps some prisoners pass dead time.

Every unit in USP Atlanta has at least one "casino" where prisoners can play cards for different stakes. In some card games, prisoners walk away after a day of playing where the range between winnings and losses is in the hundreds of dollars. Besides cards, the prisoners might play dice, chess, or other table games for money.

Some ingenious prisoners even run their own lotteries, charging participants a mackerel or more for numbers that must correspond in some way with national lottery numbers. These winner-take-all lotteries usually result in 10-to-1 payouts, sometimes more.

Other prisoners hold their own raffles. They purchase a $40 radio from the commissary, then sell the numbers one through one hundred, each for one can of mackerel. On a given day, a neutral party will pull the winning number out of a hat. Eager for an opportunity to win, the prisoners gladly fork over a mackerel to participate in the 1-in-100 chance of winning something; the raffle entrepreneur walks away with a healthy profit for providing the participating prisoners with this ounce of hope.

Gambling contributes to significant problems within the institution. Prisoners who find themselves on the losing side of a bet may choose not to pay. When this happens, the winner's manhood is challenged. In the explosive world of the penitentiary, where emotions run to extreme levels, any perceived sign of disrespect, like lack of payment, is a serious breach of prison etiquette. Expect violence, in some form, to result.

Jake and Spoon During the holiday season of 1993, Jake and Spoon, two middle-aged prisoners were engaged in their regular chess game on the third tier of D-cellhouse. The men spent a lot of time together and their friendship was well known. Jake was scheduled for release soon after the new year. The men customarily bet two mackerels on each game. On this particular evening, just before the guards called lockdown, everyone on the tier heard Jake screaming. "I ain't paying, you muthafucka. You gots to touch and move. Can't touch a joint den not move it. I ain't paying."

Spoon responded. "Better git me mine, Jake. You know I ain't one to fuck wit. Don'chu dis me like dat."

"Fuck you, nigga" Jake said as he slammed the chess set on the floor of the tier. "You ain't shit," he concluded while walking away.

Within minutes after Jake had walked away, Spoon grabbed a long prison-made knife made out of sharpened plastic and plunged it into Jake's abdomen. Jake died that evening, less than three months away from the expiration of his sentence.

Was it the few mackerels that caused Spoon to murder Jake? No. Long-term prisoners understand that Jake had disrespected Spoon on the tier in front of every other prisoner watching or listening. Spoon could have let the insult go, but in his way of thinking, peculiar as it might seem to the reader, doing so would have made him less of a man. Long-term-prison thinking creates a constant need for prisoners to redefine themselves as men. Spoon certainly proved that he's not willing to accept an insult. And he's doing it while serving a new life sentence for killing his one-time friend, Jake. A simple game of chess? Nothing is simple once gambling enters into the penitentiary equation.

Fly and Blade Gambling is also a mechanism predators use to lure victims into their trap. One young prisoner, Blade, told me how Fly, another prisoner in the world of nicknames and profanity, attempted to use gambling to lure him into sexual submission.

Blade, a 19-year old bank robber from Atlanta's inner city, was designated to serve his twenty-year sentence in the penitentiary. Several people from the housing projects in which he was raised were on the compound, so he had "backup" upon his entry into the prison. But instead of being housed with his friends, Blade first had to proceed through unit B-1, the new A&O unit through which all newly arriving prisoners must pass. Blade was assigned to room with Fly, a long-term prisoner who had arrived recently from USP Leavenworth.

On Blade's first night in the cell, Fly lured Blade into a game of dice. Fly sized up Blade and probably figured he had nothing to lose. Blade was young, small, and probably scared on his first night in the penitentiary.

Fly, on the other hand, was older, taller, and had been training with weights for the past several years. If Fly lost, he could shrug off the debt to the inexperienced Blade; winning, though, either would result in a payoff or leverage he could use to manipulate Blade.

By the end of Blade's first night, he owed Fly over $200.

"Wussup, bro? How you goin' git my money?" Fly demanded.

"Chill homes," Blade said. "We just started. You won today. I'll win tomorrow. Ain't nothing but a thang."

"Yo, don't come with that bo-shit," said Fly in his singsong voice. "You better git my money. Or you ain't got it, we go'n work it out, just you and me."

Although Blade was new in the penitentiary, he wasn't as green as most. Coming from a rough housing project background, he completely understood the danger in Fly's tone.

"Yo, my man, you want your money. Cool. Tomorrow, I'll call my peoples and work everything out. Just chill, aw-ight."

"Aw-ight, aw-ight. We'll straighten this out tomorrow. But I need to talk to ya peeps," Fly said.

"Look man. I got this. Just chill."

Blade says he went to sleep, knowing that he'd have to respond to Fly the following day. When he woke, he saw some of his friends on the compound. He told them his problem and they provided him with a knife. That evening, before Blade went to his cell, he prepared himself by hiding the knife in a sheath he had sewn into the waist of his pants.

About 8:00 P.M., Blade said he was sitting at the desk in his cell when Fly walked in. The guard came just behind Fly and locked the door.

"You been duckin' me all day, boy. I tol' the guard to lock us in early sos we could get some sleep. It's just you and me boy. Now wassup?" Fly said, approaching Blade in a threatening manner.

Blade said he stood up and had his back to the bed. Fly was closing in on him from the front. The entire cell measured only 12' × 8', so there was hardly any space to begin with. Blade said he told Fly to back off, but Fly kept coming at him.

When Fly tried to put his hands on Blade, in one swift move Blade pulled the knife out of its sheath, raised it over his head then brought it down hard, driving it into Fly's upper chest.

Blade says Fly began screaming. It was too late. Blade had turned the tables in another penitentiary case where predator becomes prey, and they were locked in the cell, with the guards well out of hearing range.

"Yo, das enough, muthafucka," Blade says Fly was crying. "We can work dis out."

"My ass we workin' dis out," Blade told him. "You better start pounding on that door, bitch, and git da fuck out dis cell 'fore I kills yo ass," Blade ordered.

"Yo, c'mon playa. I been down too long. I ain't never checked in. Les jus' chill on dis here," Fly pleaded.

"Ain't no chillin' here nigga. You git da fuck out, cuz if yous in here at count time, I'm cuttin,' you heard," Blade told him.

At that point, Blade said that Fly patched up his wound, then banged on the door for the guard to open up. Soon after he was released from the cell, Blade says that Fly walked to the Lieutenant's Office and told the lieutenant he couldn't remain on the compound because his life was in danger. Blade was never called to answer for the incident, and he never saw Fly again.

Not all gambling results in these problems, but—along with homosexual activities and drugs—it brings a share of violence into the prison, especially when one's manhood is challenged. In the subculture of prison, any perceived disrespect requires a violent response. Otherwise, the victim may become a mark predators regularly target for abuse.

Homosexual Problems

Homosexuality contributes to violence in the prison because of the high emotions created by love triangles. Everyone has heard the old jokes about not bending over to pick up the soap, but sexual predators represent a different type of problem—one that has little to do with romance or love.

Sexual predators are rapists, more concerned with obtaining power or leverage over others than sexual satisfaction. Indeed, sexual predators express anger when others accuse them of being homosexuals. They prey on nonvoluntary homosexuals with expectations of turning these weaker individuals into prostitutes, *punks* whom they can later manipulate to obtain money or drugs.

On the other hand, voluntary homosexuals create a huge problem when they engage in open and romantic relationships with other prisoners. These homosexual men prefer to be called by feminine pronouns and adopt feminine names. They exaggerate their femininity, talking with heavy lisps and elaborate hand gestures.

In homosexual relationships, the effeminate partner will call the masculine partner "her" husband, and the masculine partner will call the effeminate partner his "wife." These prison "marriages" are unwelcome and frustrating to many heterosexual prisoners for the reasons that follow.

Effeminate coquettishness heightens the volatility in the prison because "husbands" become enraged with jealousy when they perceive their "wives" have been unfaithful or disrespected. An example of one such eruption occurred in the chow hall in 1994.

Zeke had taken Bubbles as his wife. Zeke was a high-strung weight lifter, Bubbles a flirtatious instigator of problems. Bubbles walked around the unit with shaved legs, and she used a Kool-Aid mixture or colored pencils for makeup. Bubbles constantly flirted with others who would engage in her coquetry. Another prisoner, Ike, started flirting back with Bubbles, and that brought him some unexpected grief. When Zeke heard about it, he accosted Ike in the chow hall.

In front of hundreds of other prisoners, Zeke approached Ike's table. "What da fuck you doin' wit my bitch?" he demanded.

"Wha'chu talkin' bout," Ike feigned ignorance.

"Don'chu fuck wit me. Dat bitch's all I got. I'll kill you you come 'round her 'gain."

Not wanting any part of Zeke's rage, Ike didn't respond, and from that point forward, he kept his distance from both of them.

Countless pressures exist inside the penitentiary, and homosexual love affairs exacerbate the tension. Prison transfers can occur at any time, and when two lovers are separated, or when one becomes aware of the other's promiscuity, emotional outbursts occur, and violence frequently erupts with them.

Homosexuality also is frequently linked with prostitution. After receiving homosexual services, some prisoners refuse to pay. Like unpaid gambling debts or any other showing of disrespect, such actions provoke violence behind Atlanta's walls.

Drugs in the Prison

One wouldn't expect drugs to be so prevalent in a prison surrounded by doublewide fences that in turn surround 40-foot walls. In the early 1990s, however, USP Atlanta was infested with drugs.

Scores of prisoners contributed to the drug rackets. Some operated as couriers working to smuggle the drugs into the prison; others assumed the responsibility of stashing the drugs in various hiding places. Another group might work as distributors, while still others worked as enforcers to ensure drug debts were paid.

Drugs enter the prison in two ways: through corrupt staff members or through the prisoner visiting room. To bring drugs in through the visiting room, a prisoner might convince a female visitor to insert drugs into previously lubricated balloons, then carry the balloons with her into the prison. When the female visitor was ready to transfer the drugs, she would put the balloon in her mouth, then pass it to the prisoner while kissing him.

The prisoner would swallow the balloon during the kiss and allow it to pass through his digestive system. He would retrieve the drug-filled balloon by sifting through his waste once the balloon passed. The stench of excrement, apparently, did not diminish the contraband's value. Some prisoners would do anything to escape this deprivation—even smoke shit.

It was not uncommon to open the door to one of the individual showers in the unit and find a pile of excrement on the floor. Prisoner smugglers would have their bowel movements in the shower in hopes of recovering their treasured balloons. Without a second thought, some left their piles of evidence behind.

Sometimes, though, staff members would suspect a prisoner of being involved in bringing drugs in through the visiting room. When they did, they might stop the female visitor prior to her entry and require her to allow a strip search, or even a body cavity search, before the visit. Or, the guards might allow the visit to proceed, then detain the prisoner in a "dry cell" for three days after the visit while guards would sift through the suspected prisoner's bowel movements in their search for contraband.

Prisoners worked in food services, in maintenance departments, in clerical positions, and as teachers. Their mobility in the prison kept them in constant contact with one another, and their visitors provided a direct link to the community outside. Although staff members strip-searched prisoners before they entered the visiting room, and again after the visits concluded, they were unable to stem the flow of drugs into the institution.

Staff members were constantly on the prowl for prisoner informants to help them identify which prisoners were involved in the penitentiary drug rackets. Despite their efforts, drugs always seemed to be available, as hardly a day would pass without the distinctive smell of marijuana lingering somewhere in the institution. Besides marijuana, it wasn't uncommon for a prisoner to die of a heroin overdose.

Not all drugs found in USP Atlanta passed through smugglers' bodies after visits. Sometimes, the guards busted bulky quantities of drugs that were carried into the prison by corrupt staff members acting as couriers. Several staff members were arrested on drug trafficking charges while I was in USP Atlanta. Apparently, like the prisoners they were in charge of "correcting," these erstwhile guards were supplementing their incomes by participating in the underground economy.

Aware of all the drugs inside the penitentiary, the captain—who is in charge of the prison's internal security and custodial operations—specifically assigned at least one staff member to administer drug tests to randomly picked prisoners. The custody staff also worked to cultivate informants in its efforts to stem the drug problems. The drug problem got so out of hand during the early 1990s, that federal law enforcement officers entered the prison on a few occasions to make drug-trafficking arrests of both prisoners and staff. After these busts, rumors circulated for weeks over what transpired. Everyone was excited because of the activity. Hard news of these events, however, was never easy to come by, as administrators weren't usually eager to expose corruption inside the walls.

Hooch

The manufacturing and distribution of prison-made alcohol, *hooch*, is closely related to the drug rackets. A significant portion of the prisoner population escapes their predicaments by intoxicating themselves with drugs or alcohol.

As one of the largest prisons in the federal system, USP Atlanta provided countless hiding places for prisoners who wanted to supplement their incomes by cooking hooch. Other prisoners told me that the process was both simple and lucrative.

First, the hooch entrepreneurs accumulated large quantities of fruit, sugar, and some yeast from the kitchen. If they couldn't get yeast, which was essential to the fermentation process, they substituted raw bread. They then made the appropriate mixture in either a bucket or a plastic bag and left it in a warm, dry place for a few days to ferment naturally. The mixture was hidden in ceilings, crawl spaces, lockers, or any hiding places the prisoners thought guards wouldn't find it. After approximately seventy-two hours the concoction was ready to distribute. At $5 a serving, a 5-gallon mixture netted the entrepreneurs about $50. With no shortage of demand, busy wine merchants had several 5-gallon mixtures cooking at any given time.

Thievery

To break up the monotony, some prisoners make a habit of breaking into the personal lockers others have in their rooms. The thieves usually work in two- or three-man crews. One or two prisoners stand outside the cell watching while the other partner breaks open the bicycle-type lock on the prisoner's locker.

These locker bandits cause a particular problem for the victim. If the bandits break into the locker without being detected by anyone else, the victim simply loses the goods he was storing inside. On the other hand, if someone actually sees the thieves, or even if someone hears a rumor about their identities, the victim is suddenly in a precarious position. Prisoners who learn the identity of a thief have two options: either they can confront the thief, or they can let the incident pass. Consequences will follow either decision.

If the prisoner allows such an incident to pass, within hours word will spread quickly that the prisoner is a "punk," a "bitch," a "sucker," that "he's got no balls." It is tantamount to an announcement of open season in the penitentiary. Numerous predators will recognize the victim as an easy mark unless or until he does something about it.

On the other hand, the victim can respond. Talking is not an acceptable response, as the thief has broken into the victim's "house" and made a gross invasion of the prisoner's space.

Neither can the prisoner call the police as a citizen would do. Even notifying the guard would place the "snitch jacket" on the victim, from which everyone knows there is no escape. In the penitentiary, if the victim chooses to respond to his problem, whatever that problem may be, he must use force or the threat of force.

Saying one must use violence to respond to problems in the penitentiary is an understatement. No prisoner can respond to a problem with a fistfight. It doesn't mean that fistfights don't occur. They do. It's just that fistfights aren't planned responses to a problem. Gene didn't plan to hit Snake over the assignment of a room. It just happened. Both parties knew, however, that the problem could have escalated to lethal levels.

Fistfights may break out in the gym or on the basketball court. When they do, others around the situation try quickly to stop the issue from escalating further. When a prisoner is forced to respond to a problem, on the other hand, he must make a categorical statement to everyone in the know that he is a "good guy," ready to go all the way. For example, everyone knows how Smoke will respond to a problem.

If a prisoner isn't willing to kill, or if he doesn't have the backup of other killers, then he will never escape the vulnerability of being victimized. This common knowledge throughout the penitentiary is what drives so many prisoners to seek "protection" by joining gangs or to form alliances with others.

Thieves don't break into lockers at random. Indeed, no victim is chosen at random. Since predators know that many prisoners are deadly, they choose marks they think won't respond. Had I not enjoyed a friendship with powerful forces within the penitentiary, I have no doubt that I would have been put into situations that would have exposed me to an even more severe prison term.

Substitutes for Women

Despite the disruptions caused by sexual predators and problem homosexuals in USP Atlanta, the vast majority of prisoners in the penitentiary are heterosexual. Their lack of access to women, however, encourages some entrepreneurs to engage in the underground business of helping prisoners find romance.

Several prisoners purchase catalogs featuring photographic ads of women from around the world who are seeking love in America. The catalogs offer page after page of pictures of women. On a separate sheet, subscribers receive addresses that match the pictures.

Recognizing the craving for women in the penitentiary, these entrepreneurs carry these catalogs with them around USP Atlanta and let others know they have addresses of women for sale. When I was there, prisoners could purchase one address for a mackerel, or three for two mackerels. In addition to selling the advertisement, the prison entrepreneur might leverage his business by offering to write a love letter as well.

Other prisoners rent pornographic magazines. There are even rumors that some prisoners bore holes in their mattresses. They then insert plastic lining in the holes, which they can pack with a piece of liver coated in baby oil. All this to simulate sexual intercourse. Life behind the walls of USP Atlanta takes abnormal turns indeed.

Policies that deny prisoners access to women contribute to the sexual tensions and perversity that exists within each prison. Although some state prison systems use conjugal visits as an incentive to encourage good behavior, prisoners in the federal system must adjust to policies that deny them interactions with women. Some prisoners are able to work around the rules and use their writing skills to open new relationships with women through correspondence, yet the vast majority spend year after year in the wastelands behind walls, separated from the beauty and warmth of women, while the rigid, abnormal community of men fossilizes their emotions.

CONCLUSION

Some taxpayers might argue that administrators are remiss in allowing prisoners so much freedom within the walls of the penitentiary. Yet administrators need prisoners' cooperation to operate and maintain the prison within budget. Prisoners work as plumbers, electricians, cooks, and clerks. Indeed, prisoners perform virtually all of the labor inside the walls to maintain the institution, and they perform their labor at costs that are a fraction of what labor would cost in a free market. The highest paid prisoner earns less than $2 per hour while the vast majority of prisoners earn less than 50 cents per hour.

If staff members kept prisoners locked in their cells, administrators would have more control and thus lessen the volatility and perversion of the penitentiary, but they would need to hire outside labor to maintain the prison and care for the thousands of men behind the penitentiary's walls. Already swelling prison budgets would escalate quickly if 50-cents-per-hour prisoners were replaced with prison guards who earn more than $20,000 per year.

Recognizing the prohibitive costs of locking prisoners in their cells, administrators allow a degree of freedom within the penitentiary. The threat of further punishments and atmosphere of deprivation helps control the men within the walls. Yet, this setting contributes to the abnormal subculture governing the penitentiary's prisoners. It is a difficult and constantly volatile balance.

6

Managing Chaos

Previous chapters underscored the ongoing tension behind penitentiary walls. In this chapter, I'll explore the warden's response to the problems a community of felons can present. Because the penitentiary is a total institution, one that controls nearly every aspect of the prisoners' lives, administrators have many tools at their disposal. Primarily, they look for opportunities to reduce idleness and increase the accountability of the nearly three thousand prisoners behind the walls. In their efforts to keep the peace, administrators control the men's movements; they assign the men to individual work details; and they promote programs.

IDLENESS AND ACCOUNTABILITY

Many prisoners cut their ties to the community when they come inside the walls. Some do it because they find it easier to build their lives completely inside. They don't write letters. They don't make phone calls. They don't communicate outside. It's almost as if they become a part of the institution itself, with no goals other than to see the calendar page turn. Such prisoners live their lives one day at a time and express no hopes or expectations for change. Administrators are concerned that when these prisoners have too much free time, they may engage in disruptive behavior. Accordingly, they institute policies designed to keep staff members in the know and control the prisoner population.

The Bureau of Prisons requires every prisoner who is medically able to work. Some of these jobs take all of a prisoner's time. But with well over twenty-five hundred prisoners on the compound, there aren't enough full-time jobs available that require a whole day's work. Accordingly, many of the jobs are makeshift and don't require prisoners to do anything but show up. Other full-time jobs require no more than a few minutes work (or attendance) each day. Despite the jobs, then, hundreds of prisoners still have virtually all day, every day, to find their own way to spend time. Prison guards make it their business to figure out what these men are doing.

The administration keeps prisoners accountable by using systems to control their movement, conducting regular census counts, confining them to the segregated housing unit as a disciplinary action, performing regular shakedowns, monitoring their telephone conversations and mail, regularly rotating guards' assignments, and instituting lockdowns when violence erupts.

Controlled Movement

One step administrators take to enhance prisoner accountability is to control their movement. When a prisoner isn't assigned to a particular work detail he is required to be in his own housing unit. The exceptions are when the prisoner is on a callout requiring him to be somewhere else, is on a visit, or has a pass issued by an appropriate officer authorizing him to move to a different area of the facility.

This strict movement system enables the staff to contain the prisoners in a given area. That way if a disturbance occurs, or if a need arises to ascertain which prisoners were in a given area at a particular time, the pass system provides a record and place from which guards can begin their investigations.

Passes are issued during a ten-minute window beginning at five minutes to the hour and concluding at five minutes after the hour. The pass system is in place on weekdays between 8:00 and 10:00 A.M. and then again between 1:00 and 3:30 P.M. After the 4:00 P.M. count clears, and on weekends, prisoners can move from one area of the prison to another during the ten-minute hourly moves without an officer's written pass.

Besides providing a record of a prisoner's movement, the pass system accomplishes another goal of exposing prisoners to staff members. To obtain the pass, the prisoner must present his identification card to the issuing officer. Once he receives the pass, he must have the Officer in Charge (OIC) of the area to which he's going sign it within ten minutes of the time the pass was issued. This pass system helps staff members become familiar with prisoners' names and their activities. Because the prisoners need to see guards to move from one area to another during the day, the guards have opportunities to learn which names match which faces and which prisoners associate together.

This pass system serves the needs of security-conscious administrators, but it frustrates the daily life of every prisoner. Some men avoid leaving the unit because they don't want to reckon with the hassles and lines associated with passes and controlled movements. The system results in many gates and checkpoints through which one must pass to move from point A to point B. When I walked from my housing unit to the recreation yard, I had to present myself through eight separate gates or metal detectors for inspection.

Census Counts

In addition to the pass system, the institution conducts random census counts a few times each week. These counts are in addition to the regularly scheduled daily census counts, which take place each day at 5:00 A.M.; 4:00 P.M.; 9:00 P.M.; and 12:00 A.M. There's also a regular morning count on weekends and holidays between 7:00 A.M. and 10:00 A.M. Yes, there's a lot of counting in the penitentiary.

During these random census counts, all prisoner movement stops. The gates are locked and units are secured. The guards direct each prisoner to a particular area, then match their official records against his pass or identification number to ensure the prisoner is in the appropriate place. Those who are caught out of bounds receive disciplinary infractions. But a prisoner who has committed himself to living inside the walls doesn't have too much concern over receiving incident reports. He's more concerned with passing his time the way he chooses to pass it. To him, keeping a little control for himself justifies the risk of receiving a disciplinary infraction.

Prisoners who receive disciplinary infractions for moderate-severity offenses usually receive sanctions like loss of telephone or commissary privileges or loss of visiting for a particular period of time. If the prisoner isn't a regular problem, the lieutenant or unit team may agree to grant the offender an opportunity to perform ten to twenty hours of "extra duty" in exchange for expunging the disciplinary infractions. On the other hand, if the offender is known as a troublemaker, he may be sent to the segregated housing unit, the *hole*, for a length of time.

The Hole

In the segregated housing unit, SHU (pronounced *shoe*), a prisoner lives under much harsher conditions. He's confined to a small cell for at least twenty-three hours each day. He may take one hour out of the cell for "recreation," but this only means he's being put into a separate enclosed cage with fresh air. The prisoners in the hole aren't allowed access to their property, don't have access to the telephone, and have limited access to reading materials. In Atlanta, prisoners in the hole receive only three showers per week and before they walk to the shower, the guards put them in handcuffs. Guards deliver the prisoners' meals to them when they're in the hole. But by the time the food arrives it is usually cold.

More than anything, being sent to the hole is a disruption to one's time. The hard-core prisoner doesn't want to spend time in the hole but recognizes segregated housing as another part of the penitentiary and accepts that he'll serve some portion of his sentence there.

Prisoners may be sent to the hole for any disciplinary infraction or, in some cases, for an investigation. Generally, those charged with minor infractions are sanctioned in some lesser manner, with a commissary restriction or extra duty. But if the prisoner is a persistent problem, defiant or insolent, he may serve time in the hole for the most trivial offense, or for no offense. Prisoners may be held for several months or years in segregation without ever being charged with a disciplinary infraction.

Shakedowns

Since the federal courts have ruled that prisoners don't have rights to privacy, guards regularly search prisoners' property and person. These searches are called *shakedowns*. Guards have keys to all cells and a universal key that opens all prisoners' lockers. By going through a prisoner's belongings several times each month, the guards can gather information about him. They may look through his literature to see what interests him, look through his photographs to determine what type of community ties he has, and sift through his property to ascertain whether he's storing any contraband or objects that might suggest wrongdoing. The guards want to know everything possible about him.

In addition to the cell searches, prisoners can expect to be stopped at random and frisked. A prisoner may be told to stand against the wall with his arms and legs spread while a guard runs his hands across his body. Or the prisoner may be taken to a nearby room and ordered to strip naked for an inspection. These regular shakedowns help the guards control the flow of contraband and give them an idea of the different prisoner interests. They also force prisoners to exercise more caution when engaging in unauthorized behavior.

Telephone and Mail Monitoring

Staff members monitor prisoners' telephone conversations and mail. This constant surveillance over their lives helps the administration stay alert to what's going on inside the institution. And it's important for them to do so. With fewer than six hundred employees inside the prison, the prisoners outnumber the guards by at least a 3-to-1 ratio; the ratio is actually larger, because only a percentage of these staff members are on duty on a given shift. Staff members, therefore, take every precaution to ensure they know what's going on behind the walls. Prisoners, on the other hand, make it their business to evade the constant scrutiny of the guards. And the scrutiny is thorough.

On any given evening, prisoners can look through the small window in their cell's door and see the guard sitting at his desk. Prisoners aren't allowed to seal their mail before placing it in the outgoing mailbox. Instead, the guard must seal it. Before he does so, however, he sits at his desk during the late-night shift and reads through the prisoners' thoughts. If the guard determines the thoughts are appropriate, he'll seal the letter and allow it to proceed through the mail system. If not, he'll pass the mail along to an investigating lieutenant for further action.

Sometimes a guard will comment on the prisoner's letter, thereby destroying any illusion the prisoner has of privacy. For example, Chris described how he wrote a letter begging his wife not to leave him. The next morning, as Chris was on his way to work, the guard suggested to Chris that he ought to let his wife go and do his time on his own. Other prisoners complain of putting unsealed letters in the mailbox and having guards switch the letters. It's a particular problem for prisoners who correspond with more than one woman.

It's not only outgoing mail that's monitored. All correspondence a prisoner receives from people in the community is opened before the prisoner receives it. If a staff member deems the mail inappropriate, the mailroom personnel will reject the correspondence. *Playboy* and *Penthouse* magazines, for example, are deemed inappropriate reading material for federal prisoners. So are pictures that show nudity. But restrictions aren't limited to nudity. Even some types of literature are rejected. For example, *PC Magazine* and books that describe computer programming are unauthorized. One prisoner, Sean, regularly has his mail confiscated because he receives pictures of friends who are wearing emblems from his motorcycle club. Sean's motorcycle club, prison guards have determined, is a criminal organization and so photographs of its members represent a threat to the institution. They're rejected.

Even I had a problem receiving a book I had ordered. I was studying corrections and ordered a book on administrative practices. Instead of the book itself, I received a notice from the mailroom telling me the book had been rejected because the textbook presented a threat to the security of the institution.

Whereas it may take days for a prisoner to know whether his mail passed on, the telephone monitoring is immediate. Staff members working in the gun towers that surround the prison listen to prisoners' telephone conversations. The guards have the authority to disconnect a prisoner's telephone conversation at any time. Conversations frequently are terminated in midsentence, especially if they're sexually graphic.

Being deprived of normal heterosexual relations, many prisoners engaged in regular *phone sex*. Some prisoners complained about the guards' disconnecting their conversations and invading another aspect of their lives. Others grew calloused and indifferent to the utter lack of privacy, recognizing, that as a prisoner, the only opportunity one has to share private thoughts with family or friends outside of prison is through a visit. Other than in-person conversations, all prisoner communications are subject to monitoring.

Quarters Changes

Every three months marks the beginning of a new quarter at USP Atlanta—and the reassignment of guards to different posts. By rotating the guards on a regular basis, they have an opportunity to gather information on prisoners in different housing units. While on their shifts, guards spend time flipping through the picture cards that identify every assigned prisoner. By searching through these men's belongings and monitoring their actions, alert guards can determine which prisoners spend time together. It also enables them to cultivate informants from the prisoner population. By taking these security measures, the guards increase their awareness.

Institution Lockdown

Despite the pass system, eavesdropping, and shakedowns, violence frequently erupts on the compound. When it does, the warden may respond with an institution lockdown, thereby converting the entire penitentiary into one complete segregated housing unit.

During institution lockdowns, there's no prisoner movement on the compound. Guards direct the men to their cells and then lock the doors. The cell doors have small trap doors cut in their center, about 3 feet up from the floor. Guards pass the men's meals, mail, and medications through these trap doors so the heavy steel room door never needs to be unlocked. On lockdown, the prisoners have no access to work, no telephone access, no television, no commissary. They receive showers at the guard's discretion.

Whenever a lockdown occurs, staff members interview every prisoner in the penitentiary in a private room. Guards escort the prisoner from his cell to an interview room where a staff member waits with his interview questionnaire. After collecting identifying data on the prisoner, the staff member asks him direct questions about the incident.

Joe's Interview Joe described his interview after Billy was murdered on the yard.

"First of all, Stewart asks me, 'Where were you at 1:30 this afternoon?' I tell him I was in the gym. Then he says, 'Did you have a pass?' I tell him I did. 'What have you heard about today's incident,' Stewart says. I tell him that I don't know nothin'. 'You haven't heard that Billy Bright was murdered on the yard today by multiple stab wounds?' Stewart asks. I tol' 'em I hadn't heard nothin'. Then he asks me, 'Would you tell us if you did know sumpen'?' I ain't got nothin' to say to you peoples, I told him."

The guards conclude every interview with that question, "Would you tell us if you did know something?" Joe says it's important to let the guards know he wouldn't contribute to their investigation under any circumstances.

"Once you let them know you'll cooperate," he says, "they'll be callin' ya down to the Lieutenant's Office ev'ryday lookin' for information. I ain't 'bout that. They can do their own muthafuckin' work."

WORK PROGRAM

Despite the emphasis on control within the institutions, prisoners have an opportunity to influence the job to which they're assigned. Some jobs are less desirable than others, but all offer certain advantages that staff members use to entice and keep workers. Employment opportunities exist in every area of the prison; they include factory and nonfactory positions.

Approximately 25 percent of the prison's population hold jobs in one of the various prison factories. The factory jobs provide the men with a higher pay level and add structure to their day. Prisoners who seek jobs in the prison factories have tangible reasons to avoid activities that could lead to disciplinary problems.

UNICOR

UNICOR, the peculiarly named (no known acronym) federal prison industries program, receives the most attention of all work programs in the institution. In fact, no Bureau of Prisons program receives as much support or as many resources.

During the 1987 riot, the prisoners in Atlanta destroyed the original UNICOR factories. The BOP replaced them with a massive 100,000 square-foot building within its walls. Several separate factories operate inside the UNICOR Building. Among others, Atlanta has a factory that builds mailbags for the U.S. Postal Service; a uniform factory where prisoners sew battle fatigues for the military; and another factory that supplies the prison system with mattresses. Together, the UNICOR factories in USP Atlanta employ approximately one thousand prisoners, more than 30 percent of the prisoner population. Nationally, UNICOR employs over thirty thousand federal prisoners. These job programs become a way of life for many of the UNICOR workers—an acceptable escape from the prison's monotony.

Prisoners choose to work in the UNICOR program for a variety of reasons; one is that it offers the highest wages in the penitentiary. At nearly $1.25 per hour, top earners in UNICOR exceed $200.00 per month in regular pay, but they can earn three to four times this amount by working excessive hours of overtime. Some UNICOR prisoners work double shifts each day, seven days each week. They find structure through the UNICOR program, and their pay shields them from having to rely on prison hustles to support themselves. UNICOR provides some order in their chaotic world.

Supporting the administration's theory that keeping prisoners busy reduces problems among the prisoner population, UNICOR workers are less likely to participate in prison disturbances. In fact, many will go out of their way to keep the factory running.

Soon after the new factory was built, for example, some prisoners began disrupting the operation by starting fires inside the building. They would light the corrugated boxes on fire that were supposed to be used to ship finished products. Recognizing the fires as a threat, the UNICOR manager announced a $50 reward to anyone who helped extinguish the fires. This simple reward offer put a stop to the fires. The arsonists must have realized that they couldn't disrupt the factory when so many prisoners would be working as sentries for the man in exchange for a $50 reward.

Most UNICOR workers consider their jobs a privilege and recognize that receiving a disciplinary infraction could result in their being reassigned to food services or another less desirable work detail. Not only would they lose their relatively high income, but they also would lose the stability that comes from their jobs.

Mark, a Model UNICOR Worker Mark, a friend of mine who had worked in the UNICOR factory for several years, used to say that even if Congress or administrators cut the UNICOR budget and eliminated the higher prisoner pay system, he still would work in the factory. He's become attached. When he's working in the factory, he says, it's like he's not in prison at all. That's why he accepts all of the overtime work available to him, sometimes working for three straight shifts, or nearly twenty-four hours in a row. With all of his overtime work, Mark has had months where he realized over $800 in net earnings.

Since Mark is working so many hours in the factory, he has no time remaining to participate in disruptive activities. Other prisoners walk around the prison filled with anger and bitterness, but Mark just stays focused on his job and doesn't concern himself with what he calls the "nonsense." Although he hears about blood being shed regularly, it's no different from if he were to hear about it on the evening news. He's learned to sidestep the waste.

UNICOR absorbs Mark. He eats every meal in the prison's chow hall and only spends money on coffee. Mark has no contact with the world outside of prison, but surprisingly, he also has little contact with the prison itself. Unless the person works in UNICOR, Mark hardly notices him. Indeed, if Mark's not sleeping, he's in the factory, grateful for the purpose it provides his life.

When I was in Atlanta, Mark had over fourteen years of tenure in prison. He served the majority of his sentence at USP Leavenworth but transferred to Atlanta in 1993. While in Leavenworth, Mark says he kept the same routine, working in Leavenworth's print factory.

Within three weeks after arriving in Atlanta, Mark secured a clerical position for himself in the mattress factory's Quality Assurance Department. The job provides Mark with a desk, a comfortable office chair, and clearly defined responsibilities. His constant work and frugal living habits have helped him accumulate a prison commissary balance in the mid-four figures; it's enough, he reasons, to help him adjust when he is released.

Few of the prisoners in Atlanta are as consumed with their prison jobs. Perhaps fifty guys spend their time like Mark, accepting all the overtime available and competing against each other to see who receives the highest monthly pay. Hundreds of the prisoners, however, work double shifts a few days each week.

UNICOR workers frequently express their hatred of the weekends and holidays. For them, any extended time away from their routines is like receiving a new prison term. Threatened food or work strikes present a particular dilemma to the UNICOR worker. They don't like placing their jobs in jeopardy. Being prisoners first, however, most of the men confined in USP Atlanta support all prisoner-organized strikes.

Many prisoners who don't work in the prison industries program deplore UNICOR and mock all who support it. To them, UNICOR is one of the reasons prisoners are serving such lengthy sentences. UNICOR, a wholly owned government corporation, was initiated in 1934 during President Franklin D. Roosevelt's term and was strongly supported by then first lady Eleanor Roosevelt. Its goal: to reduce prisoner idleness. Don't tell this to some nonworking UNICOR prisoners. To them, the factory is owned by a mysterious coalition of judges and politicians engaged in a wicked conspiracy to incarcerate the poor and turn them into complacent UNICOR slaves.

In the early 1990s, the USP Atlanta UNICOR factories exceeded $20 million in annual revenues. Because all prisoners assigned to the factories earn less than half the nation's minimum wage, many prisoners believe UNICOR is a profit machine giving those in power an incentive to expand the prison population and the fat UNICOR profits.

Several publications declare that administrators use UNICOR profits to fund educational and recreational programs throughout the Bureau of Prisons. There even have been times when the BOP paid a portion of the UNICOR profits back to the U.S. Treasury as a dividend on the Treasury's initial investment in the program. The cynics in USP Atlanta, however, don't buy it. Prisoner folklore holds that UNICOR gains are added to the substantial profits generated by prison commissaries and telephone services. Together, the prisoners will tell you it is self-evident this money is used to enrich President Bush's family and cronies.

My Own UNICOR Experience I worked in the prison library for the first few months that I was held in Atlanta, but sometime during my first years, I transferred to a job in a UNICOR factory. I performed some clerical work for transportation and billing functions, enabling me to earn enough money to live in prison. More important, my UNICOR job enabled me to escape from the madness that is the penitentiary to a comparatively peaceful office environment for several hours each day. Further, after I had completed my assigned duties, my staff supervisors authorized me to use the modern typewriters toward my personal academic goals. The UNICOR job, I found, was helpful in my initial adjustment. I needed that structure. After my fifth year, however, I found myself wanting less formal structure, so I transferred to a job that freed me to focus exclusively on my independent study projects. For me, UNICOR was like a guide I used to bring me through those most difficult years of my early imprisonment. For others, UNICOR becomes a way of life.

Redneck Rick Redneck Rick is another prisoner who has made UNICOR the focus of his life. Rick transferred to Atlanta from another penitentiary in 1989. He was about seven years into his sentence and expected to be released in 1992. He began serving his time as a young man, when he was 20, and from the beginning he worked in UNICOR. "I ain't about spendin' my time with a whole bunch a people. I'm prejudiced and proud of it. I stick with my own kind. I work in UNICOR 'cause I stick with my own people. We work together. We eat together. We do our time together, and we ain't rennin' 'round with all the animals in this place."

Rick, about 27 when I met him, was covered with tattoos. His entire back featured a mural of a 4-by-4 supertruck weaving its way through the trees on a steep slope; the rebel flag flew prominently from the truck's antenna. His forearms were covered with the requisite swastikas, lightening bolts, and skulls that adorn so many prisoners. When he brought his two fists together, one could read BORN TO LOSE on his knuckles; two tattooed teardrops fell from his left eye.

Rick and his crew's routine were predictable. They all worked in UNICOR from 7:30 A.M. until 8:00 P.M. Between 8:00 and 11:00 each evening the four of them would drink hooch and play poker in one of the rooms. They didn't get stumbling drunk, but their intoxication was obvious.

Yet none of them seemed to interfere with the other problems in the penitentiary. They lived as stand-up guys.

In 1992, as expected, Rick was released from prison. The others in his crew received a postcard or letter from him every few weeks, and they shared those letters with others on the tier who had known Rick. Each letter sent the same message about how Rick's parole officer was riding him hard and how he was tired of the parole officer trying to run his life. About eight months after Rick left, he came back to USP Atlanta and was assigned to the same tier in B-cellhouse from which he left.

"What happened?" I asked. "Did your parole officer give you a violation?" (Rick had been convicted before the federal system had abolished parole. As an old law prisoner he was released from his prison term after having served one-third of the sentence; he was supposed to serve the remainder of his time in the community under the supervision of his parole officer. Parole is not available to new law prisoners convicted of federal crimes after 1988.)

"You can say that," Rick answered. "Besides gettin' violated I got a fresh twenty-five."

"For what, drugs?" I asked.

"Naw. Don' fuck with that shit. Robbed a bank," he said.

"How'd that come about?" I asked.

"Man, you don't know what it's like. Every day my parole officer was up my ass. He's asking me if I got a job, where I'm looking, who I talked to. He wants to know how much money I got in my pocket, what I'm spending it on. He's orderin' me 'round like a bitch. Tellin' me to take urine tests every goddamn minute and the faggot motherfucker's lookin' at my dick while he's join' it. Fuckin' asshole won't let me live my life. I got tired a that shit."

"Yeah, but what's that got to do with the bank?"

"That's what I'm sayin'. I was late getting in to see him one day. And I didn't want to listen to his shit no more. So instead I just walked into this bank across the street from his offices with a paper bag and told the teller I had a gun and that I wanted her to fill the bag with money. She did what I tol' her, but she also put an ink bomb in the bag and hit a silent alarm. I walked out the bank with no problem. I was fixin' to buy me a car and drive on down to Mexico. Fuck this shit, you know what I mean? I had to serve seven years on paper anyway, and I wasn't gonna listen to that nigger parole officer tell me what to do all day. But the goddamn ink bomb exploded in the bag and covered me with that dye shit. And the cops were on me within two minutes after I left the bank. That was the end of my parole."

"So I guess you pleaded guilty?" I asked.

"Hell yeah I pleaded guilty. I had the money in my hands and ink all over me. Motherfuckin' judge gave me twenty-five motherfuckin' years."

After his return to the penitentiary, Rick spoke with his former UNICOR boss. Within a couple of weeks of his return to Atlanta, he resumed his job in the factory and his regular poker games in the unit. To others, it looked as if Rick was happy to return to the routine that had become such an integral part of his life.

I asked Rick why he couldn't have found a low-paying factory job in the community—one that would have provided him with enough money to live in an apartment where he could continue his drinking and poker in his spare time but that also would give him freedom and the opportunity to enjoy the companionship of women, maybe even start a family.

"I would have. But that motherfuckin' nigger parole officer wouldn't stay off my motherfuckin' back."

It seemed that the outside world didn't have enough interests for Rick. He preferred the monotonous but predictable life of prison to the frustrations of living as an ex-convict.

The Hustle Shift

If a prisoner doesn't take steps to find his own job, his counselor will place him in a position. These prisoners usually are placed on the early-morning kitchen shift. They report for duty at 4:30 A.M. and remain on the job until approximately 12:30, when the noon meal ends. Some prisoners accept the detail because it helps them hustle.

Lou "I prefer the 4:00 A.M. shift," Lou says. " I been working for Smiley since I got here and I ain't changin' now."

"Wouldn't you rather have one of the later shifts?" I asked.

"Fuck no," said Lou. "This job's the best. I get here 'fore anyone else. Smiley lets me in and we kick it for a while. He's from my neighborhood and so we know a lot a the same cats. I mean, he's still a hack and all, but he's a good dude, let's me get my hustle on."

"What if you don't wake up?"

"That's on me. I gotta be here 'fore the 5 o'clock [count]. Otherwise, the unit cop'l fuck wit me. If it's an asshole on in there, he'll write me up. But I'm used to it. I been here for two years and ain't had no problem."

"How does it help your hustle?"

"Shit, I get whatever I need," Lou says. "I says to Smiley, 'Yo, let me get some eggs up off you.' He unlocks the fridge and I take a whole box a dem muthafuckas out. I give 'em to my peeps for a dollar a dozen and they take 'em back to the block and hustle 'em six for a dolla. Most a the cops don't get here 'till 7:30 or 8. By that time me and my homies a'ready made ten bucks each. And that's just for eggs. I can get anything. This is my house."

"How much do you make out of the kitchen each month?" I asked.

"At least five hun-ert. I never have to get money sent in. Shit . . . I send it out. I gets paid in stamps, macks, and tuna. And I got some eye-talian boys who buy everything I got. I ain't smoke, but I buy a little wine ev'y now and den. This job lets me do what I want. And I eats good. I ain't lookin' to change. Not 'less Smiley does.

"Sometimes dey puts him on da midnight to foe A.M. shift. When he switches I switch. And dat's even better. Der ain't hardly no cops on durin' dat shift. And der's only 'bout ten utter cats workin' wit me. I cook for everyone, Smiley too. And since der ain't no cops in da corridor, we all walk back to da block strapped wit food. I mean we carryin' everythin' dey got in da kitchen.

"Der's a-hun'ert and ninety-eight pieces a chicken in a box. I just says, 'Yo, Smiley, my peoples gotta eat. Let me get some chicken up off you.' He unlocks the door, tells me to grab what I need and says to just wrap ten up for him. Me and my boys take da rest up to da block. And you know chickens go for two bucks a bird. By the time me and my boys wack it up we all sittin' fat."

"What about the guard in the unit?" I asked.

"Shit," Lou says. "All I gots ta do is bring him a big brea'fast. I fix 'im up a cheese omelet, some bacon, potatoes, and buttered toast . . . man, dat niggas mine. He ain't fixin' to search me and my boys if he knows I'm bringin' 'em da hot plates. Not at foe in da moenin'."

Lou has the same reason for holding on to his job as everyone else. It helps him reach his own goals, and he gets along well with his supervisor. The administration could stop Lou from running his food business, but it doesn't. In fact, as Lou said, his supervisor lets him take what he needs. And as long as he feeds the unit officer, he has no trouble on that front, either.

It's easy to see how a job in food service benefits a food hustler. Some of the other work details don't provide such an obvious answer. For example, why would a prisoner choose a job in some of the more labor-intensive areas of the prison? The maintenance shops, for example, struck me as odd departments for a prisoner to seek employment. I spoke with long-time employees from each department, however, and learned that those jobs provided unique perks that weren't available on other work details at USP Atlanta.

Ron After I asked about his motivation for working in plumbing, Ron said "I go wherever the fuck I want, when I want. Whenever someone needs sumpin, they knows I can get it done and I keep my mouth shut."

"Don't tell me any names," I said. "Just explain why a guy could use a plumber in here."

"Simple. Let's say your toilet backed up. You can report it to the hack and he'll fill out a work report. By the time the work order goes through all the bullshit, five to ten days will pass. On the other hand, someone can kick me two bucks and I'll fix the toilet today."

"So you're willing to carry all those heavy tools around with you, climb all the stairs, stay on call to fix the kitchen pipes when they break, and do all the dirty work just because you make a couple of bucks whenever you fix a toilet? You can earn money in here a lot easier than that," I said.

"It ain't just fixin' toilets, my man. These tools are a gold mine. How do you think the liquor gets made 'round here?" Ron asked.

"Tell me."

Ron smiled, flashing a golden grill—a mouth full of gold-capped teeth. "I got the liquor business sewed up," he said. "With these tools I'm able to pull toilets off the wall and get into the crawl spaces. Ain't no cops shakin' down in the crawl spaces. After I remove the toilet, I build my little still back there. And every weekend, the still produces 'bout a quart of clear liquor."

"How do you make it?" I asked.

"It's Lucky's design," Ron explained. "He showed me how to build the still using some PVC pipe, a peanut butter jar with a vitamin bottle attached. I need 'bout 15 feet of quarter-inch copper tubing that I wrap in a coil. Some stoppers, clear plastic tubing, fresh dryer sheets to filter the smell, and a couple of buckets. After making a regular batch of hooch, I run the shit through my still. And every weekend I end up with the clear stuff."

"But how do you make the hooch in the first place," I asked.

"Making hooch is simple," Ron said. "You just mix orange juice, tons of sugar, and some yeast. The chemical reaction causes the mixture to ferment and after a few days it turns into wine. But I don't like the taste. That's why me and Lucky built the still. Once the shit runs through the still it comes out clear and tastes like vodka.'"

"Do you drink it or sell it?" I asked.

"Both. Me and my crew always keep ours, but I built stills for guys in every unit. Some guys sell some and I get a piece of that, others just pay me to build and maintain the still. Either way, I gits me mine," Ron said.

Other Jobs Ron's extracurricular activities weren't unique. Without exception, everyone with whom I spoke looked for jobs that would ease their time in prison. Some of the other prisoners who worked in maintenance would use their access to tools as a means of making *shanks*, prison-made knives. Prisoners in landscaping might use their access to the yard to hide shanks or drugs that one smuggled into the institution. Prisoners who work in the hospital might procure syringes—a valuable commodity on the compound for those who like to shoot heroin into their veins.

The guys developed routines, even became protective of them. The administration's goal was to divide the large prisoner population into small, manageable work details where staff supervisors could keep a close watch on the five to twenty prisoners assigned to the individual work details. Within many of these details, however, staff members develop quasi-personal relationships with the prisoners. Those relationships sometimes result in tacit *I-won't-bother-you-as-long-as-you-don't-bother-me* understandings.

Few staff members would openly condone Ron's using his position to build mini-distilleries, but neither are they eager to put forth the energy to follow Ron—and all the others assigned to their details—as he performs his work around the institution. Through constant observation, the prisoners figure out what's necessary to manipulate their jobs into positions that will help them ease their time. Sometimes it's about furthering a hustle; other times it's about using the jobs to open opportunities that aren't otherwise available in the prison.

Jerry Jerry, a glib prisoner serving a lengthy sentence, always has sought positions that place him in close contact with female staff members. "Psychology, education, health services, even the commissary are good places," he says. Jerry tells me that he looks for clerical positions because they allow him to keep clean and provide him with opportunities for conversation. "Once we're conversing regularly, we relate as human beings and not just inmate and hack. You know what I mean," Jerry says.

"I tell her good morning when I come in, tell her I like her outfit, her new hair style, whatever," he continues. "It's easy to notice everything in here because I don't have anything else to look forward to besides the time I spend with her at work. And I do look forward to it. Hell, I've fallen in love with three different staff members since I've been in."

"But how do you cross that line? How can you persuade the staff member—someone who easily can make your life even worse in here—to become involved with you romantically?" I asked.

"It just happens. The first step is to make that transition, to get her to stop thinking of you as a prisoner. Once she sees me as a man, and our conversations move from the general to the personal, we develop a level of trust between us. And our dialogue changes. Instead of calling me 'Inmate Prater,' or 'Mr. Prater,' she starts using my first name. And when no one else is around, I might use her first name. We talk about her family, about my family. I show her pictures of my life before prison. Our conversations move from the superficial to something meaningful. I develop a real interest in her feelings and the complexities of her life. In time, she, too, becomes interested in me and what goes on here.

"When she tells me that she's talking about me with her friends outside, then I know I'm in her mind. I know she's thinking about me just like I'm thinking about her. And everything kind of changes from there."

"What do you mean?" I asked. "How does it change?"

"Well, now I'm no longer a prisoner clerk. Now I'm a friend, someone who will listen to her in confidence. And, who's going to be more interested in her than me? I'm thinking about her every minute of the day. No one on the street can give a woman that much attention.

"If she has a good position, she can arrange to keep me with her during the 4 o'clock count or some other time when we'll have time to ourselves. The first step is usually pretty difficult; I mean the whole room is charged with electricity. We're talking closer. I smell her perfume, her hand might brush against mine, and maybe even rest on my shoulder for a second while she's standing behind me.

"Let's say her name is Kate. If we're working alone, which isn't uncommon if I'm working as her clerk on a weekend or during the evening shift, and the opportunity comes where we're close together, I'll say, 'Look, Kate, I'm feeling kind of nervous right now.' She'll ask why. 'Because,' I'll say, 'I'm not feeling like a prisoner right now and I'm not seeing you as a staff member. I'm a man seeing you as a beautiful woman—a woman I want to touch.'

"If it's right, she won't say anything. Instead, she'll show me I'm not alone in those feelings and we take it from there."

"Don't the bonds become too tight?" I asked. "I mean, you've got to grow more attached than she does."

"Hell yeah I do. I get so tied up in these relationships that I lose my mind. Especially when they realize the absurdity of it all. And they always do. My longest affair was only two months. But those two months . . . let me tell you . . . they completely consumed me. All my emotions. Hers too. We fell in love, and the whole thing became too much for her. She'd start crying at work. We talked about how this couldn't work between us, how she needed her job and such. I had to leave the job because there got to be too much tension. We couldn't go back to the prisoner-staff relationship after we'd been lovers. She eventually transferred to another prison."

"How about the other times?" I asked.

"The other times it was just me. I got emotionally involved. For them it was just physical. We had our thing, then they woke up, I guess, and just turned on me. Started becoming real distant. Called me 'Mr. Prater,' and shit like that. Now it's like nothing ever happened."

My Other Jobs Like every other prisoner with whom I spoke, I've also looked for employment opportunities that would help me with my time. In my case, I needed a place that would provide me with space alone. My first job was working in the library. After I'd been in Atlanta for six months or so, I started to get a feel for what life was like in prison and recognized the need to find a better job—one that would allow me to concentrate more on my goals.

I was fortunate to find a clerical position in one of the institution's business offices. My detail supervisor supported my educational program and informally allowed me to focus on my schoolwork as long as I had completed my clerical duties. In time, I became more proficient at my job and was able to finish my work in about two hours each day, thereby leaving me with the remaining six hours on the job to read my texts or type my papers. The job was so good it allowed me to study full-time in two university programs. I continued my work in Ohio University's correspondence program. And in 1989, when the new education building opened at Atlanta, Mercer University began offering courses inside the prison. I simultaneously enrolled as a full-time student there. This schedule enabled me to earn my bachelor's degree in June 1992.

For me, there was nothing more important than building a record that would help me earn freedom. I kept my distance from activities that could have exposed me to problems with the staff or other prisoners. Working, studying, and looking for opportunities to distinguish myself was my way of doing time; my thoughts always focused on steps I could take to prepare myself for the life I would lead upon release. And during the first ten years of my sentence, I never deviated from that goal.

After my first decade passed, I began to realize that regardless of what I accomplished in prison, nothing would help me advance my release date. No administrative mechanism existed for a prisoner to earn freedom more rapidly.

Instead of focusing all my energy on keeping a clean disciplinary record, I began concentrating my energies on preparing for leading a successful life upon my release. And that shift in goals resulted in my initiating independent education projects.

The Importance of Choice

Some may find it ironic that prisoners are given a degree of choice in their job assignments within these institutions of absolute control, yet a job assignment represents one of the few incentives that a staff member can offer a prisoner. These are men whose convictions have resulted in their loss of normal heterosexual relationships and distanced them from their families and communities. They have very little more to lose. The administration's main goal seems to be to prevent escapes, disturbances, abuse of staff, assaults on other prisoners, and unauthorized behavior within the institution. By allowing the prisoners some degree of choice in choosing their job assignments, they develop an attachment to something. They then have an interest in keeping it.

Accordingly, administrators may use those job assignments as an incentive for prisoners to refrain from the most outrageous violations of prison rules. Work details and quarter assignments are perhaps the two most crucial factors in a prisoner's time. They're important because they dictate where an individual serves his time in the prison and with whom. If a prisoner has a good job assignment and a quarters assignment that offers some degree of peace, he may be more inclined to behave in a way that won't result in his losing these privileges. And staff members make sure prisoners don't forget that both job and quarters assignments are privileges. As prisoners, most of our rights are subordinated to the administrator's discretion and institutional need. Prisoners can be reassigned to different jobs at any time, and a counselor has the authority to change our quarters assignment whenever he deems it appropriate.

PRISONER–STAFF RELATIONSHIPS

The job assignments in food services, maintenance, health services, education, clerical positions, or most of the other jobs in the penitentiary place prisoners in close daily contact with a single staff supervisor. Consequently, relationships develop between the prisoners and the staff. Having a good relationship with a staff member can result in the prisoner finding ways to make it through his bid easier. Lou was able to use his easy relationship with Smiley, his staff supervisor in food services, to further his hustle. Consequently, Lou made sure that he performed all of his required duties and did everything he could to keep Smiley happy. Ron took care of whatever his staff supervisor required of him. Consequently, Ron's supervisor gave him enough freedom of movement within the penitentiary to further his own activities.

Staff administrators don't condone these types of quid-pro-quo relationships between prisoners and staff, and they take safeguards to limit them. A warden perceives any violation of prison rules as a threat to the orderly running of the institution, and it is obvious to see how allowing a prisoner to supplement his income through the thriving underground economy by stealing food or giving prisoners enough free time to engage in the making of alcohol or manufacturing of shanks disrupts the administrator's objective of keeping control.

Administrators in USP Atlanta try to control these relationships. The controlled movements, pass system, and shift rotations help them control staff-prisoner relationships because they limit the amount of time staff members spend with a particular individual. SOP (standard operating procedure) policies discourage familiarity between staff members and prisoners.

Also, the administrators promote an esprit de corps between staff through frequent staff-member meetings. These meetings represent an effort to ensure that all staff members understand the administration's objective of order, by constantly reaffirming the fact that all prison personnel are correctional officers first, and they must remain united and ever vigilant against the wiles of the convicts under their supervision. Administrators also require all staff members to participate in regular training courses. They send staff members to other institutions to audit operations in other facilities, and they invite staff members from other prisons in for internal audits.

Besides this constant checking and rechecking, administrators encourage an informant system. Staff members might advance their careers by informing on their colleagues and thus performing a service that results in a more secure prison. Accordingly, they offer incentives to prisoners, hoping that some will betray their fellow prisoners for an extra phone call or perhaps a transfer to a desirable institution in exchange for information about corrupt staff members who work with prisoners in some inappropriate way. Treachery runs high behind penitentiary walls.

Indeed, administrators use any means necessary to maintain order inside the institution. Despite their efforts, however, some staff members will overlook rule violations if doing so makes their job easier. At the same time, other staff members enforce every rule at every opportunity, thereby creating an enmity between themselves and the prisoners around them. Indeed many guards seem consumed with the activity of prisoners and take a sadistic pleasure in frustrating the men around them. For example, mail can be withheld without consequences; blankets might be confiscated on Fridays to prevent a prisoner from receiving a new one until the laundry opens on Mondays; guards might not tell a prisoner he has a visitor waiting. Guards have an incredible amount of power over each prisoner's life. The Bureau of Prisons' motto is to be firm but fair. Some guards who see the prisoners in cages, however, can't resist the urge to poke them to exacerbate the tension.

Administrative Remedies

Prisoners have their own responses to abusive guards. The administration would prefer that prisoners use the administrative remedy procedures to report problems they have with staff members. The first step in this feckless process is for the prisoner to attempt to resolve the matter informally. If he can't come to a satisfactory resolution, he can then file paperwork against the staff member at various levels in the bureaucracy in sequential stages: first, the prisoner can appeal to the warden; next, he can appeal to the regional director; then, he can appeal to the director of the Bureau of Prisons; last, he can seek relief through the federal courts.

But, prisoners rarely achieve satisfaction through administrative remedy procedures. They perceive the responses received as rubber-stamp denials. Many continue to file administrative remedy procedures, however, because they are convinced that these complaints hinder a staff member's chance for advancement within the Bureau of Prisons. There may be a degree of truth to this belief, or perhaps the administrative remedy procedure is just an unwelcome interruption. Either way, staff members abhor having to respond to these prisoner complaints.

Although some prisoners relish the opportunity to "file" complaints against staff members, finding the administrative remedy process therapeutic, others prefer to take a more personal interest in responding to their problems with staff. Some responses to aggressive staff members include smearing the officer's telephone with excrement, hurling urine balloons at him from a distance, or setting off fire alarms in the guard's area of control. Prisoners also may collaborate to rid themselves of a troublesome guard.

Bullethead   Bullethead, for example, was the name prisoners gave to a particularly abusive guard. Prisoners perceived him as hating anyone wearing khaki clothing, but black prisoners were convinced that he also was a racist who took particular pleasure in harassing them. Blacks said he would stop them for random searches and go through their belongings before they had a chance to pass through.

One time, after he stopped a group of six blacks on their way to the yard for a random search, he had one prisoner's arms spread and was frisking him as the other prisoners watched. The prisoner being frisked said, "What? You called me a nigger?"

Bullethead protested, "I didn't say nothin'."

The prisoner said, "Yes, you did. You called me a dumb nigger."

The other blacks then joined in. "Yo, we heard ya."

"You called my man a nigger. Waz wit dat?"

"Bullethead you ain't right. Is we all dumb niggers now, is dat what you sayin' we is?"

"How you gonna call my man a nigger like dat?"

Bullethead protested, "Hey, wait a goddamn minute. I ain't say nothing 'bout no nigger."

"Man, call a lieutenant. You just can't be callin' me a nigger like dat. How you goin' let some shit like dat come out yo mouth? Ain't nobody call me no nigger. I want a see the muthafuckin' lieutenant."

By that time several other prisoners stopped by to ask about the commotion.

"Yo slim, what up?"

"Ain't nothin' but the usual. Bullethead called my man a nigger right here front a me and my boys. Now he's tryin' a say he din't do it."

"Thats some fucked up shit. Racist mothafuckas 'round here. Make a nigga wanna kill again."

The crowd continues to grow. Soon the lieutenant comes and disbands the group, instructing them to file an administrative remedy. The one prisoner who made the accusation does so, and the other five prisoners sign sworn affidavits stating they heard Bullethead utter the epithet. Bullethead can do nothing but deny it.

The result was that Bullethead was transferred from his post, and the prisoners rejoiced in their victory. Filing a standard grievance against Bullethead for frequent shakedowns and perceived harassment wouldn't have gotten too far in the administrative process. By making allegations of racism and introducing several corroborating witnesses, however, the prisoners were able to strike back and rid themselves of a guard whom they perceived as being particularly abusive.

PROGRAMS

In addition to the control techniques and the job assignment requirement, USP Atlanta also offers several programs to occupy the men's time. Some of these programs are formal, like those sponsored by the education department. Others are less so, like hobby craft programs sponsored by the recreation department. Religious services also sponsor programs that help prisoners develop their spirituality. And some community programs exist like the Mercer University program, which works together with the education department to offer courses that could lead to a university degree. Visiting programs also give prisoners something to look forward to. The administration authorizes these programs in an attempt to reduce prisoner idleness. If prisoners have something to work toward, administrators recognize, they may be less likely to engage in disruptive behavior.

Education

In the late 1980s, the Bureau of Prisons made it compulsory for all prisoners who didn't have a twelfth-grade education to participate in educational classes designed to lead them to a high-school equivalency certificate. Those who failed to pass the general equivalency exam couldn't earn the higher pay grades from the various prison jobs. Those who did obtain their high-school equivalency, however, could move forward and continue studying in college or vocational training programs. For motivated prisoners, those who are able to avoid the frequent distractions, educational programs offer opportunities to develop skills and prepare oneself for the future. They have been particularly helpful in my own adjustment to prison.

In 1989, USP Atlanta opened a new education building that featured several classrooms, a large leisure library, and typing rooms. During the evening, professors from Mercer University came into the prison and taught courses from a structured curriculum that would lead successful participants to an undergraduate degree. Yet, of the 2,700 prisoners in Atlanta, fewer than 200 participated in Mercer's program, despite the fact that government grants sponsored the courses and students had no financial obligations if they participated.

Relatively few prisoners appreciated the value of a college education. They were unable to see how college would contribute to their lives. I consider myself fortunate to have earned my undergraduate degree from Mercer University in 1992, because by 1994, the U.S. Congress abolished access to Pell grants for prisoners. When Congress cut off access to funding, Mercer University was forced to stop offering higher education programs inside the prison.

The education department also allows prisoners with special skills to design and teach courses on a voluntary basis. Such courses are part of the Adult Continuing Education (ACE) program. Prisoners designed ACE courses on managing small businesses, developing communication skills, accounting, understanding the stock market, and a number of other areas to help prisoners grow during their confinement.

Prisoners who design these ACE courses, generally, are proactive and find a measure of personal satisfaction or accomplishment through taking the initiative of leading a class. Those men who led conventional lives prior to their confinement experience a kind of sublimation through teaching; they find that imparting knowledge helps them escape, if only for a few hours each week, the regular monotony that is confinement. One ACE instructor who was an accountant before his money-laundering conviction told me that he identified with staff members more than the prisoners around him. "When I see the guards running in response to an emergency," the prisoner said, "I feel inclined to join them. But as a prisoner, I can't. Teaching these classes gives me at least the illusion of distinction, and I guess I need that in here."

Although administrators verbally expressed support for these educational programs, the reality is that many of the policies actually discouraged prisoners from participating. For example, prisoners would encounter problems being released from their housing units in time for the classes to begin. They would encounter problems from guards who wouldn't allow them to hold too many books or papers in their possession—regardless of whether the books were part of a course. Prisoners might not be excused from work assignments to participate in classes in which they wanted to enroll. And there was no formal distinction between a prisoner who worked to educate himself and one who made no effort to improve his skills beyond the GED. Accordingly, many of the prisoners found it easier to avoid the frustrations by not participating in programs associated with the education department.

Recreation

Recreational programs, on the other hand, differed in that they didn't have formal enrollments or present courses. The Recreation Department offered pool tables, foosball, hobby craft projects like painting, and leatherwork. It also sponsored the weight-lifting equipment, basketball tournaments, racquetball, tennis, and outdoor sporting events. Recreational programs are among the most popular in the penitentiary.

In the spring, all of the units organize softball teams that play against one another. Each evening, at least two softball games are played on the field. Hundreds of prisoners sit on the bleachers to watch the games, and bookies take bets on the various teams. Some prisoners may even recruit exceptional players to their teams, agreeing to pay them in commissary or to have money sent to their accounts. In the society of deprivation, significant bragging rights come with being a part of the prison's winning teams. Not only softball, but all the organized sporting events generate considerable enthusiasm on the compound. Softball and basketball bring the most spectators, but all competitive sports in the prison offer excitement, gambling, and a break in the monotony.

During the sixteen years that I've been confined, I've observed that basketball and weight lifting represent two of the most popular recreational programs in prison. Indeed, entire subcultures revolve around them. Several basketball teams exist within each prison, and some players take the sport more seriously than any other aspect of their confinement—more important than visiting with family, than outside correspondence, than preparations for release. Incarceration eliminates autonomy from many aspects of a prisoner's life, and since opportunities to distinguish oneself formally or favorably influence one's custody and classification scoring, much less one's release date, many prisoner's build their lives around prison recreational activities, with basketball and weight lifting the most popular among them.

Religion

A full-time chaplain worked in Atlanta to coordinate the religious needs of those prisoners interested in practicing their religion or developing their spirituality. The chaplain conducted religious services each week and arranged to have members of the clergy from other faiths come into the prison and lead religious services for the prison population. Individual study programs also were available through the chaplain, as well as a religious library offering literature and video and audiocassettes of a religious nature.

Many of the men sought sanctuary through some of the religious groups in the prison. A large community of the prisoners worshiped together, and many recognized that joining that community of worship provided some protection from the considerable number of predators on the compound. At the same time, some of these large religious communities were suspected by the administration of being fronts for racial gangs or predatory themselves.

Guards wouldn't allow prisoners to gather in groups of more than six without staff supervision unless they were participating in an authorized program. One way for prisoners to avoid this prohibition on gathering was to meet in the chapel. In the chapel, groups were allowed to meet for worshiping purposes. When lieutenants responsible for investigating prison gangs suspected that some of these groups were nonreligious, like the Identity Christians or

Five Percenters, they would accost the members, suspend their mail, search their lockers frequently, or order them to strip so gang investigators could photograph and record their tattoos and identifying marks.

Hundreds of prisoners, however, were active and dedicated participants in USP Atlanta's religious programs. Each evening the chapel offered religious study programs and a quiet place where people could pray and develop their spirituality.

Visiting

USP Atlanta offers visiting privileges five days each week. Through the visiting program, prisoners are allowed to spend up to thirty hours per month in the visiting room with visitors who have been approved previously by the individual's unit team. Prisoners can have up to ten family members and ten friends on their visiting lists at any given time; those whom the prisoner's unit team have approved may visit during regularly scheduled visiting hours. However, unless the warden makes an exception, the prisoner and the proposed visitor must indicate that they had a relationship prior to the individual's incarceration. For some unexplained reason, the Bureau of Prisons discourages prisoners from developing new community ties during their incarceration.

Visits are important to the prisoners in Atlanta. The visits take place in a large sterile room; yet it comes alive during visiting hours. Prisoners object to being strip-searched on the way into the room, but once they see their visitors the experience seems to remove them mentally, at least temporarily, from the penitentiary. Prisoners are allowed to embrace and kiss their visitors upon entry into the visiting room and again when they leave. They may hold hands during the visit, but, after the initial greeting, no more kissing or embracing is allowed.

At least three guards are present in the room for monitoring during the visiting hours. Cameras in the ceiling can be rotated to provide those outside the visiting room with a view of the room. Despite all the surveillance, overt and clandestine, prisoners still managed to evade the rules while I was there.

The most serious violation, of course, was using the visiting room as a means of escape. One prisoner who had been serving a fifteen-year sentence succeeded in his escape from Atlanta in the early 1990s. The exact method of his escape was never officially revealed to the prisoners, but the rumor mill had it that the escapee had his visitors smuggle in an extra set of clothing. The prisoner sneaked into one of the civilian bathrooms and put the street clothing on over his prison garb. When a crowd of visitors gathered around the door to leave, the prisoner mixed in with the group. Either he was able to transfer the infrared stamp from his visitor's hand onto his own, or more likely, he succeeded in having someone on the outside make an agreement with the guard responsible for checking departing visitor's hand stamps. Whatever the case, the other prisoners of the penitentiary, me included, were not released from our cell that night because the count didn't clear.

There was only one escape from the penitentiary during the six years I served in USP Atlanta. But several violations occurred through the visiting room. It was used for introducing drugs into the prison, and several prisoners were able to find ways to "get their freak on" despite all the guards. On a crowded day, it was easy for a prisoner to slide into the civilian bathroom with his female visitor and enjoy some quality time in the privacy of a public bathroom stall. Romantic. Behind the vending machines was another popular spot. Any area that blocked the guard's view provided an opportunity to violate the rules on sexual contact between prisoners and their visitors.

MY MOVE OUT OF ATLANTA

By 1994, the level of violence and chaos in the penitentiary had reached a high level. There were contract killings inside the prison, alcohol and drugs were everywhere, and steel and hard plastic shanks measuring as long as 18 inches were frequently found in the prisoners' cells. After a guard who had been sitting at his desk was bludgeoned to death with a hammer, *The New York Times* published a story that identified USP Atlanta as the most violent penitentiary in the federal prison system. The prisoners ran the joint.

I was then studying through correspondence at Hofstra University with hopes of earning a master's degree. I was seven years into my term, had a disciplinary report that was free of any infractions, and was working my way toward developing a record that I hoped would help me persuade others that I was a worthy candidate for support of my efforts to earn freedom.

Although I had several powerful friends inside the prison, I recognized that the highly charged environment meant that anything could happen at any given time. My two closest friends, Dan and Paul, were about to transfer to a new prison much closer to their home in St. Louis. With them leaving, I recognized it probably would be a good idea for me to request a transfer.

During the several years I served behind Atlanta's walls, I was fortunate to have had an easy relationship with both prisoners and staff. My unit team at the time was led by Mr. Chester and Ms. Forbes, both of whom were supportive of my efforts to educate myself. I had heard that Dennis Luther, the warden at FCI McKean, in northwestern Pennsylvania, was very supportive of educational programs, so I asked Ms. Forbes, my case manager at the time, to submit me for transfer to that prison. Although my records indicated that I wasn't from the appropriate region for placement in McKean, Ms. Forbes and Mr. Chester agreed to submit my transfer request to further my educational goals. I also called upon others from a strong network of support I had been developing over the years (which included several of America's leading penologists) and asked them to lobby the appropriate personnel to approve my transfer. Soon thereafter, Ms. Forbes came by my cell and told me my transfer request had been approved. I was on my way out of Atlanta.

CONCLUSION

In this chapter, I discussed the ways USP Atlanta's administrators managed the nearly three thousand prisoners serving time behind the walls. Nearly all of Atlanta's prisoners are serving sentences well in excess of ten years, and many of them have extensive criminal backgrounds and violent histories. They perceive themselves as having very little to lose. Accordingly, the warden and his associates write and enforce management policies designed to reduce prisoner idleness and increase accountability. They also offer activity programs for the prisoners and encourage staff members to remain loyal to the administration's management objectives through frequent meetings and cross training.

Despite its efforts, when I left Atlanta in 1994, one of America's most influential newspapers had dubbed USP Atlanta the most violent prison in the federal system. Drugs were rampant. Someone had escaped through the visiting room. Gangs were prevalent, and many staff members were corrupt. If the Bureau of Prisons' mission was to operate as a "correctional system," it was failing miserably in Atlanta. In the next chapter, I'll visit the very different culture of confinement fostered by Warden Luther's management policies at FCI McKean.

7

FCI McKean:
A New Experience

After ten years in USP Atlanta I was very excited about the possibility of a transfer to the medium security facility, FCI McKean. In this chapter I will describe my arrival at my new "home" and my amazement at the contrast with my prior incarceration. Warden Dennis Luther ran a very different type of prison, perhaps unique to the federal prison system.

HOW I GOT TO McKEAN

Within a few days of Ms. Forbes's telling me that my transfer to the Federal Correctional Institution at McKean had been approved, I was called to R&D (receiving and discharge) to pack out. I placed all of my belongings in boxes, recruited a few people to help me, and began my transfer out. It was exciting for me, a step in a new direction. And, I expected the transfer to offer new opportunities and an improvement to my quality of life.

In leaving USP Atlanta I'd be moving from a maximum-security prison to a medium-security prison. That means I would be around less severe offenders. In USP Atlanta, many offenders were serving life sentences and had no expectations of going home. In fact, as I was preparing to leave I ran into Frank B. again; he had just transferred to Atlanta from USP Leavenworth.

"Frank, how you doing," I asked. "Remember me?"

"No, I can't quite place you," he said.

"We met at MCC Miami back in 1987. I was just coming in and facing continuing criminal enterprise charges. You told me to fight 'em all the way."

"Oh yeah, I remember," Frank acknowledged. "How'd you make out?"

"I got forty-five years," I said.

"Sweet Jesus. I'm sorry to hear that," Frank responded. "But I know how you feel. Judge gave me four life sentences."

But, he wasn't the typical lifer serving time in Atlanta. Frank was a refined businessman from Palm Beach, Florida. Very articulate and clean cut, if he weren't wearing khakis behind Atlanta's walls, one might imagine him to be a leader in his community. Many people in Atlanta had sentences like Frank, but their behavioral patterns and backgrounds were much more like Smoke's, who considered himself a peaceful man but wouldn't hesitate to "peel a nigga's skull" or plunge a prison-made weapon through a man's heart if he felt he had been disrespected.

Atlanta remained a place where the men cheered when one of their own had "the balls" to beat a hack's head in with a ball-and-peen hammer. I was glad to leave, even felt blessed to have received the transfer I had requested. I was also glad that Paul and Dan, my friends from St. Louis, were being transferred out at the same time. They, too, would be transferring to a medium-security prison, one that would make family visits easier for them. Still, I felt sorry for Frank and many other prisoners like him that I had known in Atlanta. The structure of their sentences would require them to serve all of their time behind those walls, as BOP classification policies require all prisoners serving life sentences to remain in maximum-security unless special circumstances are made. For many, the penitentiary would be the last stop.

McKean wasn't only a medium-security prison, it was one that I had hand-picked from all the federal prisons. It was my first choice, and I was grateful to my unit team for using its influence to help me transfer there. I had first heard about McKean in a *USA Today* article by Tom Peters, the management guru famous for writing books about innovative leaders. He wrote about Warden Dennis Luther at McKean, describing him as a maverick, one who had the courage to lead rather than simply manage. From what I had read in the article, not only was Warden Luther supportive of educational programs, he also was willing to grant prisoners a degree of autonomy in managing their own lives.

After I read about McKean, I asked one of my mentors to see what he could learn about the prison. Dr. R. Bruce McPherson had then been working with me as an educational adviser for several years. I met Bruce through another prisoner in 1990. Our relationship began when I wrote him a letter expressing my eagerness to educate myself during my confinement. Bruce and I began an intense correspondence through which he would critique mercilessly my ideas and writing. In the process, he became a very close friend, a father figure to me. He began visiting me regularly, introduced me to his family, and helped me to become a better man.

When I read about McKean, I expressed my interest in that prison to Bruce. On my behalf, he made contact with Ms. Sylvia McCollum, the education administrator for the Bureau of Prisons at its Washington head-quarters. Bruce sought permission from her to visit FCI McKean to evaluate and contribute to its educational program. Bruce was a professor of education at the University of Illinois and at the University of North Carolina, responsible for motivating other professional educators. To her credit, Ms. McCollum was happy to arrange for Bruce to meet with Ms. Celia Barto, the supervisor of education at McKean.

Soon after, he drove from his home in Chicago to Bradford, Pennsylvania, where McKean is located. He spent a day visiting with Ms. Barto and several prisoners whom Ms. Barto said were active in McKean's educational program. And immediately after his visit, Bruce wrote me an outstanding report. He told me that when the time was right for transfer, McKean should definitely be my first choice.

It was important for me that Bruce not only spoke with Ms. Barto but also with prisoners participating in the educational programs. As a staff member, I reasoned, Ms. Barto would paint a glowing picture of the institution and her department. To get a clearer picture, I needed to hear what the prisoners had to say. But everything I heard about McKean came back extraordinarily positive.

Later, I had my own opportunity to get some firsthand information. USP Atlanta's education department was the subject of an internal audit where a team of staff members from education departments in other BOP institutions came to Atlanta for a week and inspected its operation. I was working as a clerk in education at the time and learned that Ms. Barto was coming as one of the auditors. I made it my business to identify Ms. Barto and see whether I could arrange an opportunity to speak with her.

On the morning of the audit, a team of perhaps fifteen staff members from other prisons came into the institution. I learned through my detail supervisor which one was Ms. Barto and was surprised to see that she was an attractive, well-dressed young woman, probably about the same age as I am. This was surprising, as the supervisor of education is at the level of department head in the BOP's organizational chart; my limited observations during the course of my confinement suggested that department heads usually were much older. I took this to be a good sign, one that suggested the warden at McKean was promoting people on the basis of competence rather than seniority. I approached Ms. Barto.

"Good morning," I said.

"Good morning," she responded.

"My name is Michael Santos. I understand you are the supervisor of education at FCI McKean."

"Yes, I am," she responded.

"I was hoping that I could speak with you at some point during your visit. I am considering a request to transfer and would like to learn a few things about McKean and the educational opportunities in that facility."

Ms. Barto listened to my request, probably surprised to have been approached by a prisoner. She said, "I have a bit of work to do this morning.

But later this afternoon I'll speak with you. I'll ask you some questions about the education department here for the audit, then you can ask me what you want to know about McKean."

"You're very generous. Thank you. I'll be here when you're ready to speak with me." I went about my duties and waited. Later that afternoon, when we had an opportunity to speak, she asked her questions for the audit—whether I found the staff responsive to the educational needs of the prisoners, any complaints, any suggestions, and so forth. Then, she asked me what I wanted to know about McKean.

I asked about access to computers, about the warden's support of educational programs, about prisoner-teaching opportunities, about the library, and whether she could confirm a rumor I had heard indicating that prisoners were allowed to purchase their own memory typewriters. Everything she said convinced me that when the time was right, I would work to arrange my transfer to McKean.

When I finally decided to transfer, a few months after meeting Ms. Barto, I asked Bruce to help me by writing a letter to the BOP's regional designator. I also called upon help from others in my network of support. In particular, I asked Norval Morris, a distinguished law professor from the University of Chicago with close ties to the Bureau of Prisons to help me. I had read several of Norval's books during the course of my studies, and after writing him to exchange ideas, he and I had developed a friendship through correspondence. He called the BOP's regional director on my behalf. I am convinced that Bruce and Norval's intervention were instrumental in my request to transfer to McKean being approved.

The Move

To avoid redundancy, I won't provide the minute details of the actual transfer. Suffice it to say that although several years had passed since I last went through the BOP transit system, the dehumanizing process hadn't evolved. I was awakened before dawn, chained, and directed through all the hurry-up-and-wait procedures necessary for transfer. This time, though, my spirits were significantly higher. By then, I had several years of experience in the federal system and I knew I was on my way to a place that my research suggested was going to bring significant improvements to my life. I found it difficult to contain my enthusiasm.

One thing I didn't consider, however, was that since I had come behind Atlanta's walls in 1988, my body had never moved at a speed faster than I could run. When I was loaded onto the bus, and the bus started to move, I started gripping the seat. I felt like I was on a roller coaster, or in a Formula One race car, totally unaccustomed to the speeds at which I was traveling. When we finally made it to the airplane, I felt relieved to be leaving the frequent stop-and-go and the swaying high-speed turns of ground transportation. I boarded the marshal's plane at a nearby air force base; got off the plane in Harrisburg, Pennsylvania; made an overnight stop at USP Lewisburg; and then traveled by bus to FCI McKean.

FCI MCKEAN

When the bus finally pulled in front of McKean, I was happy with what I saw. Instead of the massive stone structure that was USP Atlanta, McKean was designed like MCC Miami with several two-story buildings spaced along acres of green grass. Most important, there was no 40-foot wall enveloping the prison. It did have the double fences and coils of gleaming razor wire, but it was a noticeable step down in security. Eight other people were with me on the bus as I made my way into the prison. We were led to a holding cell for the expected fingerprinting, mug shots, and processing.

While waiting in the holding cell, I learned that a few of the other prisoners also were optimistic about the transfer to McKean. Within the BOP's northeast region, it turned out, McKean had a reputation as an easy place to do time. Prisoners called it the *Dream McKean*, and many would have liked to transfer there. The other prisoners were talking about what they had heard.

"The 'pound's got open movement on weekends and after the 4 o'clock count."

"I heard guys can buy hot plates from the store and cook in their cells."

"Man, niggas up in here can has they own TVs in days cell."

"My homies' here. He says McKean's da bomb."

I didn't talk to them but sat on the bench listening. Their conversation kept my spirits high, but I wasn't ready to reveal my own information. I was just glad to be taking in more that confirmed what I already had heard. Prisoners who appreciated the privileges of McKean, I thought, would be less inclined to cause trouble in the prison. And in an easy environment, I'd have more opportunities to develop myself. While I continued the wait, the other prisoners who hadn't been talking spoke up.

"Ya all niggas rappin' like you're goin' to Dinseylan'. It's still muthafuckin' jail."

"True dat, true dat," another confirmed.

The cold sound of reason. I was glad I hadn't spoken. Clearly not everyone was enthusiastic about this transfer to McKean. His comment made me realize that despite all the perks I'd heard about, I'd still be around a group of people who bitterly resented their confinement and those who held them.

We finally made it onto the compound around 2 o'clock that afternoon. Before reporting to my assigned quarters, unit 4A, I asked someone where the education department was located. Then, I walked over and was glad to see Ms. Barto easily accessible in her office.

"You made it here," she said after recognizing me.

"Yes. I just got in this morning. I stopped by here to say hello and to ask whether there was an opportunity for a job."

"What would you like to do?" she asked.

"Well, I type pretty well, but I can do anything," I said. "I'd like to find a position that would allow me to work on my studies."

"How much longer until you complete your program?" she asked.

"I'm writing an ethnography right now. It's a long report that describes USP Atlanta from the perspective of the prisoners. Once I finish that paper, I'll have to write my thesis. Then I'll be finished. I expect to complete all my work within a year, but I could work at a full-time position while I'm doing it."

"Could you work as a tutor in our computer lab?" she asked.

"Absolutely."

Ms. Barto then introduced me to Ms. Dillick, the teacher in charge of computers. Ms. Dillick hired me as a tutor, and she gave me permission to use the computer to work on my studies. So within an hour of being on McKean's compound I had resolved an important issue: finding a job. And the right job in prison is crucial to one's adjustment.

I then began walking toward unit 4A, to which I was assigned. While I was on my way there I ran into Flaco, a Colombian guy I had known in Atlanta. Flaco brought me some shower sandals, soap, shampoo, a razor, and other supplies to help me settle in. He also introduced me to some of his friends in the unit. I was assigned to a bed in the common area as there weren't any beds in the rooms available. By the time I settled in, the guard began walking around the unit shouting "Count time! Report to your room for the stand-up count! Count time!"

I was surprised to see how slowly most of the prisoners moved. Everyone laughed as one of the prisoners yelled out "Count these nuts, muthafucka!" These guys obviously didn't realize how privileged they were to be in McKean. The prison was as close to freedom as a medium-security prison could be, I thought. I wondered why they didn't appreciate it.

Later that afternoon, I met with Flaco again and he showed me around the compound. About one thousand prisoners were confined at McKean. While walking with Flaco I spoke with a dozen or so who had been confined with me in Atlanta previously. I also met with Jim, John, and David, the prisoners with whom my friend Bruce had spoken during his reconnaissance visit to McKean. They were all students in the University of Pittsburgh's Bradford campus; the university sent professors into the prison. The program was similar to the one Mercer University used to operate in Atlanta in that professors came into the prison and taught undergraduate courses that could lead to a degree. Somehow, McKean's program didn't terminate with the abolition of the Pell grants for prisoners.

Luther's Belief about the Treatment of Inmates

One of the most conspicuous differences between the management policies at USP Atlanta and FCI McKean was that the warden posted framed plaques throughout the institution identifying "Warden Luther's Belief about the Treatment of Inmates." In Atlanta, the warden hardly communicated with the prisoners. The warden in USP Atlanta made himself available by occasionally standing in the lunchroom, but when prisoners came to him with problems, he would patronize the men, making clear that he was boss.

I was standing by Alex when he approached Atlanta's warden to explain his problem in finding a law book he needed to complete a brief he was preparing for court. "Warden, a law book is missing from the law library. The rules on prisoner law libraries state that we're entitled to this book. I need it to complete a brief I'm filing. Every time I speak with the librarian, he tells me that he's not replacing any more books. I need your help in getting this book."

The warden stood listening to Alex's complaint. An underling stood on each side of the warden as they listened to the prisoner make his request for the law book. When he finished, the warden responded by calling one of the nearby lieutenants.

"Lieutenant Ramos," the warden called out.

"Yes warden," the lieutenant obediently answered.

"Lock this man up in SHU. Send him out west to Lompoc. Maybe he'll find the law book he's looking for out there."

Alex tried to protest, saying his family lived in South Carolina and that he didn't want to transfer to California. It was no use. Alex's protests went unheard as he was led away in handcuffs. I never saw him again.

In McKean, the warden's ubiquitously posted plaques made clear that not only were he and his staff approachable, but they took each prisoner's complaint seriously. The warden's creed listed over twenty-five numbered statements such as:

- Inmates are sent to prison as punishment, not for punishment.
- We will not tolerate abuse of inmates.
- Inmates are not an interruption of your job, they are the reason for your job.
- Inmates should be treated courteously and with respect.
- Staff must respond to all written inmate requests within five days.
- Inmate status does not imply that the person is less than human being.
- Do not be intimidated by an inmate's intelligence.
- McKean is not a place for those with insecurity problems to boost their self-esteem artificially by abusing inmates. . . .

Every statement on the warden's plaques made clear that he expected all staff members at McKean to treat the men with dignity. In return, the warden expected the men to act responsibly. As a prisoner, I knew that I couldn't ask for a better atmosphere. For several years I'd been living as a number, one who was suspected of acting treacherously on every occasion. Now, the plaques and my initial impression indicated I could expect to be treated as a human being. During that first week in McKean I saw two men walking through the unit inspecting for cleanliness. I heard one of the people around me comment that he's the warden. "Which one?" I asked. The guy told me the warden was the one on the right. I got a good look at him and prepared myself to approach him at the next opportunity.

First Meeting with Warden Luther

A few hours later when my unit was released for chow, I saw Warden Luther standing in the cafeteria with a couple of other staff members. I went to introduce myself.

"Good morning, Warden. My name is Michael Santos."

He returned my greeting.

"I'm a long-term prisoner in my seventh year of a forty-five-year sentence. I have been in Atlanta since I began and just transferred here earlier this week."

"Did you know Fred Stock while you were in Atlanta?" he asked, inquiring whether I knew the warden.

"Yes, I did. In fact, I spoke with him about my specific request to transfer here after I read about your support for educational programs," I said.

"We have an excellent education department here. Have you met Ms. Barto?" he asked.

"Yes, I have. She arranged for me to work as a tutor in the computer lab."

Our conversation continued in the middle of the chow hall while hundreds of other prisoners around me were waiting in line for their food, looking for tables, or sitting down.

"I wanted to speak with you about a specific request."

"What can I do for you?" he asked.

"Since I've been in I've been committed to an education program that I hoped would help me upon my release. I earned my undergraduate degree while I was in Atlanta and then I began working toward a master's. I'm hoping for your permission to purchase a personal word processor so I can complete my course work and correspondence while I'm in my cell."

"What kind of machine did you have in mind?" he asked.

"There's a portable word processor with a twenty-page memory available in a catalog I saw in the education department. It would help my academic program significantly, and I have the funds available in my commissary account to purchase it," I said.

"You know the Bureau doesn't allow inmates to have their own disks. I don't have any problem with them but I have to comply with the policy."

"I understand. That's why I looked for a machine with a large memory but no diskette," I said.

"If there's no disk I don't have any problem with it," he said. "What do you need me to do?"

"I need you to sign this request authorizing me to order it."

Warden Luther then signed the request and wished me well with my studies. The conversation went easily as he was very relaxed and spoke to me person to person instead of warden to prisoner. Prior to my transfer to McKean, I would have expected a warden to reject my request at once and dismiss me. Instead of looking for a reason to deny my request, he listened to my need and easily granted it. Luther was much more than a bureaucratic manager. He was a leader.

THE MENTORS PROGRAM

Over the next few weeks, I got to know the prisoner leaders on the compound and learned about the most influential programs. I became good friends with Joe Hargrave from upstate New York and Wayne Davis from Harlem. Joe and Wayne both had been down for about ten years and had a lot of influence. Many of the prisoners at McKean were from New York and idolized Joe and Wayne for the reputations they brought with them from the streets. In prison, Joe and Wayne were leaders, and as such had the respect of both staff and prisoners. As long-term prisoners, they recognized the benefits of Warden Luther's management style and so used their influence to persuade others not to engage in disturbances that would end the privileges at McKean. When younger prisoners from urban areas came into the prison, looking to bring excitement and the problems that accompany it, Joe and Wayne would pull them aside and describe the significant advantages of serving time in McKean as compared to other prisons where they had been held. Every man had an interest in keeping the peace, in reducing the volatility, because if they didn't, the administration would tighten security at the prison and eliminate privileges.

Joe and Wayne led me to the *mentors program*, which the psychology department sponsored together with the warden. The mentors comprised a group of long-term prisoners with demonstrated leadership abilities. Every Wednesday afternoon, the psychology department would sponsor a seminar on a different issue of coping with confinement. But instead of the seminar being led by a staff member, a mentor would lead the discussion group. It was a communications group. Through it, accepted leaders from the prisoner population would describe their experiences in other prisons and encourage the population not to create problems so the management wouldn't be forced to tighten the security at FCI McKean.

I recognized the mentors program as a valuable tool and readily accepted an invitation to participate. And I saw the positive influence of McKean's mentor group during an incident when the institution's captain began complaining about the quantity of rule violations rising and indicated that he was going to recommend the end of open movement on the compound.

The Mentors' Influence

Warden Luther called a meeting with the leading mentors in his conference room. This in itself was a change from the way I had come to expect wardens to treat prisoners. While in Atlanta, I watched the management style of two different wardens, neither of whom included the input of prisoners in their policy decisions. Warden Luther certainly was a maverick. With the prisoners seated at the conference table, Warden Luther entered the room, assumed his position at the table's head, and addressed the mentors.

"I called you here today to let you know we're about to implement some changes on the compound. The level of disciplinary infractions has increased to an unacceptable level. Accordingly, we will be eliminating open movement on the compound. And if the disciplinary infractions do not plateau, we will begin eliminating other privileges. I'm calling upon you as the inmate leaders to spread this message, and I'm counting on you to use your influence in persuading others not to ruin what we've got going here."

Joe Hargrave spoke up. "Warden, we appreciate your calling us in here and sharing your concerns. This is the only time we've heard about this. I'm confident we could have addressed this issue if given a chance. Have you already etched this new policy in stone?"

"Well," Warden Luther began, "the numbers pretty much speak for themselves. Over the last two quarters disciplinary infractions have increased by 8 percent. We're getting a lot more prisoners in from the penitentiaries, a lot more first-time commitments to an FCI. We've seen a difference in their behavior, and we need to respond. My budget is only so much. I can use it to initiate more programs, or I can use it to hire more officers and install more fences. It's your choice. As I've always said, I'll manage this prison according to how the prisoners behave."

Wayne said, "A-yo warden. How 'bout if we not only cause the level of disciplinary infractions to plateau, but we cause them to decline. Would you give us back the open movement then?"

"I was hoping I could count on you guys to do something about it. What do you propose?" the warden asked.

"If you give us a chance, we can spread the word to our peoples," Wayne said. "No one here wants to lose the open movement as that's part of the freedom that keeps the stress level so low. I'm sure once we spread the word and bring everyone up to speed we can make things right."

"I tell you what," Warden Luther said. "We're going to move to the ten-minute move system for the next three months. We'll evaluate the quantity and type of disciplinary infractions then. If they're brought down to the level we had in the year-ago period, we'll resume the open compound. It's on you."

Then Joe spoke. "Do you think we could post a tally of how many infractions are being issued—just to see if we're on target as time passes?"

"That's reasonable," the warden responded. "I'll instruct the associate warden of custody to list the quantity of disciplinary infractions for each severity level from last year and this year. I'll have the numbers available for you to pick up from the captain's secretary each Friday after count."

As I became more familiar with Warden Luther's leadership style, I recognized that his meeting with the mentor group was vintage. There were no secrets; there was no hidden agenda. Everything was placed on the table, an open book for the prisoners to see. His concern was to have a smooth-running prison, one with minimal disciplinary problems. By sharing his goal with the prisoners and communicating with them openly, he was able to make the prisoner leaders partners in his strategy to reach his objectives. The warden wanted an easily manageable prison; the prisoners wanted to serve their sentences in an environment that was free of stress. Luther encouraged a symbiosis between prisoners and management. And it worked.

The mentors announced to the entire population that they were scheduling a blitz of seminars to discuss the need to act responsibly. Because the message came from Wayne, Joe, and other mentors who had served ten years or better already, people who were respected in their communities inside and outside of prison, the message was well received. During the meetings, the mentors discussed the differences of life at McKean as compared to life inside other federal prisons. To continue the privileges, the men would have to cooperate in helping bring down the level of disciplinary infractions. "Otherwise we won't only lose the open movement," the mentors advised, "but we'll also lose everything else that makes McKean such an easy place to serve time."

There was a lot to lose. At McKean, Warden Luther made clear that he wanted no escapes, no suicides, no assaults, and no drugs. As long as he could contain these usual prison problems to manageable levels, he would allow privileges that would make life easier inside. Warden Luther allowed extensive commissary selections. He allowed twenty-four-hour television and telephone access. He even allowed the prisoners to purchase food from community restaurants once each month. If the prisoners didn't cooperate in minding their behavior, these privileges would vanish. But the prisoners got his message. When the designated time came at the end of the quarter, the numbers verified that the quantity and severity of disciplinary infractions had dropped significantly. Indeed, after the mentors' push, the level of disciplinary infractions dropped to its lowest level since the institution opened in 1990.

Issues and Choices

During that first quarter I spent at McKean, I really began to appreciate the culture of open communications and the warden's willingness to include prisoners in his management decisions. Indeed, by openly expressing his management objectives, Warden Luther was able to enlist support from the prisoner leaders and through them, the population. An atmosphere that was less stressful and therefore safer for both prisoners and staff was the result. Yet, it bothered some of the other mentors and me that others took the privileges we had for granted. We all had to live behind the same fences, but the actions of a few had the potential to ruin things for all of us. When someone was caught with a shank, or whenever I heard of another serious infraction, I remember thinking to myself that the McKean way of life couldn't last. The only hope for its continuation, I realized, was to persuade other prisoners to go along with the program. I suggested an idea to the other mentors that I thought might help spread the word.

FCI McKean dedicates one channel on all of the unit televisions for videocassette recordings. The prison rents movies from a local video store and uses this reserved channel on the television sets to show these VCR movies. I proposed to use the institution's video equipment to film a bimonthly information video that we could show over the movie channel when the movies weren't being shown. The videos would describe different issues at FCI McKean and the choices prisoners could make in response to them. The host of *Issues and Choices* would interview department heads in the prison and long-term prisoners. Through these shows, *Issues and Choices* would describe the management's position and long-term prisoners would comment on their experiences in other prisons. The goal of the show was to remind all the prisoners at FCI McKean how the management policies resulted in a low-stress atmosphere, and how we as prisoners had an interest in preserving it.

With the mentor group's support, I proposed the *Issues and Choices* program to Warden Luther. He authorized it, and we filmed the first show by interviewing the staff member in charge of the Inmate Benefit Fund (IBF) and one of McKean's most influential prisoners, Joe H. The show explained how the IBF provided a win-win situation for prisoners, staff, and the community. This McKean program allowed prisoners the privilege of purchasing clothing, athletic supplies, and food items from local vendors. The IBF added a small surcharge to all purchases, and profits were used to sponsor programs inside the institution for which no other funding was available. Vendors benefited by increasing their revenues through sales to the 1,000-man population at McKean. Prisoners benefited by gaining access to goods that otherwise wouldn't be available. The administration benefited by creating this tension-reducing program. As a long-term prisoner, Joe H. was effective in persuading others to support the IBF and in encouraging them to behave in a way that would ensure the stress-free life at McKean continued.

The *Issues and Choices* program succeeded because it provided a forum for discussing topics on the compound that impacted every prisoner's life. Warden Luther was so enthusiastic about the program that he appeared on the show whenever his presence was requested. Indeed, Luther supported every program that furthered the unique culture that his policies encouraged.

Breaking Down the Barriers

Another innovative program initiated by the warden required all new staff members to participate in a meeting with the mentors so they could learn about McKean's culture from the prisoners. Luther called this program "Breaking Down the Barriers." I sat through a few of these sessions during which each mentor introduced himself and explained his background and his activities in the prison. The new staff members then asked questions about prison life.

This open communication encouraged by Luther's Breaking Down the Barriers program discouraged the us-versus-them atmosphere that existed in USP Atlanta. Instead, the meetings helped the newly arriving officers understand that McKean was a different kind of prison. Every person behind the fence—whether that person went home after an eight-hour shift or remained behind the fences indefinitely—was treated like a human being.

With programs like Breaking Down the Barriers and the Mentors, Luther worked to ensure that everyone behind McKean's fences lived or worked in a safe, clean environment. By providing incentives that kept prisoners motivated to abide by the rules of the prison, he was able to keep the level of volatility considerably lower than that of other federal prisons. At McKean, for the six years that Luther ran the prison, there were no prisoner-on-staff assaults; there were no suicides; there were no escapes. Even the level of violence between prisoners was low. During Luther's time there was no gang problem, and I never knew of any arson or fights with weapons. Compared to USP Atlanta, FCI McKean was problem-free. Every prisoner had a vested interest in keeping things running smoothly.

"EARNING FREEDOM"

In addition to participating in the mentors and the *Issues and Choices* program, I also was busy working to complete the requirements of my own academic program. Within a few months after my arrival at McKean, I completed my final term paper. Only my thesis separated me from earning my master's degree.

I wrote to my graduate committee at Hofstra and proposed a unique idea. I wanted to explore the concept of earning freedom and asked permission to write my thesis in the form of a utopian novel, one that would contrast this idea of requiring prisoners to earn freedom through merit with the traditional concept of using the calendar to measure an individual's punishment. My committee at Hofstra approved my proposal and I began my work.

Realizing that I needed more information about prison management, I sent Warden Luther a copy of my thesis proposal and asked for an opportunity to discuss his ideas about the management of prisons. I knew it was a long shot, but Luther struck me as being so open that I thought he might answer a few of my questions if I presented them to him in writing. He surprised me by summoning me to his office the day after I submitted my proposal to him.

After making my way through the security gates that separated the warden's office from the prison's compound, I was led inside. I greeted him and he asked me to sit down.

"I read the proposal you submitted to Hofstra and I'm really enthusiastic about it," the warden said. "The truth is I'm considering retirement sometime in the next five years—probably sooner rather than later."

"I'm sorry to hear that," I said. "I don't expect these policies will last with another warden."

"That remains to be seen," Luther said. "I think we've got a good thing going here and I'd like to see more written about our policies. Perhaps your thesis can be a start. Why don't you prepare a list for me of the issues you'd like to discuss. Submit them when you're ready, and I'll set aside a block of time for us to talk."

"This is really a welcome surprise," I said, "and I appreciate it. Actually, I've got a pretty good idea of where I want to go with my work. If you have the time available, a brief discussion right now could really help me set the tone for 'Earning Freedom,' the title of my thesis."

I didn't know whether the warden was ready to talk with me when I came in, but I recognized this opportunity as a rare one. In all the years I'd been confined, I'd never heard of a warden permitting a one-on-one discussion with a prisoner in his office. Who knew whether he might change his mind? I was happy when he asked me how he could help.

"I suppose the easiest way would be to move forward with a kind of informal discussion," I said, "one that would help me understand your career and how you came to form your beliefs about the management of prisons. The nearly eight years I've served in the prison system lead me to believe they're unusual but very effective."

"Well, if I'm not mistaken, I've held the position of warden longer than anyone else in the federal system," Luther said. "I've been doing this for better than twenty-five years. Through my experience I've learned a lot, and I've come to realize some of the traditional methods of management could stand some improvement."

"What influenced your management policies? Were you in the military prior to joining the Bureau of Prisons?" I asked.

"No, I was never in the military. After graduate school I took a job as a case manager in Lewisburg. Readings, my educational background, my faith in God influenced my direction. I've always believed in the power of communication, and I think it's helped me here."

Luther leaned back in his chair to reflect for a minute, then continued, "Norm Carlson, one of the earlier directors appointed me warden of MCC Chicago. He was supportive of programs and so I felt comfortable beginning to develop my ideas under him. I was a warden in Chicago for a few years, then I moved around a bit, serving several years as warden in Eglin and Danbury. With each stop, I learned more about people. I also learned that providing incentives was an effective tool to keep prisons operating smoothly."

"Did you implement these same policies in all of the prisons you ran?" I asked.

"No, I would say my system evolved over time," he answered. "I had some ideas of what I wanted to do, but in order to implement those ideas I needed to open a new facility. That opportunity presented itself here. By coming on board from the beginning I was able to play a role in building the staff that shaped our culture. Our supportive staff has been an integral part of the success we've enjoyed at McKean. We may have had more difficulties trying to implement change in an existing prison. Here we had an opportunity to shape the culture from day 1."

"But your policies differ significantly from the policies at other federal prisons. Instead of depriving prisoners of access to goods they want, you seem to make everything available. How do your colleagues respond to these progressive management policies?" I asked.

"I've been doing this for a while," Luther said. "A warden with less experience might not have the confidence to try these policies out. It's much safer to toe the line, to manage rather than lead. I wanted to try some new ideas here, and they seem to be working out all right."

"As far as I know, McKean is the only medium-security prison that offers open movement, twenty-four-hour television and telephone access, extensive commissary selections, and many community programs. I'm curious how your superiors respond to all the privileges we have here?"

"By every internal measure McKean comes out on top," the warden responded. "It's hard to argue with our success. Since we opened this prison in 1990 we've had no escape attempts, no inmate-on-staff assaults, no murders or suicides. Objectively, we have a well-managed prison. We also have the lowest staff-turnover rate in the Bureau. This tells me that our staff members enjoy working in this environment we've created. Despite the cowboys out there, I think our record reveals that we're doing all right here."

"Why then do you suppose other wardens manage their facilities so much differently? Why do they encourage that enmity between prisoners and staff?"

"I don't think other wardens set out to create hostile atmospheres. Their policies are just different from mine. As I've said when addressing the mentors, wardens are allocated a certain amount of money each year to operate their prisons. Some use their funds to install more fences and security measures. Such policies can't help but make life more difficult for the people inside. Inmates and staff. I've found it more effective to look at the big picture."

"What do you mean by the big picture?" I asked.

"Prisoners were sent to prison for a certain amount of time. There's nothing I can do about that. It's my responsibility to keep them in prison, but I'm not here to punish people further. That job belongs to a judge. My job is to incarcerate them for the length of their sentence, and I hope that at the very least I'm doing everything I can to ensure the men don't leave here worse than when they came in. I try to reduce the level of tension by making it as easy as possible for an individual to make something useful of his life so that when he does leave prison, he'll be able to find his place in society. Besides that, I'm convinced that a less stressful environment makes our prisons safer for staff members and less costly for taxpayers."

"What flaws do you see in your plan?" I asked.

"The biggest flaw is that we're kind of at the mercy of the people this prison holds. Some people are so full of hate that they're bent on destroying a good thing. I was walking through segregated housing the other day and an inmate yelled out at me, 'Who the fuck are you asshole?' I told him that first of all, we don't talk to people like that in here, and to answer his question, I am the warden. The guy said 'I ain't give a fuck, that's the only way I know how to talk.'

"Some people don't know how to communicate. There are a lot of prisons better equipped to manage those bent on causing disturbances. But we can't choose our clientele. And too many bad apples can spoil the whole pie."

"Can't you request the region to send you the type of prisoner you're looking for here?" I asked.

"That would be nice," the warden said. "But our system doesn't work that way. McKean is a medium-security prison, and we're prepared to receive all prisoners who have been properly designated. And again, all has been going well since we opened. We've got a pretty good system for spotting the troublemakers and we've been able to respond before things get out of hand."

"When I first arrived here," I said, "there was a move to close down the open movement system. Was that your idea or were other members of the staff urging you to tighten things down?"

"That was a response to a change in the behavior of our population. We manage our numbers pretty closely. During those months we noticed an unacceptable increase in disciplinary infractions. And it was consistent with our management plan to do away with privileges if the men can't act responsibly; the privileges exist only as long as the inmates allow it. If people act responsibly, our staff will treat them responsibly. If they want us to micromanage them, we can do that, too. But I'm pleased with the way things turned out. I am convinced that an open system fosters a safer environment for inmates and staff."

"As I wrote in my proposal," I said, "I expect to write my thesis in the form of a utopian novel. I will use dialogue to juxtapose your beliefs about the treatment of prisoners with those of a well-known prison scholar who advocates a much stricter approach to managing prisons."

"To what prison scholar are you referring?" the warden asked me.

"John DiIulio," I said, and the warden smiled. "He's a professor at Princeton who has published several books on prison management," I continued.

"I know John," the warden said. "He's a friend of mine."

"John DiIulio's a friend of yours?" I asked incredulously. "That strikes me as odd. How do you reconcile the liberal way you manage McKean with the tight policies Professor DiIulio advocates?"

The warden chuckled. "John and I aren't as far apart as you think. And what makes you say my policies are so liberal?"

"Well, look at the perks prisoners have here," I said.

"But those privileges exist only as long as the inmates abide by the prison's rules. It's quid pro quo. As far as I'm concerned, the men earn these privileges by acting responsibly. Nothing is given. Swift and certain punishment is part of my philosophy. But it's only part. Another part is rewarding those who act responsibly."

"I suppose you're right," I said. "After so many years in prison, I'm just not used to hearing prison administrators express these thoughts."

"Well, why don't I let you get back," the warden said. "I've got a meeting to attend. When you need some more information, let me know."

"You've given me a lot to work with," I said. "I'll keep you informed of my progress. And thank you again for giving me so much of your time."

"You're quite welcome," the warden said as he led me to the door. "And good luck to you with your writing."

DiIulio's Visit

Professor DiIulio and I had formed a correspondence back when I was in Atlanta. I read an article he wrote in the *Wall Street Journal* about the need for tougher prisons. I wrote to tell him why I disagreed with his article and that began a dialogue through the mail. After speaking with Warden Luther and learning that he and DiIulio were friends, I wrote to the professor and told him that I had transferred to McKean and had met his friend the warden. That letter opened a new opportunity for me.

DiIulio wrote me back and told me that the warden was indeed a friend of his. "Dennis Luther is perhaps the best warden in the business and perhaps the only warden who could make his policies work," DiIulio wrote. He then suggested that he bring a group of his students at Princeton up to McKean for a visit during which time I could discuss my experiences in prison with them.

This was an outstanding opportunity for me, I thought. As a long-term prisoner, I always welcomed the opportunity to meet people who weren't standing up for the 4 o'clock count. But I especially welcomed the opportunity to discuss ideas with these students and DiIulio.

DiIulio made arrangements with Luther, and several weeks later I was summoned to the warden's office early on a Saturday morning as we waited for DiIulio to arrive with his students. When they finally did arrive, about fifteen students and the professor, we spent time in one of the warden's conference rooms and listened as Luther explained his responsibilities as a warden. The students asked me questions about life in prison, and then we toured the facility. We then returned to Luther's conference room where the warden and I responded to the students' questions.

During that meeting I obtained more information from both Luther and DiIulio that I was able to use in my thesis. For one thing, I learned that Luther believed the prison system was filled with too many people who didn't belong behind fences. When DiIulio asked him how many of his prisoners he thought could safely be returned to society without endangering their communities, Luther contemplated the question, then surprised me with his response. "Thirty percent of these people don't belong in prison. It's a waste of taxpayer money and human life to continue their confinement. And it's one of the reasons I've decided to retire from this position."

The Thesis

Learning that Luther expected to retire within the next year, I was disheartened. I had been serving time at McKean for less than a year and had hoped to remain there for the next several years of my sentence. I decided to concentrate on writing my thesis as I wanted to earn my degree before Luther left. There was no telling what changes might come with a new warden. And if I were transferred to another prison, I couldn't be sure whether I'd have access to a word processor to complete the extensive writing project. I finished the thesis in the early spring of 1995 and felt honored when Hofstra University awarded me my Master of Arts degree, the second degree I had earned from prison. Luther announced that he would be retiring later that summer.

Before he left, the warden told me he would be interested in exposing more people from the academic community to the unique culture at FCI McKean. I told him that because I had studied prisons from behind prison fences, I had come into contact with many of America's leading penologists. I told him that, with his permission, I could contact those professors and see whether they would visit McKean for a discussion on prison issues. The warden gave me permission to move forward, and over the next couple of months professor Marilyn McShane came from the California State University as did Professor Timothy Flanagan, then from Sam Houston State University.

LUTHER'S FINAL DAYS AT FCI McKEAN

Warden Luther was an aberration from most prison wardens in that he recognized the prisoners were a part of his community. He made efforts to give us a degree of control over our destinies. If the prisoners complied with keeping the level of disciplinary infractions down to a manageable level, the warden would authorize programs that would ease our way of life. And he authorized many.

Besides the Inmate Benefit Fund, another program that Luther supported was a video program through which prisoners could purchase a videotape and film a greeting that could be sent to their family. Luther authorized outdoor cookouts to provide the prisoners with a simulated picnic. He also authorized a program called "Family Day," where well-behaved prisoners could bring their family members into the prison for a full day of less structured outdoor visiting. And he allowed all types of programs from the community into the prison.

One prisoner at McKean had close ties to the music industry. The prisoner asked the warden whether he could arrange to have Willie Nelson, the famous country singer, come into McKean for a one-time performance. The warden agreed, and, just before his retirement, we had Willie Nelson Day at McKean where the singer performed a live two-hour concert on the recreation field for all.

Because of Luther's management style and the culture he created behind McKean's fences, 1,000 convicted felons whom the Bureau of Prisons designated as needing medium-security were able to serve their terms in relative harmony without presenting a danger to staff members, to each other, or to government property. All were disappointed to see Luther go in the early summer of 1995.

WARDEN MEKO'S FIRST VISIT

About a month before Luther was scheduled to retire, he called Joe H., Wayne, and several other influential prisoners on the compound to his office for a meeting. Luther wanted to introduce the mentors to Mr. Meko, the new warden at McKean. Mr. Meko explained that he wouldn't be taking control of the facility until the following month, but he had come to McKean for a tour of the prison. He said that he was very impressed with the culture warden Luther had created and that he didn't expect to make any changes upon his arrival.

The mentors had been hoping that Luther's able assistant warden, Craig Apker, would take over the warden's position. But word had it that Mr. Apker was transferring to another institution. So there was a fear of the unknown. How were things going to change with a new warden? When the mentors heard the new warden express his support of Dennis Luther's policies, however, everyone was relieved.

All long-term prisoners knew and understood the quality of life in other prisons—or lack thereof—and expected a new administration to abandon the unique programs and way of life that Luther had created. But Meko made clear that he respected the environment Dennis Luther had built and gave his word that he wouldn't change anything; in fact, the ubiquitous plaques describing Luther's belief about the treatment of inmates would remain on the walls. Meko even appeared on the *Issues and Choices* program to make this announcement to the entire population.

CONCLUSION

Warden Dennis Luther administered FCI McKean according to his belief that a culture can be created in each prison. His overriding philosophy was that "If you want people to behave responsibly and treat you with respect, then you treat other people that way." During his six years as warden there were no escapes, no murders, no suicides, and only three serious assaults against guards and six recorded against inmates. With Luther's retirement, Warden Meko assumed the helm. From what the mentors heard during their meeting with him it appeared that McKean's new chapter wasn't going to be so bad. Or so they thought.

8

A Prison Disturbance
at McKean

Warden Meko arrived at McKean toward the summer's end in 1995. He had previously worked as an administrator in the BOP's central office. With him came Associate Warden Nuss, who replaced Warden Luther's protégé, Craig Apker. Contrary to what Warden Meko had said during his interview on Issues and Choices, *upon their arrival, Meko and Nuss began implementing changes on McKean's compound. And, the changes weren't gradual. In this chapter we will see how the culture of McKean changed as a result of both the policies of the new warden and the political environment outside of the institution.*

THE NEW WARDEN

Almost immediately, the new administrators dismantled the Inmate Benefit Fund. This was a strike at the core of Luther's programs, as the IBF did more than allow the men confined in McKean to purchase items from community stores. It also was the source of funding for the many extracurricular programs inside the prison and so was a key source of incentives for the prisoner population.

For example, prisoners elected to the IBF management committee purchased several video monitors with a self-contained VCR machine for each housing unit. The prisoners also purchased several videocassettes. Staff members inspected the housing units each week, and those with the cleanest cells were rewarded with access to the incentives so they could watch movies in the privacy of their cells.

Profits from the IBF also contributed to the college program, paying for guest speakers from the community, and for recreation and educational programs that otherwise wouldn't have been available. Losing the IBF funding resulted in the direct loss of several programs.

More noticeable than the dismantling of the IBF program was the manner in which the change was implemented. Meko didn't announce his change to the mentor group. He didn't discuss it with prisoner leaders on the compound. He provided no reason at all; he simply ordered the disbanding of the group. If reasons existed for canceling the IBF, Meko didn't deem it necessary to share them with the population. This approach to change was very different from the one Luther's leadership team had encouraged.

During the first weeks of Meko's administration, he initiated a change in policy restricting the places where prisoners could be photographed. He also now required prisoners to leave the television rooms during count times. Prisoners were no longer allowed to wear clothing with any colors on the compound. We also were required to wear khaki uniforms to the dining room, education department, and chapel until after the 4:00 P.M. count, whereas before we could wear personal clothing purchased through the IBF programs. All of these policies were normal operating procedure on other prison compounds. While Luther ran McKean, however, he relaxed these regulations in an effort to ease the tension and discourage prisoner disturbances.

Luther, however, had retired and was no longer leading the policies that governed FCI McKean. Luther's plaques stating his beliefs about the treatment of prisoners were taken off the walls soon after Meko assumed control. Rather than governing his prison through the use of incentives and open communication, Meko chose to use a much more punitive approach to management, taking away privileges and threatening stiff sanctions. Further, Meko and his staff were adamantly opposed to open communication or any interaction with prisoner leadership groups. The new management style that Meko introduced, combined with coincidental societal forces (described below), resulted in a pressurized atmosphere that soon exploded into a dark morass of violence.

THE CRACK COCAINE ISSUE

By October 1995, the federal prison system had swelled to well over one hundred thousand prisoners. The vast majority of these prisoners were serving sentences for convictions related to the distribution of illicit drugs, and the skin color of the population was becoming disproportionately dark. Black prisoners that were serving time for distributing "crack" cocaine were serving sentences significantly longer than the white prisoners that were serving time for distributing "powder" cocaine.

In fact, under the 1987 U.S. Sentencing Guidelines, offenders who were convicted of distributing 5 grams of crack cocaine received the same sentences as offenders who sold 500 grams of powder cocaine. Since crack cocaine was predominantly restricted to black communities, the vast majority—well over 80 percent—of offenders selling crack were black and received proportionately longer sentences than their white counterparts who, for the most part, sold powder cocaine. Many Americans—especially those in prison—perceived racial undertones in the sentencing disparities.

In October 1995, black prisoners throughout the federal system were paying close attention to federal legislation addressing the disparity between crack and powder cocaine sentences. Prisoners complained that both substances were cocaine and the U.S. Congress shouldn't authorize the huge 100-to-1 disparity between crack and cocaine sentences.

When journalists reported that lawmakers had elected to maintain the significantly higher sentences for defendants convicted of crack cocaine offenses, federal prisoners in Memphis, Tennessee, and Allenwood, Pennsylvania, began rioting. By early Friday afternoon on October 20, hundreds of prisoners on McKean's compound were talking about the riots in other federal prisons. Hundreds began talking on the compound about "settin' it off" at McKean. Meko responded by shutting the prison down for a few days.

Lockdown

After the 4 o'clock count cleared on Friday afternoon, the unit manager from each unit called a "town hall" meeting to address the prisoners. I was assigned to unit 1B, the honor dorm, with about two hundred other men. Those of us in the honor dorm had been assigned there by application, and because each of us had a long history of disciplinary-free conduct. Ms. Kennedy, our unit manager, announced that the warden wanted to lower the tension inside the prison. Accordingly, he was confining the men to the housing units until further notice. We weren't confined to our rooms, just inside the buildings. The lockdown prevented prisoners from communicating with those confined in other units. Meko also was stopping our access to the telephones. He allowed VCR movies but ordered maintenance personnel to disconnect cable reception so that prisoners couldn't watch television; Meko wanted to filter all information coming into McKean about the other federal prisons that were rioting over the crack issue.

Although we didn't have access to television, prisoners could listen to news reports over the portable radio we had purchased from the commissary. Every hour we heard reports about prisoners causing massive amounts of property damage in several federal prisons. The more militant prisoners in each unit were gathering in small huddles and openly expressing their contempt over the injustice of their sentences for convictions related to crack cocaine. Informants found a way to communicate with staff members about which prisoners were initiating a disturbance, as every few hours guards would come around to escort one or two guys to segregation.

On Sunday evening, about forty-eight hours after the lockdown began, Ms. Kennedy, the unit manager, held a second town hall meeting. She said that the warden had decided to hold a holiday schedule on Monday. This meant the entire compound would be free to meet in the dining room for meals, on the compound, and in the recreation area. It would be the first opportunity all prisoners would have to communicate with one another since the unit lockdown began on Friday. And by Monday, a lot of news and rumors had spread through McKean's compound regarding the disturbances in other federal prisons.

A lot of the staff members at FCI McKean were expressing their opinions that although other federal prisoners were rioting, nothing would happen at McKean. The prisoners, these voices said, were too complacent with the lives they were living. Anyone who mistakenly held this opinion didn't take into consideration the significant changes Meko's administration had brought to the institution. Prisoners might have considered it the Dream McKean under Luther, but now it was no different from any other medium-security prison. There was a lot of hostility in the air—and a lot of open talk about orchestrating a disturbance.

The Disturbance

By Monday evening, everything seemed chaotic on McKean's compound. People were congregating outside the units in large clusters. Ordinarily, staff members would have broken up the groups, but the noticeable rise in prisoners' anger caused the guards to allow more things to slide than usual. With the changes that Meko had brought to the institution, I had been trying to keep a low profile, purposely staying away from the action. But even I had heard prisoners talking about taking over the prison. I didn't believe it, but I heard the talk.

My normal routine would have been to rise early in the morning, before dawn, then go to the gym for either an early-morning workout or a run. But I had heard others talking about going to breakfast and then "settin' it off in the chow hall."

Despite the heated talk, initiating a riot seemed foolish to me. The BOP seemed well equipped to handle any type of violence behind the fences. After all, the administration controlled the flow of food and water, so the prisoners couldn't hold out for too long without obtaining cooperation from administrators. And that was unlikely. Besides, I couldn't make the connection of how participating in a massive prison disturbance would translate into relief from long prison sentences. If anything, it seemed to me that a prison riot would encourage taxpayers to scream for even tougher sentences. I decided to stay in my cell on that cold October morning.

Mark, my cellmate, was a UNICOR worker. We had spoken about the rumors of a disturbance before we had gone to sleep on Monday night. Neither of us believed anything dramatic would happen, but we weren't really connected with the guys doing all the talking, so we couldn't be sure.

Mark left the cell about 5:30 Tuesday morning and quickly returned telling me there were fires burning in the unit's common area and that no guard was in the unit. I got out of bed to see what was going on.

Most of the people assigned to the honor dorm were long-term prisoners who chose not to take part in the disturbance. The few people involved were in their early twenties and didn't have much direction. The fires Mark was talking about were contained to two trash cans, and once they burned out, nothing else happened. This was not the case in six of the other housing units. In fact, every unit except the honor dorm and the unit for UNICOR workers was engaged in a massive property destruction campaign in protest of the disproportionately longer sentences that crack-cocaine defendants received.

X's Unit   I later had an opportunity to speak with X, who was confined in unit 3B when the riot jumped off. X, a Nation of Islam militant, had adopted the single-letter name as a show of defiance to the "slave name" he said he had been inappropriately christened with at birth. I asked him what he remembered about the disturbance.

"Fa' real," X said, "I thought cats was fakin'. My mans an 'em kicked it wit' me Monday night 'bout settin' it in the chow hall at breakfast. Cats heated 'bout dat crack shit."

"How were they going to set it off?" I asked.

"Just tear shit up—ya heard? I'm sayin', cats be on some bullshit. Niggas be doin' a lot of fakin'. Everything real—Detroit and Clevelan' niggas stepped to me like, 'yo, NY rollin' or what?"

"Come on son, we wit whatever." X told the others that his group from New York would join forces with the groups from Detroit and Cleveland.

"That night me an' my mans an 'em stayed up on some late night shit." Word, we broke nite watchin' da videos. I'm sayin' a nigga got tired so I tol' my mans an 'em I'll get wit 'em later on, tol' 'em to holla at me when da doors pop. If cats fakin' then fuck it.

"A yo, 'fore da kid could crash out, it was on. Cats was doin' they thing. Niggas had da fire 'larm on blast, mad niggas rennin' 'round tellin' cats to suit up and lace up. Mad cats was rockin' da khakis and da hat piece runnin' 'round da joint. I'm sayin', shit was bananas. Word! Niggas was like, 'Fuck dat breakfas' shit. I'm sayin', da kid said fuck it. I put my shit on and slid downstairs. A yo. When da kid got downstairs, it was like—yo, cats was outta control. Cats was tyin' da doors down wit buffer cords. Niggas flipped da pool table, put da shit in front a da door so Jake couldn't get in. Yo, son, niggas was amped up. Shit was real propa. Niggas just started gettin' caught in da hype. We laced da floor wit mad baby oil an' crazy ice in case Jake came runnin' up in da piece. Dat way they bus' they shit. And you know how dem German cats move. . . ."

"What do you mean Germans?" I asked.

"My bud," X explained. "Up in N.Y. we calls Spanish cats Germans," he continued. "Da Germans was tearin' da laundry room up kid. Word! Dem niggas was takin' da cheddar out da machines an' da whole shit. Then niggas tried to get up in Jake's office, know what I'm sayin', burn da bed books an' shit."

Translation: X explained that while most were tearing apart the units and barricading the doors early on that Tuesday morning, others were taking apart the coin-operated laundry machines and robbing the quarters inside. Still others had broken into the guard's (Jake's) office and were destroying the paperwork. He continued his colorful description.

"Outta nowhere dis other cat jus' came an' smashed the windows. Word, they started burnin' shit up. This one stupid-ass muthafucka lit da wooden console. You know, da shit days in da center of da unit. Anyway, da nigga smoked us out. Had niggas on some real fireman shit, ya heard?"

"Yeah, I hear ya," I said. "I didn't think it would blow up like it did myself. Do you think it was just the crack thing that set it off?"

"Naw. It was more than that," X explained. "First, cats wasn't feelin' dat warden no how, know what I'm sayin'. He come to da pound on some real tough-guy shit an' just flip shit. Niggas wasn't feelin' dat at all. Then you had mad cats kickin' same shit you kickin' now—ain't shit gonna happen, niggas wakin' up in here, ya know. It's like ya'alls shittin' on a nigga's character. So cats got in they feelin's and shut shit down."

"But what were you tryin' to do?" I asked. "You're not even in here for crack."

"Yo, check this out," X explained, "I'm in da struggle and my mans an 'em in da struggle. Ain't a whole lot ta dat. We goin' hard t'gether, ya heard? I'm sayin', da kid definitely wasn't gonna jump out there an' set it. But once it was on, it was on."

"So how long did it last?" I asked.

X thought about it for a second. "I think it jumped off 'bout 5:00. Yeah, some shit like dat. But one thing fa sure. It was light out when we finished; Jake come up in there 'bout 6:30."

"There was no cop in the unit when you woke up?" I asked.

"Crazy! Jake was out there," X recalled. "By da time I got up, niggas had shit locked down. Doors an' everything was shut down. Jake had to bus' da glass. Word, them niggas had da bullhorn an' all dat. Talkin' 'bout yo, move da barricades so they can get in. Niggas was like 'Beat it. Get da fuck outta here wit dat shit.' Word!

"Then my mans an 'em took da buffers up stairs to da second floe so they could smash them niggas out if they tried ta come through da front door. My man Smooth got on some real warrior shit. He was on top of da tier with a bandana 'round his head. He started kickin' his own beat. 'Who's my brutha?' he'd scream. And my niggas would holla back, 'You my brutha!' Smooth would answer: 'What we need?' and we'd all holla back 'Unity!' Within a few minutes the whole unit's joinin' in with Smooth's rhythm:

'Who's my brutha?'
'You my brutha!'
'What we need?'
'Unity!'
'Who's my brutha?'
'You my brutha!'
'What we need?'

'Unity!'

"Yo!" X continued, "Niggas was really feelin' dat shit minute. Then Jake got up in there. Them niggas came through the door. My man dropped da buffer but he missed. Word. Muthafuckin' Jake started tear gassin' da joint up. Niggas started breaking out, bouncin' back to they rooms. Yo, when I looked out my room window, dem Ninja-Turtle niggas was comin'. Them muthafuckas was suited up an' ready fa war. Fa real."

"Is that when it ended?" I asked.

"Hell no," X said. "Da cats sleepin' in da common area was fucked up by da gas. Jake rushed in screamin' an' shit, tossin' them niggas in da two-mans, ain't carin' dat da room's full. They tol' 'em niggas to sleep on da floor. Word, da shit was mad crazy!"

"What happened after they cleared the unit out?"

"They locked us down, then bounced to da other units dat flipped," X said. "A little after 9, mad Jake come poppin' da doors one at a time. Word! Tyin' cats' shit behind they back wit them plastic handcuffs. Them shits was hurtin', too. They didn't tie y'all cats in da honor unit down?" X asked me.

"Our wrists were tied in front. I guess since there was hardly any damage in our unit they weren't too concerned about us," I answered.

"Yeah, well Jake punished us," X said. "They had da kid's shit tied fa two hours. My shoulders was killin' me. They didn't switch shit up 'til they brung lunch. Den they tied my shit in da front. I was still fucked up, but you know, shit got better. After dinner they untied niggas. You know, they had to do dat interview shit—axin' a nigga who did what, dis dat and da other. I tol' 'em I was sleep. Them niggas was like, 'Yeah, okay.' They locked my ass up da next day. You know how they move."

"Did they take you to the hole?" I asked.

"No. Them cats in unit 4B went hard fa real," X said. "Them niggas had Jake hostage fa a minute. But my man Big Red tol' 'em we ain't gonna get down like dat. So they cut 'em loose. But cats did crazy damage. Jake had to shoot tear gas through the ceilin' to get up in da house. Word. They came through da skylights. Them cats in 4B was not playin'. After shit was dead they cleared out 4B and used it as a new hole. They locked me down in it, talkin' 'bout mad rat muthafuckas sayin' I was down wit da movement. I know they was full of shit. But I didn't have no wins. So I just layed down. Me an this German cat from uptown was locked down together."

"How long were you in 4B?" I asked.

"A-yo, I was down for a minute, 'bout two months. They had kangaroo court up in there. After I done seen da kangaroo judge, they said ain't 'nough proof to charge a nigga, but they gonna ship me anyway 'cause all da cats dat said I was down. I was like 'Good lookin'. Let me out dis camp.' I wanted to get da fuck outta there anyway."

"In my unit we were pretty much sealed off from what was going on in the other units," I said. "But from my room we could see buses lined up outside the fences on the same day as the riots. Who were they taking out?" I asked.

"Just mad cats. Shit-list niggas. Cats dat niggas tol' on," X answered. "It's fucked up 'cause a lot a dem cats thought it was a game. I mean, cats got they shit pushed back. Niggas went to da 'burg. Atlanta. I even heard cats got shipped to Marion and dat max joint out West. A-yo, son, dat shit was real!"

"How many people from your unit would you say were involved all together?" I asked.

"Nigga don't even know, 'bout 70 percent," X said. "It's hard to tell. Everybody was wearin' da same shit so Jake couldn't tell who was who. Niggas had da muthafuckin' ski-mask thing happenin' like it was a bank job, ya heard. But it seemed like everybody was doin' they thing."

"Isn't Joe Hargrave in your unit?" I asked.

"Yeah, him and Tamer had the last joint on the tier," X said. "They just sat shakin' they heads. You know I got mad love an' respect for 'em cats. Wayne and Bump, too. We kicked it for a minute. They just said we was on some kiddy shit.

"I ain't gonna front. They was right. But a nigga was caught up in da hype. All the old heads like Joe and Tamer, da genies, and da crackas wasn't down wit it. I'm sayin', 'bout 70 percent were doin' they thing."

"What do you think the group wanted to gain from it all?" I asked.

"It wasn't 'bout what I thought," X said. "I'm sayin', it was 'bout what they thought. An' fa real . . . shit happened so quick I don't think nobody thought. Niggas was just rollin' wit da punches. All them other joints flipped . . . maybe if this spot was still sweet shit wouldn't a went down like dat. But Meko turned da joint from sugar to shit in a minute, so niggas was like fuck it. Shit got us heard. Ya heard."

After the Riot

The administration resumed complete control of McKean by 1:00 in the afternoon that Tuesday, fewer than ten hours after it began. All the prisoners were locked back into their cells. The men who had been assigned to common areas were randomly thrown into two-man cells and ordered to sleep on the floor. We were confined in those conditions for the next few days while staff members were conducting their investigations to determine which prisoners would be charged with inciting and participating in the disturbance.

Since all the prisoners were locked down in the cells, staff members were responsible for preparing all the meals and delivering those meals and necessary medications to the prisoners. Mail wasn't delivered.

After a few days of total lockdown status, staff members began escorting the men to the chow hall one unit at a time for meals. Uniformed and armed members of the National Guard were present on the compound. Video cameras had been installed and were recording all movement on McKean's compound. And during the brief time that we had been on lockdown status, new fences had been installed on the compound separating the housing units from other areas of McKean's compound. Everything had changed.

Within a week after the riot, the compound resumed normal operations. But normal was to be significantly different at McKean. All incentives and privileges that prisoners had grown used to under Luther's leadership were no longer available. Guards locked the doors to the individual cells every day at 4:00 P.M. for the census count and didn't open the doors again until it cleared. The prisoners also were locked in their cells at 11:30 P.M. each weeknight, and the guards wouldn't open their doors until 6:00 the following morning. Late-night television or telephone access was no longer available. The honor dorm, which only used to accept prisoners with clean disciplinary records reverted to "regular unit status," meaning that there would be no more preferred housing units on the compound. Warden Meko tightened down the joint.

Many prisoners speculated that the administration knew the riot was coming and actually welcomed it. Numerous informants live on the compound. It is inconceivable that they didn't provide information to staff members about so many people discussing their plans to initiate a riot. More tangible proof that the staff had been forewarned about the disturbance was the fact that staff members had evacuated the housing units before dawn on Tuesday morning. In all the years I had been confined, I'd never seen a unit completely abandoned by staff members. But on the morning of the crack riot at McKean, all unit officers had evacuated their posts, leaving the prisoners' rooms unlocked and unsupervised.

News stations had been broadcasting that other federal prisons had been rioting, and the administration obviously was concerned about the volatile situation at McKean because the warden had ordered the partial lockdown on the weekend prior to the riot. When Meko opened the compound for the holiday schedule on Monday, there was so much talk about a disturbance that even I heard about it, and I wasn't involved with anything disruptive. If someone like me had heard about a planned disturbance, I can't believe that the informants wouldn't have already told staff members what was going on. If Meko and Nuss wanted to foil the plan, they easily could have locked the doors to the prisoners' cells late Monday night. But they didn't. Instead, the guards evacuated the units and allowed the prisoners to "set it off."

Local papers reported that the disturbance had caused over $1 million damage to McKean's compound. Perhaps the bigger issue to the new administration, however, was finding a reason to dismantle the unique culture that Warden Luther had worked to build at McKean. After all, a riot offered conclusive proof that incentives had no place in the management of prisons.

If Luther still had been the warden of McKean in October 1995, my guess is that no riot would have taken place. For one thing, he wouldn't have increased the tension inside the prison by dismantling programs. And as soon as he heard any signs about prisoner unrest over an issue that was beyond his control, he would have addressed the entire compound at once.

Luther's open-communication style would have been to explain to the population that he, too, disagreed with lengthy sentences being imposed on nonviolent drug offenders but that there was nothing he could do about the legislation. What he could do was exercise control over the ways in which people served their sentences at FCI McKean. He would have reminded the population of the privileges and incentives available at McKean. Then, he would have painted a picture of what prisoners could expect to follow any type of disturbance. Meko and Nuss, on the other hand, were all about ending these incentive programs. And what better way than a riot causing $1 million worth of damage to accomplish their goal?

THE NEW McKEAN

Prior to Meko's coming to McKean, I had been highly visible on the compound. Leading at least two seminars each month, I actively participated in the mentors group. I actively taught courses in education. And I frequently hosted *Issues and Choices* programs. I contributed to the culture Luther was building at McKean because as a long-term prisoner, I had a personal interest in keeping his incentive program alive.

After Professor DiIulio brought his students from Princeton University to McKean, Warden Luther suggested that I write to other academics about McKean and invite them to learn more about the unique culture he had established. By then, I had earned my master's and was working toward a doctorate through my correspondence at the University of Connecticut. My independent study program had helped me develop relationships with several academics, and I was pleased to write them about the progress federal prisoners were making under Luther's leadership. I invited those professors to contact Warden Luther about the possibility of visiting the institution. Since the professors with whom I corresponded wrote extensively about prisons, many welcomed this invitation.

Professor Marilyn McShane, from California State University, authored *The Encyclopedia of American Prisons* along with several other articles and books about the prison system. Marilyn, a prison scholar, worked with me as a mentor. When I wrote her about Luther's invitation she happily accepted and scheduled a visit to McKean. When she came, she toured the facility and then gave a seminar to the prisoners about ways they can help Americans better understand the prison system and the people it holds.

Dr. Timothy Flanagan, a distinguished professor from the criminal justice program then at Sam Houston State University in Texas, now at the State University of New York, also responded to the invitation. I had dialogue with Dr. Flanagan because he had given me an opportunity to contribute a chapter to his book *Long-Term Incarceration*. He, too, accepted Luther's invitation to tour the prison, and he also gave a seminar to prisoners and staff about correctional issues.

After Meko came, however, it became obvious to me that he had rethought his earlier statement about continuing to operate McKean in the same manner as Luther. As a prisoner, I wasn't privy to what influenced his management decisions. Perhaps his superiors in Washington, D.C. or at the region wanted to bring McKean more in line with other medium-security prisons. All I knew was that life was going to be different. And the more I saw of Meko's management style, the more I realized that I needed to lower my profile.

Yet even after Meko came, professors were still responding to the several letters I had written about Luther's invitation for academics to participate in McKean's correctional program. Professor John Lee from the University of Maryland wanted to open a dialogue between his students and prisoners at McKean; Lee believed that motivated people in prison could contribute to community programs that help adolescents living in high-crime areas. Warden Luther encouraged this type of collaboration with community members, and when I spoke with him about Dr. Lee's proposal, Luther gave his approval to move forward. By the time Dr. Lee was available to proceed, however, Luther had retired and Meko had assumed control. Citing security concerns, Meko cancelled the program.

Meko's cancellation of Dr. Lee's program was a good sign that he wasn't supportive of prisoner-community collaborations. The next sign I received was his letter telling me that I couldn't read a book. Professor McShane sent me a book on prison management and asked me to write a review for one of the academic journals with which she was affiliated. Meko's letter denying my access to the book stated that such a book was "a threat to the security of the institution."

These were indeed ominous portents that things had changed at FCI McKean. I began lowering my profile by resigning from all programs that required me to interact with others. I still had my typewriter in my room, and that privilege afforded me the quiet space I needed to concentrate on my efforts to educate myself further.

McKean was a long way from my home in Seattle, but I was more interested in making preparations for release than I was in receiving visits. And as far as I knew, there were few other federal prisons where I could make as much progress as I could at McKean, even with Meko's changes. I wanted to concentrate on reaching my own goals. I would operate like a submarine, quietly working my way toward my objectives while staying out of sight from those around me. Like a submarine, I would keep my periscope up to know what was happening around me, but I'd also do everything possible to stay away from the spotlight.

After the disturbance, Meko's administration began transferring scores of prisoners. The transfers were without notice. Prisoners were packed up and shipped out. I noticed that those being transferred weren't only guys like X, people suspected of being involved in the disturbance, but people like Joe H., Wayne, and Curtis, too. These guys were leading mentors, guys who used their considerable influence on the compound to support positive programs. It became apparent to me that anyone considered a leader under Luther's administration was vulnerable to a transfer. The prisoners weren't given notice. They simply were ordered to pack their property and report to R&D for transfer. No one knew where they were going.

I had hoped that my recently adopted lower profile would help me escape this mass transfer. But a few days before Thanksgiving, less than a month after the riot, I asked my counselor for access to my central file for another reason. When I began looking through it, I saw that Associate Warden Nuss had checked out my folder recently. This concerned me. There was no reason for an associate warden to review my file—not unless he wanted something specific. I became concerned that I was a target for transfer.

On Thanksgiving morning, I saw Nuss in the chow hall. I had never spoken with him before, but I thought if I introduced myself, I might be able to find out whether he intended to transfer me.

"Good morning Mr. Nuss," I said as I introduced myself.

"I know who you are, Mr. Santos," Nuss told me.

"We've never spoken before, but I wanted to speak with you about something I noticed earlier this week," I said.

"What's on your mind?" he asked.

"Last week I had an opportunity to look through my central file. I noticed that you had signed a log indicating that you had checked out the file. That concerned me."

"Why should my reviewing your file concern you? You're an inmate in my institution. Any staff member has access to your central file," Nuss interrupted.

"I'm aware of that. But you're not any staff member. You're the associate warden, and I thought you must have a specific reason for wanting to review my file," I said.

"I certainly did, and my reason is no concern of yours," Nuss said.

"That's true," I said in deference, wondering why my approach had brought on such hostility. "But I have noticed that a lot of people are being transferred from this institution," I continued. "I'm concerned that you might think it necessary to transfer me. If so, I'm hoping I can persuade you otherwise. I'm engaged in a correspondence study program. I recently completed the first phase of this program, and I'm about to enroll in the second. I don't want to enroll if there's a possibility that I'll be transferred."

"Well," Nuss said, "I wouldn't invest any more money in an education program while you're here."

"So you're saying I'm going?" I asked.

"You're going," Nuss said.

"Is there any chance of my persuading you to leave me here? I want to stay because I have my own typewriter here, and I've been able to make progress toward my goals."

"I know all about you, Mr. Santos," Nuss said. "As far as I'm concerned you've done a little too much. I've got a prison to run. And I'm not prepared to make special accommodations for you or any other inmates."

"Do you have any idea how much time I'll have before the transfer?" I asked, realizing I was in a no-win situation.

"I can't tell you when you're going. But you're going," he said.

"Can I at least have some input into where you're sending me?" I asked.

"Where do you want to go?" he asked.

"Well I'm from Seattle," I said. "If I have to leave here, I'd like to move closer to home."

"That's not up to me. It's up to the regional designator."

Going to the Hole

After speaking with Nuss, I stood in line for my meal and sat down to eat. I watched Nuss as he was leaving the dining room. Before making it out the door, I saw him stop to talk with a lieutenant. As soon as I finished my meal, the lieutenant came to my table and said she wanted to speak with me outside. I thought that was strange. If the lieutenant had something to say to me, she could have said it there. Instead, she escorted me outside. Once I was outside, she told me to put my hands behind my back. She then handcuffed me and escorted me to segregation. I said nothing, and she said nothing.

After taking my clothes and issuing me an orange jumpsuit, the guards led me to a cell. My handcuffs were then removed and I was locked inside. Another prisoner was there already, one whom I hadn't seen before. He was situated on the bottom bunk so I set myself up on the top. It was a sterile cell and cold on that late November morning. I began reading a magazine that was lying on the bunk. No one came to speak with me. There was no word of the reason I was being held. About six hours later I received an official-looking paper saying I was being held for an investigation. The paper didn't say for what I was being investigated.

A lot of anxiety fills a prisoner's mind when he doesn't know what's happening. I did nothing inappropriate, and that made the waiting even worse. I've read so much about the prison system that all the worst things began going through my mind. I worried that Nuss was drumming up charges against me. Whatever they were, as a prisoner I wouldn't be in a strong position to refute anything he said. Indeed, when a person wears prison clothing, he can't give his name without being suspected of being a liar.

Nuss's attitude toward me seemed aggressive, almost like he felt offended that I have used my time in prison to educate myself. And a person in his position could say whatever he wanted about me. For example, he could say that I was instrumental in causing the disturbance. Such a statement would have exposed me to severe punishment within the BOP, and it would have raised my security level; it also could have exposed me to further criminal prosecution. I didn't know what to expect, but I knew it couldn't be good. After all, I had been sent to segregation without explanation.

That was a long night. Not being able to sleep, I read a complete book. About 5 the next morning, a guard came by the room and told me I was leaving.

THE TRANSFER

Julius Caesar said that as a rule, what is out of sight disturbs men's minds more seriously than what they see. The morning that the guards placed me in chains and began moving me closer to the bus, I realized the timeless validity of Caesar's statement.

My anxiety had no limits as I thought of everything that could be happening. The fashion in which the prison machine was arranging this transfer shook me. It let me know my insignificance, reminded me that I had very little control over what happened to me. I could only control how I responded to the obstacles that confronted my life. My responses, however, could have other ramifications—like how long I would remain in prison.

At this point, I already had served eight years of my sentence. During that time I had met several people who had had relatively short sentences extended because of their behavior in prison. One individual came in with five years to serve. He killed another prisoner in what he calls self-defense. Now he's serving a life term at USP Atlanta.

Essentially, I, too, am serving a life sentence. But I had been working exceptionally hard since my term began to build a record that might merit relief at some time. I had so much of my life invested in my prison record that I became paralyzed any time I came into a situation where something might jeopardize all that I've been working toward. I had become neurotic, fearing that one disciplinary report would void all of the support I'd built over the years, rendering my accomplishments irrelevant. I could control my own behavior but not the actions of people around me.

After being processed out of McKean, I was marched to the bus with no idea of where I was going. Other prisoners being transferred with me told me they were going to Lewisburg. I was hoping that I wasn't being returned to a maximum-security prison.

Lewisburg, like Atlanta, is a notorious federal penitentiary. If Nuss had arranged my transfer there, I knew I wouldn't be making too much progress with my studies. Instead, I would have to remain focused on keeping my head alert to all the snakes and predators around me.

My experience of living in Atlanta convinced me that predators preyed on easy targets. Accordingly, a prisoner would have to be perceived as one who would let nothing slide, that he would respond to even the slightest offense immediately and with extreme violence. It's an environment to which I didn't want to return. Yet while I was riding that bus, not knowing when my stop would come, I had bad feelings, tremendous anxiety that Lewisburg would be my destination.

Prisoners with more "street" awareness or closer criminal ties wouldn't have the same anxieties when entering any prison. To them, prison is an accepted and expected part of their lives. Nothing that happens inside gives them any reason to pause. They might be well connected inside the walls and the strength that comes with their numbers shields them from any problems. They might ride through prison with superstarlike criminal reputations and thus avoid confrontations. Or they might come to prison well prepared to respond to the violence inside. I had none of those characteristics, and I knew it.

In Atlanta I had the friendship of Dan and Paul. Both were of the upper-echelon organized-crime type. In many ways, prisons have a caste system, and "wise guys" or people perceived as connected to organized crime represent the Brahmin class. By virtue of my friendship with Dan and Paul, I escaped confrontation behind Atlanta's walls. But if I was committed to Lewisburg,

I couldn't ride on their respect. I knew my "square john" demeanor would expose me to problems within days if not hours of admittance to a maximum-security prison. And I knew my response would determine how I spent the remainder of my time inside those walls. Despite having served eight years already, an impending test for which I knew I wasn't prepared awaited me.

I was silent the entire bus ride. I wouldn't allow the others around me to know what was going through my mind. I know enough about my fellow prisoners to keep my mouth shut. They try to get information about everyone and anyone. They then use that information. They exploit it. Information is power in prison, and I wasn't going to empower anyone with information about me.

After about three hours—my thoughts were dark; they made those three hours seem like three days of torment—the bus pulled off the highway and moved through a small town. It turned at a sign that read Allenwood Federal Correctional Complex. It is a complex holding prisons of several different security levels; the bus pulled in front of Allenwood Low—a low-security prison.

The prison is brand new, all red brick and glass as I recall. I hoped that I'd be getting off there. But when the bus driver called the names of who would be departing, my name wasn't among them. The bus pulled off again. And this time I knew it was heading toward Lewisburg, about thirty minutes away.

Those were a long, long thirty minutes. The bus moved in through the rear entrance to Lewisburg. It went through the double gates and circled the ominous penitentiary. Its design is like a monastery from the Dark Ages.

The bus finally stopped in front of the penitentiary's entrance. I could hear screams coming from the caged and screened windows. It was the prisoners inside who were screaming. They were behind mesh screens so we couldn't see them. But they saw us. We just heard their demonic voices, crazy voices. The prisoners were cussing at the bus drivers, threatening the prisoners on the bus. Demons welcoming others to hell.

After awhile, the guards began calling prisoners by their federal registration numbers. The men marched off the bus and out the door. I was the third prisoner called. As I stepped off the bus, I heard what those in the cages were screaming.

"Be ready white boy."

"Welcome to the burg."

"You be suckin' my cock tonight."

Once inside the building my mind started racing. I thought of how I'd respond to the first situation, playing different scenarios in my mind. I thought of objects within reach that I could use as a weapon if needed. Anything could happen in such a place. I knew that. I also thought of the others whom I knew from Atlanta who were now serving life sentences because of their reactions to perceived problems. I wondered whether all of these worries were only in my mind.

Then I remembered some of the episodes I witnessed earlier in my sentence and knew my concerns were valid. I thought of the possibility of spending the rest of my life in prison, knowing that with a sentence like mine, if I responded violently to any aggressor I would likely remain in prison forever. I also knew that if I did have a problem, the prisons where I'd be held would all be of the maximum-security type, where predators are like fish to the sea. I was but a few yards from constant mayhem. And I knew I had to harden myself for what was to come. My university studies weren't going to be of much help for the preparations I knew I had to make. As of that moment, I still didn't know to which prison I'd ultimately be sent. But I was feeling Lewisburg.

After sitting in that waiting room for about thirty minutes, the guards called my name. I walked to the room to where they instructed. I said nothing. I still didn't know where I was going. I didn't want to ask or give the appearance that I gave a damn. Being silent was part of my front. If I spoke, I thought, my voice might crack and reveal my fear.

The guards issued me some clothes, fingerprinted me, and took my picture. They ordered me to move to another room. I waited until a medical worker asked to see me. He asked me to complete a form. Then he looked me over and asked me to sit in yet another waiting room. This time the wait was longer.

I sat there trying to look hard with a scowl on my face, but I was tormented by my own thoughts. I noticed a large paper cutter in the corner. I could rip off the arm and use it as a sword to defend myself if need be, I thought. Then I questioned whether I really had it in me to strike another human being with intentions to kill. I remember hearing another prisoner describe how he "drove a meat hook [into a man's back]." To him it was a normal response to the situation he encountered. As he told the story, no one in the room showed a flicker of feeling that he did anything abnormal. My own mental deliberations, I realized, were a weakness inside a prison. Others in the penitentiary wouldn't hesitate to use lethal violence; they wouldn't care about human life or the consequences that follow taking it. Toughen up, I told myself.

I didn't know what was happening, but all those procedures seemed like admittance to me. And if I was being admitted to Lewisburg, that meant someone must have placed something very bad in my prison file. Yet I knew not what it was. I did know, however, the awesome power that prison administrators have over an individual's life.

Then a lady called me into yet another room of the dungeon. She told me I was on my way to Fairton, a medium-security prison in New Jersey. I think that was the first time I breathed all day. I knew nothing about Fairton, but I was relieved that I wouldn't have to battle it out in maximum-security.

FAIRTON

I stayed in Lewisburg for only a few days before I was sent on another bus to Fairton. Since I was only a "holdover" prisoner in Lewisburg, just passing through on my way to another prison, I was sent with others to a unit that is isolated from the prisoners serving time in the penitentiary. The BOP doesn't generally mix prisoners of varying security levels. Within a few days, around the first of December, I was processed out and sent on my way to Fairton.

Fairton is similar to McKean in design but operates as an ordinary medium-security prison. When my property finally arrived, I was most concerned with my typewriter. I explained to Warden Morris that I was studying in a correspondence program and urged him to allow me access to my typewriter.

"This is a prison, son, not a college." Warden Morris said. "If you were so concerned about schoolwork you shouldn't have broken the law. We don't allow prisoners to have their own typewriters at Fairton."

"Can I donate it to the prison?" I asked. "I just want access to it. Maybe you could keep it in education and I could check it out when I needed to type my term papers."

"Send it home," Morris ordered. End of discussion.

I wrote my final term paper by hand and elected not to pursue further studies. Fairton was clean and a relatively easy place to serve time—even if there were fewer privileges. But it wasn't conducive to graduate studies.

I made a friend in Fairton, Chris M., who came from a background similar to mine. He was beginning a twelve-year sentence for bank robbery. I spent my time in Fairton lifting weights and listening to Chris' hilarious stories about how a kid from the suburbs turns into what the Boston newspapers called "The Gentleman Bank Robber."

Within five months of my arrival at Fairton, though, my time remaining to serve dropped below eighteen years. When my case manager learned of this development, she told me that my security level automatically dropped to low. Accordingly, I had to transfer from Fairton to a low-security prison. She asked me where I wanted to transfer. "I'm from Seattle," I said. "In all the years I've been in I've never been close to home. Send me to California. That's where the nearest low-security prison to Seattle is." She told me she would submit the paperwork at once. A few days later I was told to pack my belongings. I had been redesignated to Fort Dix, in Southern New Jersey. I guess this was as close to Seattle as the BOP could put me.

CONCLUSION

McKean, under Warden Meko, contrasted greatly with the administration under Warden Dennis Luther. One might have thought that it would be easier for the new warden to maintain the culture and programs that had worked so successfully. My experience under both Luther and Meko raises questions about the extent to which factors such as personality and leadership skills influence prison administration. However, it is equally possible that Warden Meko was under pressure from his superiors to bring McKean in line with other Bureau of Prison institutions.

9

Fort Dix:
Low-Security Living

During the time I was confined in Atlanta I grew used to life behind the walls. I had no choice. Since it was my first time in prison I couldn't compare it with anyplace else. I heard stories about other prisons, but each day inside rendered me more cynical about what others around me had to say. On the other hand, my relationships and living patterns gave me a degree of comfort because I knew what to expect and grew used to that life. When I stepped on McKean's compound I immediately realized a difference. The level of tension that had become normal to me in Atlanta was missing. Prisoners walked easier. There were fewer metal detectors. There was more freedom.

As I grew accustomed to McKean, especially under Warden Luther's leadership, I felt much more in control of my own life. While living in the penitentiary, on the other hand, every day was like walking on a high wire. I had to keep balanced and focused on my goals constantly, or else I could slip into the abyss of life in prison, or worse. As Rico had told me, "It's easy to have respect in prison. One just has to be willing to go all the way." In Atlanta, besides my own behavior, I was linked to the behavior of every other prisoner around me. At McKean, with the significantly lower degree of tension, I became much less dependent on others. Ft. Dix proved to be another prison experience.

GETTING USED TO DIX

Soon after I walked onto the Fort Dix compound I experienced an even greater reduction of stress. There was no controlled movement, and I didn't see any metal detectors at all. Guards weren't constantly on the lookout for weapons, relentlessly stopping prisoners who might be walking around with metal shanks. It looked and felt as if I were walking through a large park. As a low-security prison, this was as close to freedom as I had known since 1987, when the gates initially closed behind me at MCC Miami.

With over four thousand men assigned to two separately divided compounds, Fort Dix is the largest federal prison in the United States. I learned during the Admissions and Orientation program that it holds people from over ninety different countries; most of the American population comes from areas between New York City and Philadelphia. Fort Dix is situated about halfway between these two cities.

The prison is located on the Fort Dix Army Base, right next to the McGuire Air Force Base. We're so close that the radio reception on our portable Walkman radios is interrupted frequently by dialogue between air force pilots and air traffic controllers at McGuire; on the other side of the compound we can hear drill sergeants leading calisthenics. The Fort Dix housing units—identical redbrick, three-story structures stretching in long parallel lines—had been used as military barracks before the doublewide, razor wire-topped fences were wrapped around the compound.

It's because the prison was previously part of the Fort Dix military compound that the closed institutional feeling of confinement is missing, at least for me. In each housing unit the guard is stationed on the first floor in a small office separated from the many other rooms on the floor serving as common areas. The regular prisoner rooms are on the second and third floors of the buildings, and no guards are stationed there. The two upper floors have 12 twelve-man rooms and 16 two-man rooms; 8 two-man rooms on a wing of the first floor are reserved for prisoners with medical problems. Each room has opening windows large enough to pass a sofa through. There are neither bars on the windows nor locks on the doors; indeed, although rules prohibit it, a prisoner could walk outside the housing units twenty-four hours each day. In every other prison where I had been held, prisoners were locked inside their rooms each evening.

Each man is assigned a large wall locker that holds four times as much property as those assigned to prisoners in the other facilities where I've been confined. And instead of sleeping on steel plates covered with mats, prisoners at Fort Dix actually have beds with springs and genuine twin-size mattresses. These living accommodations resemble low-income housing projects rather than the prototypical federal prison.

With no controlled movements, the prisoners are free to walk around Fort Dix's large prison compound; it stretches over 1,000 yards in length from fence to fence. Officially, prisoners aren't allowed to enter housing units to which they're not assigned. But if someone wants to visit a friend in another unit, the guard in charge usually grants permission.

With unlocked doors and wide-open spaces, it's obvious that staff members are far less concerned with the probability of violence. In fact, Fort Dix is so large that a prisoner can pass weeks without having any interaction with staff members. In higher security prisons, on the other hand, it's hard to pass a four-hour period (except when one is locked in the cell) without having to ask a guard permission for something.

The level of freedom at Fort Dix reflects the Bureau of Prison's assessment of the type of offender confined in this low-security prison. When I arrived, all prisoners had to have fewer than eighteen years remaining to serve. Since then, higher population levels in the federal system have lifted this sentence-length cap in low-security prisons to twenty years. As a rule, most prisoners on the compound are serving shorter terms and have limited if any histories of documented violence. Like all federal prisons, the majority of prisoners at Fort Dix are serving time for drug offenses. But the prison also has a substantial population of former lawyers, accountants, and other professionals serving time for white-collar offenses.

CATEGORIZING THE
PRISONERS AT FORT DIX

Because the level of stress, tension, and danger is so much lower at Fort Dix than at other prisons where I've been held, prisoners have more freedom in the choices they make. Without the constant threat of violence or disturbance, men at Fort Dix can choose to serve their sentences without any substantial interference from others. This isn't to say there's no threat of violence or that prisoners are completely free of tension, only that the level of volatility is less intense at Fort Dix than at the higher security prisons where I was held previously. In the remainder of this chapter, I want to describe some of the ways that prisoners at Fort Dix serve their time.

In his book *The Felon*, John Irwin suggested that most prisoners fit into one of four categories. Irwin, a well-known criminologist, described the different prisoner roles as "doing time," "gleaning," "jailing," or functioning as "disorganized criminals." Although Irwin published his findings in 1970, the categories he identified still apply.

Irwin classified those who pass through the motions of prison without trying to make any waves as prisoners that are "doing time." Such prisoners try to stay out of trouble and do whatever they can to get released the soonest. To them, time in prison represents an inevitable consequence of their criminal careers.

Another category of prisoner takes advantage of every opportunity available to develop skills during their confinement; they are described as "gleaning." Different from those who are doing time, those who are gleaning actively participate in educational and self-improvement courses, hoping they will develop the skills necessary to succeed upon release.

A third category consists of those who are "jailing." They try to cut themselves off from the outside world and concern themselves only with the happenings inside the prison. They differ from those who are doing time in that they aren't consumed with thoughts about building a record to get out of prison; they differ from those who are gleaning in that they have no desire to develop skills to help them succeed upon release. They are content with the respect or status they have inside of prison walls.

Finally, Irwin describes the "disorganized criminal." Prisoners fitting into this category might not fit into the other roles because of some type of disability, psychological or physical. Such prisoners, according to Irwin, frequently are targets of exploitation by other prisoners.

In the higher security prisons, where many of the men were serving sentences in excess of twenty years, I would have placed most of the prisoners in Irwin's "jailing" category. People in the penitentiary are concerned about their image and the amount of respect they receive inside the prison. Prospects for release are slim, and people do everything possible to make their lives easy. The following profiles briefly describe the backgrounds of some prisoners and how they are serving their sentences at Fort Dix.

Carnalito, the Hustler   Carnalito, a young prisoner, originally comes from Mexico. When he was 9, he decided that he no longer wanted to attend school. He ran away from his family's home and illegally crossed the border into Texas where he moved in with his older brother. Carnalito ran away from his brother's home when he was 12. He hitchhiked to California, where he supplemented his dishwasher earnings in a San Diego Chinese restaurant by stealing cats he could sell to the restaurant's owner for $5 each.

Carnalito eventually was arrested and deported back to Mexico. When he was 15, he crossed the border into Texas; later, he was arrested for a drug offense. For that conviction, and for illegally entering the United States a second time, Carnalito was sentenced to serve five years in prison. He arrived at Fort Dix in 2000, when he was 18.

Having no source of outside support, Carnalito, who stands about 5′4″ and weighs no more than 130 pounds organizes his life as a hustler behind Fort Dix's fences. He speaks little English, but over half the prisoners on Fort Dix's compound are Latino and so Carnalito has no problem communicating.

Carnalito begins each morning at 5:00 by performing laundry services. He washes and dries the clothes, then neatly folds them before returning them to his customers. His customers are happy to provide him with $3 worth of either mackerels, stamps, or cigarettes to pay for these laundry services. The laundry room is always crowded. By using Carnalito, the laundry customers are able to avoid the frustration of waiting in line to use the machines and watching over the clothes to avoid theft. The customers feel that $3 per load is a reasonable price to pay for Carnalito's services.

While the clothes are washing, Carnalito performs his assigned duties as a unit orderly. He's responsible for cleaning one of the common bathrooms on the first floor of his housing unit each weekday; for this work detail, Carnalito receives $10 each month in "prisoner performance pay." Other orderlies are responsible for cleaning the other bathrooms. Many of them, however, choose to pay Carnalito $15 per month to complete their responsibilities for them. Carnalito performs the duties of three other orderlies, thus earning an additional $45 each month; they pay him in commissary items.

By 8 each morning, Carnalito completes his laundry and work detail services. He then begins performing his janitorial services for the prisoners' rooms that he cleans. Carnalito charges $1.50 per day for room-cleaning services. He has many customers and earns approximately $100.00 per month cleaning rooms.

By noon each day, Carnalito finishes all of his cleaning responsibilities. But he's not finished with his work. He also cooks meals six days each week for one group of five prisoners. The five don't want to be bothered with the frustrations of eating in the chow hall in the company of hundreds of other prisoners. But neither do they want the frustration of waiting in line for one of the three microwaves that must be shared by the 350+ other prisoners assigned to their housing unit. Instead, each contributes to pay Carnalito a total of $200 per month for his services in preparing their dinners six nights each week. For this fee, Carnalito procures vegetables from kitchen hustlers. He assumes the risk of hiding the vegetables from the guards; he'll hide them under the wall lockers or secrete them in other hiding spots. Carnalito cuts and then cooks the vegetables together with the commissary items provided by the group of prisoners for whom he is cooking.

The group pays Carnalito his $200 monthly fee by sending the money to his mother's address in Mexico. All of Carnalito's other clients pay him in commissary items. After providing for his own needs, Carnalito still has approximately $200 worth of commissary each month from his earnings. He multiplies this commissary by "running a store," allowing others to obtain packs of cigarettes or bags of coffee at anytime on credit. For every two packs his customers take, however, Carnalito requires them to pay three packs back.

Not counting the $200 that Carnalito's clients send outside for his cooking services, he earns approximately $400 through his cleaning services and the store he operates. Whenever he accumulates too much commissary, Carnalito makes a deal with other prisoners who buy his commissary at 80 cents on the dollar; the purchasers send the money to Carnalito's address in Mexico. Carnalito works hard inside the prison, but through his work, each month he accumulates at least $500 in his Mexican bank account. If all continues to move along according to his plan, Carnalito expects to leave prison in 2005, when he will be 22, with nearly $20,000 in U.S. currency. He expects to use his money to open a business in Mexico.

Carnalito moves like an expert in the prison's underground economy. He wears institutional clothing and doesn't flaunt his wealth. His low profile in the prison has allowed him to serve the three years that he has been confined on this compound free of problems from either prisoners or staff. He doesn't use the telephone, doesn't use the mail, and stays away from activities that could bring him to the attention of the guards. Always with a rag hanging from his pocket or a mop in hand, Carnalito is one of the hardest working prisoners in the unit. He doesn't look at doing time behind these fences as punishment. Rather, Carnalito says that his time in Fort Dix has given him an opportunity to accumulate enough money to give him independence upon his release.

Carnalito is a hustler, but in Irwin's category of prisoner, I would say that Carnalito is gleaning. He has taken advantage of every opportunity to prepare himself for release. He's not concerned with his image in prison or the prison subculture. Instead, Carnalito focuses on his work and makes the prison work for him.

Puerto Rican Lou Lou is the opposite of a hustler. He's jailing. Lou has been in prison since 1995 and expects to be released in 2004. He began serving his sentence at the low-security prison in Loretto, Pennsylvania. Lou wasn't happy there and so was instrumental in organizing a food strike on the compound. During a food strike, prisoners refuse to eat meals in the dining room; administrators consider any type of prisoner strikes as a serious threat to the orderly running of their institutions. Lou's activities resulted in his spending a few months in the hole followed by a disciplinary transfer to the medium-security prison at McKean.

Lou was at McKean during the 1995 crack riot and was identified as one of the hundreds of participants. He was then confined in various segregated housing units for nearly a year and received a disciplinary transfer to another medium-security prison at Three Rivers, Texas. Lou stayed in Texas for eighteen months, then transferred to Fort Dix in 1998. Since arriving at Fort Dix, Lou has committed himself to lifting weights, playing chess, cheering for the Yankees, and supporting all Puerto Rican events.

"Everyday I wake up for breakfast at 6," Lou says. "When I get there, my man fixes me up with a dozen raw egg whites. I need them for protein."

"What do you do, drink the egg whites in the chow hall?" I asked.

"I drink six in the chow hall. The other six I bring out with me," Lou said.

"You never got stopped?" I asked.

"You know how them robocops are," Lou said. "They give me a pat search every now and then. I take cereal out, too. I put the cereal in a plastic bag and slide it inside the front of my pants. Ain't a cop in here that's puttin' his hands over my nuts. 'xcept Trini. That guy has a sixth sense. But he don't usually bother for food; he only looks for drugs. Since I don't use drugs I don't have to sweat Trini. Anyway, I've got my cup 'specially modified to hold the eggs. Watch," Lou said as he proceeded to show me.

The plastic cup he uses to smuggle egg whites out of the chow hall has a double lining. He removed the insulation between the two linings and fixed the cup so he could pour the egg whites in the space that originally existed for insulation. When he snaps the inner lining back in place, it seals the egg whites from coming out. That way, when the guard asks to search the cup, Lou simply flips it over like he's emptying it. Nothing falls out and Lou is allowed to proceed back to his housing unit without a problem.

Once he returns to the unit, Lou says he sleeps until about 11. He then takes a shower and gets ready for his day. His job assignment is working in the weight room in recreation. Lou is an exercise fanatic and has been working hard for several years to build a championship physique.

"I'm tryin' to get big," Lou says. "Ain't nothin' else to do in here."

Lou exercises five days each week for as much as three hours each session. When he's not exercising, he's looking for someone with whom he can play chess. Lou doesn't gamble, but he takes his chess games seriously. He began playing in 1995 when he was in Texas. Since then he's played every day and regularly reads chess books to make him a better player. As one of the top chess players on Fort Dix's compound, he talks a lot of trash to other chess players and bodybuilders alike.

The only thing that takes precedence over chess and exercise for Lou is the New York Yankees. He's obsessed with this team, and whenever their games are televised Lou is in front of a monitor, dominating the room with his loud voice if anyone says something against his team. If the Yankees game isn't on television, Lou finds a radio station that's broadcasting the play by play.

"How old are you?" I asked.

"Thirty-two," he answered.

"What are you going to do when you get home?"

"I'm thinkin' of startin' a commercial cleaning company when I get out," Lou explained. "My boy has a service in Philly and he does pretty good at that, cleaning buildings and stuff. He says he'll help me get started when I get out."

"Why don't you do something while you're in here to make yourself better prepared to run a business outside?"

"I do," Lou says. "I been readin' all kinds a business books and I took a few classes. But I ain't tryin' to tie myself down. Nothin' really matters in here anyway. Them classes ain't gonna help me get home any sooner."

"Forget about getting out sooner," I said. "I live in the same building as you and see how you spend your time. Don't you think that if you applied as much time to preparing for your future as you spend playing chess or lifting weights you'd have a better chance of successfully running this business you want to start?" I asked.

"Not necessarily," Lou answered. "I've taken most a them bullshit classes they got down in education. I ain't really learn nothin' that's gonna help me in business. The teachers don't care 'bout me. They're just tryin' to check a name in their little book. Besides, when I'm doin' this time I ain't really thinkin' 'bout business outside. I'm just gettin' through each day with what- ever comes. I like doin' time my own way. And I ain't changin'. I'm pretty sure I can take care of myself when I get out."

Lou takes each day as it comes. He's not involved in any prison hustles and passes his time in his own zone. He'll worry about the outside when he's released. While he's inside he wants to focus on "gettin' big 'cause nothin' else matters anyway." Lou sees nothing to gain by participating in programs, and with no chance of advancing his release date, he also sees nothing to lose by participating in a prison disturbance.

"All I'm tryin' to do is get through my bid," he says. "If I gotta get down with my peoples I'm ready for whatever. I don't care 'bout the hole or gettin' transferred or none a these supercops runnin' 'round here. The time keeps tickin' and come 2004 these doors are gonna open. Until then, I'm just gonna do my own thing. I ain't botherin' nobody. But if some drama jumps off, if someone messes with one of my homies, I don't care if I got one year left or one day left. I'm gonna be there. And I'm comin' with everythin' I got. That's just who I am."

"Do you see the potential for problems here?" I asked.

"Every day," Lou answered. "Some these muthafuckas ain't got no respect. They break in lockers, cut in line, shit like that. If any of 'em disrespect me or anyone I know though, they're gonna have problems. And people know it."

Because Lou cuts himself off from the outside world and lives his life completely inside the prison, Irwin would say that Lou fits the "jailing" role. He's not consumed with thoughts about building a record to get out of prison, as Lou readily admits that even if he has one day left to serve, nothing will stop him from responding to what he perceives as a sign of disrespect. To Lou, his image and the prison respect he receives is of paramount importance.

Roger Golden, an Individualist Roger Golden is a 57-year-old prisoner who has been confined for the past six years. Well over six-feet tall, he's long and lanky and kind of stands out at Fort Dix with a long white beard, bald head, and the aura of peace with which he walks. He describes himself as a lifelong hippie, "I'm in here for having too much fun," Roger says.

Roger was sentenced to a thirteen-year term after he pleaded guilty to distributing 7,000 pounds of marijuana. He says the only reason he received such a long sentence is because he refused to cooperate with the government in providing information about others. The time doesn't phase him, Roger says, as he had been expecting to come to prison since he made the choice of selling marijuana over thirty years ago.

Roger comes from a large and wealthy Jewish family in New York. His family members tried to push him into pursuing a career with one of his family's businesses, but he was determined to live his life as an outlaw. When he was 21, he began what he calls his career as a marijuana distributor by selling bags of weed in the park. That was the mid-1960s, and he really enjoyed his work. At the time, he was earning about $1,000 each week, "which was a lot of money in those days."

A friend of his suggested that he expand his operation by working with connections in Europe, where hashish from the Middle East was available. Roger agreed. He bought acid in the United States and carried it with him to sell in England. While in England he bought hashish, strapped it to his body, and brought it back with him on his flight to sell in America. Expanding his business to Europe increased his earnings to about $8,000 for every day he worked. "There was no war on drugs then," he says, "so it was really easy."

After Roger started to accumulate large amounts of money, he began manufacturing furniture in England with the hashish he bought secreted inside it. "My partner would buy hashish in Lebanon for $10 a pound," Roger explained. "He would transport it in suitcases to England, where it was worth about $200 a pound. But we wouldn't sell it there. Instead, we would insert it into furniture we manufactured. Then, we shipped the furniture to America without any problems. In America, we could sell the hashish for $700 a pound. It was like playing with Monopoly® money. Eventually, we began sending the hashish over in Jaguar automobiles. Later, I began buying boats and using them to transport large loads of marijuana and hashish all over the world."

"Did you ever come to prison before?" I asked.

"I never came to prison, but I always expected to come to prison," Roger said. "I mean, let's face it. I made the conscious decision to become a career marijuana dealer when I was 21. Since then I had nearly a thirty-year run selling pot. I fully expected to come to prison, and early on I started making preparations for the time I would serve in confinement."

"What kind of preparations did you make?" I asked.

"I began studying martial arts and yoga," Roger said. "I had to do something with my spare time. And since I expected to come to prison, I figured I'd better develop some skills that would prove themselves useful. The inner peace and discipline I could develop through yoga and martial arts, I figured, would help me cope during the years I expected to serve. I also studied lucid dreaming, astral projection, and hypnosis. These activities have been helpful in my adjustment to confinement.

"I always expected to serve ten years. But I expected to serve the time in three different installments. I planned to serve a term during each decade of my career. I figured the first time I was sent away I would serve about eighteen months. Then, I expected to get out and continue selling. The next time I would be sent away I expected that I'd serve about forty to forty-two months. I figured I'd probably give it another run, and if I got caught again, I'd serve about five years.

"The thing is, I had about a thirty-year run before being sent to prison for the first time. When I pled guilty on this charge, I received this thirteen-year sentence as my first prison term. With good time I will serve about ten years on it, so I guess I got what I expected."

"Have you ever experienced any remorse for your crimes?" I asked.

"Remorse?" Roger said in surprise, "Of course not. I'm proud of what I did," he continued. "As a young man I set out to become an outlaw, and I actually believed that I was doing the right thing. I wanted to make pot popular in America."

"I don't understand you when you call yourself an outlaw," I said. "I think of an outlaw as someone who uses violence, the threat of violence, or any means to get what he wants. Yet, you say you're nonviolent."

"I'm a nonviolent outlaw," Roger easily explained himself. "When I started selling marijuana, I did it because I thought it was better for people than liquor. People who smoke pot don't drive recklessly and beat their wives. They just laugh a lot and get the munchies. I wanted to distribute as much pot as possible. I never lied or cheated anyone. And I told all of this to the judge at sentencing."

"What did you say?" I asked.

"Well, before the judge sentenced me he asked whether I had anything to say for myself. I told him that I'm at peace and comfortable with whatever time he felt it necessary to give me. I had been sober for about a year before sentencing and so I was feeling really healthy and at peace. So I told the judge that although I used to be certain that marijuana was better than liquor, now I realize it's the same thing as saying that a punch in the nose is better than a kick in the ass. Still, I'm not ashamed of what I did. I was always honest and kept my integrity about what I was doing. And I've helped a lot of people. Now it was time to go to prison and I was prepared for this new experience in my life. I told the judge I was at peace with myself and the life I have led," Roger concluded.

"You say that when you began your career as a pot dealer you also began preparing yourself for prison by studying yoga and martial arts," I said. "Now that you've been in for six years, can you describe whether those skills have proved helpful?"

"Absolutely," Roger said. "It's been thirty-five years since I began practicing and I can't remember missing a day. I wake up every morning at 3:34 A.M. and practice tai chi for an hour. Then I begin my yoga training. These exercises bring me peace, and that's all one really needs to pass through a prison term."

"But as prisoners we're not allowed to practice martial arts. Hasn't a staff member ever said anything to you about your regular tai chi sessions?"

"On my first day here I was practicing in one of the common rooms. A lieutenant called me down to his office and asked me whether I was teaching tai chi to anyone. I told him that I wasn't teaching it, that I was only practicing the movements. Since then I quit practicing tai chi in the common areas. Now I only practice before dawn, and I do it in the darkness of my own room while everyone else is sleeping. I haven't had any further interference."

"Where do you work in here?" I asked.

"I have the best job in the world," Roger said. "I clean the patio area outside my unit during the evenings on weekends. It only takes me about fifteen minutes . . . leaves me the rest of the time during the week to myself."

"Describe how you spend your day," I said.

"After I practice my yoga and martial arts," Roger began, "I go to the chapel where I teach a class on yoga each morning between 8:00 and 9:00. Then, I usually go for a walk around the track until about 10:30; this is important for me to keep my balance. I return to the unit when they close the yard and wait for lunch. I usually go to the chow hall for a salad and some rice—I'm really conscious about what I eat. In the afternoons, I'll walk some more and then go work on my art or writing projects. In the evening, I'll do the same thing."

"What are your goals in prison?" I asked.

"I'm working to become a great prison writer and artist. In fact, I would be kind of disappointed if I got out of prison now because I haven't had enough time to fully develop my skills. I could still become a great artist or writer. But I want to become known as a great prison artist. My goal is to help people understand that regardless of the fences, anyone in prison can develop a great career. A prisoner might not be able to develop a family, but he can develop meaning in his life. Adversity doesn't have to stop someone from moving forward. I want to help prisoners understand how they can make their lives useful while they're serving time. I want to help others learn how to make something of their lives while they're serving time. That's all I really care about. I just want to be a good human being."

According to Irwin, Roger would be a cross between a prisoner who is doing time and a prisoner who is gleaning. He "fully expected to come to prison," so to Roger, prison represents an inevitable consequence of his life as an "outlaw." At the same time, Roger actively participates in self-improvement programs and shows little proclivity to participate in the prison subculture.

Poker Joe, Air Black Joe B. served the first eight years of his sentence in high- and medium-security prisons. His security level dropped to low as he moved into this second half of his sentence, and about a year ago he was transferred to Fort Dix. Joe described the differences in his life between the higher security prisons and his life at Fort Dix.

While he was in higher security prisons, Joe B. spent his time playing basketball, running poker games, or hustling food from the kitchen. "There was always something going on," Joe B. said.

He had three simultaneous card rooms operating at the same time. Prisoners could play poker at his table in recreation, in his housing unit, or in another housing unit where he had someone else looking after his interests. Up to seven people would play dealer's-choice poker at each of his tables. As the *House Man*, he provided the cards and the poker chips, and he personally guaranteed that everyone playing at his tables would pay their debts. For this service, he collected between 20 and 40 cents per hand from each pot.

To avoid interference from the guards, Joe B. used playing cards from the game UNO as his poker chips. Each UNO card represented between 20 and 40 cents. If a guard asked about the game, Joe B. and his fellow players said they were playing UNO; admitting they were playing poker could result in a staff investigation that would land each player in segregation while lieutenants tried to prove they were gambling. The pots of his games ranged from a low of $15 to a high of $60. Most hands cleared $30 to $35.

Joe B. grew up on the basketball courts of the Bronx and has played a lot of ball since being locked up. While in the higher security prisons, he organized and played on teams every day. As one of the top basketball players in every prison where he's been held, Joe B. earned the Air Black nickname early in his sentence. As reputations do in prison, his nickname has stuck with him. Prisoners always gambled on the basketball games, but when Air Black and the other star athletes were playing, the stakes were higher. Joe B. took his cut when his team won.

The higher security prisons also gave Joe B. an opportunity to earn an income from the hustling rackets. Each month he and his crew divided up the several hundred dollars they earned by bringing food out of the kitchen and selling it in the units. It was a good hustle, Joe B. said, ensuring that he never had to depend on anyone from the streets to support him. All of those activities stopped when he came to Fort Dix.

Joe B. explains that there are too many rats on this compound to do anything. When he first arrived at Fort Dix, he got his job in the kitchen and expected to resume his same activities. While in the kitchen, he noticed that there were more "inmate police" than there were guards. It was impossible to build a good hustle out of food services because there always would be someone "dropping a note" or "dry snitching." The quantity of informants at Fort Dix, Joe explained, is noticeably higher than in higher security prisons. And with so many people running to tell on each other, it was impossible to get his hustle going. So he resigned from his food service position.

It was the same thing with poker and basketball. He quit playing poker completely after his first month of card playing at Fort Dix. Instead of handling their business like men, Joe B. said, when someone starts losing he'll drop a note to a lieutenant letting him know about a card game going on somewhere.

When I asked Joe B. why someone would tell on his own poker game, he explained that a guy might tell on everyone else playing with hopes that the lieutenants would send the other gamblers to the hole so he could escape his debt. People in Dix tell for anything, he says. Guys tell in exchange for arranging a transfer to another prison, for a room change, or in exchange for a better job. They even tell because they think they will get a break, he says.

"Jake came up in our card room," Joe B. says. "I had just left the game a few minutes before. He took all the cats' names and numbers down. Later that night each of 'em got called to see the lieutenant. Lieutenant says to 'em, 'Look, you're not in any trouble as long as you're straight with me. Just tell me what you were playing.' Stupid mu'fuckas tol' the man they was playin' poker for candy bars. Each of 'em ends up with a shot for gamblin'. They tol' on themselves. That shit never would have happened up in da higher joints. Cats would a just said they was playin' UNO. When I heard 'bout that, I quit playin' poker for good."

Joe B. has adjusted his schedule completely. Now he doesn't play cards at all. He's not involved in any prison hustles. And he only plays basketball for recreation. Joe B. has about eight years ahead of him. He's now committed to developing his writing skills and currently is writing what he calls an urban novel through which he describes the street life that tempts so many young blacks. Since Joe expects to serve the remainder of his sentence in low- and minimum-security prisons, he says he will keep to himself and concentrate on improving his writing skills. He acknowledged that if he ever had to return to the higher security levels, he'd likely put the pen down and revert to his earlier ways of doing time. "There's too much shit happenin' up in them joints to be cooped up in the cell writin'," he says. "I'd still be doin' my thing here if there weren't so many rats runnin' 'round."

I asked Joe B. whether he noticed any difference between the officers at Fort Dix and the officers in higher security prisons.

"Here at Dix," Joe B. said, "the officers are way too petty. They want you to give 'em all kinds of respect just 'cause they wearin' them tight-ass uniforms. But they treat us like we little kids. I been doin' time since most of 'em was in high school and they try an' talk to me any kind of way. I just stay away from 'em."

Joe B. is assigned to a job in the labor pool, which doesn't require him to do much more than check in with an officer a few times each day. Occasionally, he might have to pick up cigarette butts, but for the most part he's free to spend time as he sees fit. When I asked Joe what annoys him the most about Fort Dix, he said that more than anything it's the rats; he prefers the "always on" atmosphere of the higher security prisons where he was held. Despite his preference, he's committed to getting out of prison as soon as possible and wants to work his way down in security level. He expects to stay in Fort Dix until his unit team approves his transfer to camp. He really wants the better visiting conditions and higher degree of freedom that most federal prison camps offer.

While Joe B. was in the higher security prisons, he was jailing, Irwin would say. While there he had cut himself off from the outside world and focused on making his time easier in prison. Once his security level dropped and he came to the less intense Fort Dix environment, Joe B. adapted a different role and began gleaning. Now he writes and looks for opportunities to develop skills that will help him upon release. Still, he admits that if he were put back into the volatile environment of higher security he would resume his jailing behavior.

Barry, the UNICOR Man Joe B., Roger, Lou, and Carnalito all have found jobs that give them the maximum amount of freedom in their day. Not everyone appreciates this freedom, however. Some prisoners look for structure. One place they can find structure is through assignment to the UNICOR factory.

Barry is in his fourth year of a ten-year sentence for a nonviolent drug conviction. He's 34 and has been working in the UNICOR factory for two years. He originally sought employment in UNICOR because it offers higher pay than any of the other prisoner-work assignments. Non-UNICOR workers usually earn well under $40 per month. Since his first year in UNICOR, Barry has worked his way up to grade-1 pay, which provides him with a base pay of over $150 per month. He works a lot of overtime, too, which sometimes results in monthly paychecks that exceed $200.

Besides the pay, Barry says his job as a clerk for one of UNICOR's factory managers provides him with a degree of responsibility that he appreciates. His duties require him to work with sophisticated computer software applications, and he recognizes that those skills will prove valuable upon his release.

"Most guys in here are completely illiterate when it comes to computers," Barry says. "When they get out they're going to find out what a disadvantage that is. Nearly every job in society requires some knowledge of computers.

I'm expecting my computer experience will help me overcome my felony conviction."

Barry explained that his clerical duties require him to work in the same capacity as a mid-level manager of any large factory. He uses word processing programs, spreadsheet programs, database programs, and even some drawing programs to complete his responsibilities.

"I do all of the work," Barry said. "My supervisor is really just around to make sure I'm not doing anything unauthorized. The factory wouldn't skip a beat without him."

Each morning Barry must report for work at 7:30. His detail supervisor takes roll and Barry sets himself to work. He works pretty consistently until just after 11:00, when it's time for lunch. After his forty-five minute lunch break, he returns to work. By then, his duties usually are complete and so he spends the afternoons "shootin' the shit" with his coworkers. He's not allowed to use the computers for any personal work. If caught even typing a letter home, this could result in his being fired and receiving an incident report. Barry says he doesn't break the rules because he appreciates the job. It not only provides him with the money he needs to live in prison, but it also keeps him current with the technological skills he recognizes that he'll need upon his release.

Barry's official work day ends at 3:30 in the afternoon, but he works overtime whenever it's available. When he's not working, Barry likes to exercise, watch movies, or read. Besides reading for leisure, Barry frequently studies application manuals to become more proficient with the software programs to which he has access. Most of his life at Fort Dix revolves around his UNICOR job.

I asked Barry whether he's been saving the money he earns from UNICOR to help him upon his release. He hasn't. In addition to his ten-year sentence, the judge also imposed a $10,000 fine on Barry. Consequently, the Bureau of Prisons requires him to contribute 50 cents of every dollar he earns toward his fine. This leaves Barry with about $100 each month. He uses this money to pay for his personal hygiene items, stamps, telephone calls, and the commissary items he needs. After those expenses, there isn't much money left over. He lives paycheck to paycheck. Striving to develop skills that will help his future, Barry represents a classic gleaner.

Jerry, the Family Man Being close to New York, Fort Dix has a rather large population of people who allegedly belong to one of the five Mafia families in New York. There are organized crime families based in other American cities, but as far as the New Yorkers are concerned, no one else really counts. As Frank Sinatra sang, New Yorkers are "king of the hill, top of the heap"; everyone else is a second-class citizen.

Those at Fort Dix who serve their sentence with the *gangster* label are usually prisoners who have been incarcerated for significant periods of time— well over ten years—already. Their good behavior in prison resulted in their security levels dropping to low and their subsequent transfers to Fort Dix.

Like all prisons where I've been held, those who are perceived to have close connections to the Gambino, Luchese, Colombo, Genovese, or Bonnano family—the Mafia—are given a special honor or respect within the fences.

Mafia prisoners represent a detached group within the prison community. People who are not of Italian-American ancestry mistakenly apply the name *wiseguys* to all alleged organized-crime members. But this is inaccurate. In actuality, I have learned, there are relatively few authentic wiseguys, or *made members*, of the five families. To become a *made man* or an authentic wiseguy, one must be accepted by his peers and take the code of silence about the family's business.

In prison, however, one doesn't have to be an authentic wiseguy to receive Mafia respect. In fact, there are many *associates*—and many who are simply friends. Besides these friends and associates, there are also scores of lackeys—those who care more about perceptions of being associated than actually being anything more. Out of the 2,000 prisoners in Fort Dix East, there may be 40 people who curry the perception of being related to the Mafia, but there are few actual leaders. One of the leaders in Fort Dix is Jerry.

Jerry has been incarcerated for sixteen years and is less than two years away from his release date. I met him through another friend of mine, and I've enjoyed his company during the time we've been confined together on this compound. Eager to leave prison as soon as possible, he passes his time rather easily and is an expert at avoiding problems inside the prison.

Jerry communicates with a natural, offhanded ease that endears him to others. In fact, his reputation as a stand-up guy leaves him beyond suspicion of being an informant or doing anything contrary to the rules by which guys from the neighborhood live. His status gives him the freedom to talk freely with any staff member; he's a man others can turn to for assistance. Jerry's personable charm makes him a natural communicator. Like a diplomat within the prison, Jerry frequently intervenes to help a friend or acquaintance find a good job or overcome a misunderstanding with others—be it staff or other prisoners. Others respect Jerry for standing by his principles.

He's the kind of prisoner Fort Dix seems designed to hold. He minds his own business. His behavior doesn't cause any problems within the prison. He's independent in that he never cries about his time or the conditions in which he is serving it. Instead, Jerry performs his assigned duties in the prison and then passes his free time without interfering with others. Not only does Jerry keep himself out of problems, but he also frequently uses his influence in the prison to keep others from disturbing the easy atmosphere of Fort Dix. Jerry brings a calming presence to the prison.

Jerry sleeps until after 10 each morning. He spends several hours during the day playing gin with others who are equally respected in prison, or he may walk around the track with one or two close friends for exercise; he's never able to make a full circle around the track without being stopped for the requisite handshakes with associates and impostors alike. Always neatly dressed in freshly ironed clothing, Jerry strolls around the compound with the confidence and assurance of a leader who is comfortable in his domain.

During the evenings, Jerry's room becomes a gathering place where friends join him for meals. Each evening, Jerry and his group eat together and pass a couple hours discussing old times and news from "the neighborhood." As might be expected, each meal includes large dishes of macaroni with well-seasoned sauces that Jerry and his friends prepare for themselves; I can verify that their meals are far superior to the food served in the prison's chow hall. Years of imprisonment have made these cooks masters of the microwave.

I frequently enjoy these meals with Jerry and his friends. As the only guy at the table not from the neighborhood, I sit as an outsider looking in. Federal prisoners don't have access to HBO television, but when I eat dinner with Jerry and his friends I imagine it's like having a front-row seat on the set of *The Sopranos*. Through our dinners and conversations, I've learned a lot about Jerry and his friends.

One topic that finds its way into every meal is the concept of honor, a code by which every guy from the neighborhood professes to live. This code requires each individual to accept complete responsibility for his actions. Ironically, accepting responsibility doesn't mean one should acknowledge wrongdoing or look for ways to make amends. Rather, it means keeping one's mouth shut about one's business. More important than anything, as an *honorable man*, one would never, under any circumstances, cooperate with law enforcement. It doesn't matter if a car is stolen or one is an eyewitness to a robbery or even a murder. A neighborhood guy will never be a witness to a crime. Society relies on law enforcement to handle its problems; neighborhood guys take care of disputes themselves.

These are men who readily identify themselves as embracing the criminal code. There's no dishonor in committing a crime; according to Jerry and his friends, dishonor comes from ratting on someone else to escape one's punishment.

To most people, this allegiance to the criminal code belies the concept of honor. But Jerry and his friends see no inconsistency. If one is "with society," then one lives by society's rules; once one chooses to live by the code of the neighborhood, however, that individual must do so all the way. These are men of principles, even if those principles are at odds with the principles of society at large. It doesn't mean that neighborhood guys can't be friends with people who abide by society's principles. It only means that business is kept separate from such relationships.

The regular community meals provide Jerry and his friends with an opportunity to forget the fences around them and celebrate the joy of life. Because no one sitting at the table bothers anyone else in the prison and doesn't interfere with the prison's operations, staff members pretty much leave the men alone to serve their time. Their miniature community is like a quasi family, one that lessens the isolation of confinement and recalls the good times to which they'll all return. According to Irwin, Jerry and his friends from the neighborhood are "doing time."

Gypsy, a Biker Gypsy is a young-looking 66-year-old convict. He began serving a forty-eight-year sentence when he was 43. Gypsy currently is within six months of his release. As a long-time convict, Gypsy is intimately familiar with the federal prison system. He transferred to Fort Dix after having served long terms in the penitentiaries at Lewisburg, Marion, and Lompoc—three of the most notorious prisons in the federal system.

Besides serving a significant portion of his life behind walls, Gypsy had a long career as the National President of the Pagan Motorcycle Club. He tells me his club is well known as the most violent and vicious motorcycle club on the East Coast.

"Is this accusation accurate?" I asked Gypsy.

"Let me say this," he said. "We'll fight when it's necessary."

I asked Gypsy to describe his perspective on Fort Dix.

"When I first got here I was disoriented. I admit that I've been institutionalized. Who wouldn't be after twenty-three years of living in prison? Where I was before, I couldn't just walk anywhere. I had to ask a guard to give me a pass, then unlock a door and let me out whenever I wanted to go somewhere. After over twenty years of living as if I were an animal, I grew used to the keeper."

"What was it like when you first got here?" I asked.

"When I got to Fort Dix, the first thing I did was begin looking for an ax or a shank. I've always had an ax built into my locker and a few shanks buried around the prison where I could easily get my hands on 'em. People know who is who in prison, and despite my age, people have always known that I'm one who won't hesitate to take a swing at someone's head with my ax or drive steel in 'em if the situation calls for it."

"Wouldn't you have cared about the consequences?" I asked.

"Hell no," Gypsy said. "Can't be thinking 'bout consequences in the joint. You've just got to stand by what you believe in. When I got here I started to feel there was a whole different attitude 'bout doing time. Nobody was about nothing. I wasn't used to it at first."

"What struck you as odd about the place?" I asked.

"There's no drama here," Gypsy said. "I wasn't prepared for that. I'm used to being on alert, knowing something can jump off at any time. It took me about five months before I began to accept that there was no threat here. It allowed me to decompress, to wind down. I think I needed this time before I got out."

"Were there some aspects of living in low-security that you didn't like when you first got here?" I asked.

"Sure," Gypsy quickly said. "I wasn't too comfortable with the twelve-man rooms. Before they let me on the compound a counselor pulled me aside and told me that I'd be living with blacks and Hispanics. Because of my history she said she had to ask me whether I was going to have any problem with that. I told her I've been living in prison for over twenty years and have learned to get along with anyone. But when they put me in a room with twelve other people, and I noticed that I was the only white guy, I felt really out of place.

"Before I came to prison I really only associated with other bikers or members of the club," Gypsy continued. "Since I've been down I've learned to get along with everyone. We're all part of the same struggle. But in the other joints whites don't cell with blacks, and every chow hall is voluntarily segregated with the whites, blacks, and Hispanics each having their own specific areas to eat. Here I was just thrown in the mix. I wasn't really ready for it. It was different, but I was willing to give it a try.

"When they put me in a twelve-man room I immediately noticed that I was the only white. This was unheard of anyplace else. But I could also tell that not one of the other prisoners were convicts. Everyone was real friendly like, offering me coffee, shower shoes, a toothbrush, and shit like that.

"It really bothered me though when I noticed that the doors didn't lock. Anyone could have walked into the room and stabbed someone in the middle of the night. I didn't like that. In fact, I think I hardly slept during my first few months [at Fort Dix]; I couldn't sleep comfortably until I began to get a feel for the people around me."

"You say that you began to get a feel for the place after a few months. What changed?" I asked.

"The level of freedom began to grow on me," Gypsy said. "For the past twenty-some odd years I've been living in pressure cookers. Every day we'd see cops running around from place to place to pick up a body or clean up some blood. We had lockdowns a few times each month. And despite the seniority a guy gets in the joint, he always knows that on any given day things can blow up.

"When I started to fall into a routine here I really started to like it," Gypsy continued. "I wake up about 4 every morning. Now I like having the door unlocked because I walk outside my cell and get me some hot water. I can sit and drink my coffee in the peace of one of the common-area rooms or I can return to my cell. I got used to this freedom."

"How do you spend the rest of your day?" I asked him.

"After I have my coffee I go take a shower and shave," Gypsy said. Then, as soon as the compound opens at 6:00 I go out and walk for about an hour. At 7:30, I volunteer in the wood shop class and I pass a lot of my time there. Later in the afternoons I exercise with the weights; I love working out with the weights. They'd taken the weights out at Lompoc, where I was before, so here I'm sure to get my workout in every day. And in the evenings I walk around the track a little more. I like staying out at night. I hadn't been out late since 1979. Here we're out every night 'till almost 10 o'clock. Standing under the stars is real nice."

"Have you had any problems adjusting since you transferred here?" I asked.

"Just one," Gypsy said. "It was a few weeks after I got here. I was in the chow hall at the salad bar. I had the metal serving spoon in my hand when some Dominican guy comes rushin' up beside me and starts dippin' his bowl into the salad dish. I tell the guy, 'Hey! Just wait your goddamn turn in line. I'm not takin' it all.' The guy starts blabbin' off in Spanish. I just smacked him in the nose with the metal spoon in my hand. After I hit him the guy just looked at me cross-eyed not knowin' what to say, then he walked away.

"After that happened I just shook my head and asked myself what the hell I was doin'. I was about to get myself in a beef and sent right back up to the penitentiary. By that time I'd already gotten used to the freedom. I like being able to walk out of my cell before dawn. I like being able to walk around without having to see a cop. I like lifting weights. And I like staying out at night. After realizing all the things I liked here, I decided to start letting the little things pass."

"Do the guys you hang around with like Fort Dix as much as you do?" I asked.

"If guys have been around the system," Gypsy said, "they know how good it is here. I mean, come on. Where else can a guy put a debit card in a vending machine and buy a sandwich at 9 at night? Where else does a guy have so much storage space? Where else does a guy have so much freedom?

"I hate having to deal with the cops for anything. But here at Dix, I have less contact with them than anyplace else I've been since that peanut farmer was in the White House. Here I don't worry about asking for passes or cops giving me permission. I can do as I please, and I can pretty much do it all day. I have a great job as an orderly that doesn't require more than ten minutes work; it provides me with freedom for the remainder of the day. I exercise five days each week and receive visits at least once each week. This isn't a good joint. It's a great joint.

"The only people who say they don't like it are people who've never been anywhere else, or they're people who like pretending how tough they are and that they get more respect in the penitentiary. Whenever I hear someone talk about getting more respect in the penitentiary," Gypsy continued, "I know they're full of shit. I tell 'em it's not the penitentiary that gives someone respect. It's the man who demands it. If someone feels they've been disrespected here, they can solve it real easily. They can solve it the same way they say that it would be solved in the pen. But guys ain't about nothing here. They just want to talk and act like killers. In reality, they're probably in here on the witness protection program.

"I know this place is full a rats and other guys who are no good," Gypsy pointed out. "And if I was in the pen I'd have to deal with them a little differently. But I've been down for too long, and I'm real close to the door. I'm willin' to overlook a lot from here because I like the freedom. Besides that, I know once I get outside I'm gonna be around a whole lot of disrespectful people. What am I gonna do? Stab everyone? Being around this camp has been good for me. It's given me a chance to mellow out and think about living the rest of my life outside of prison," Gypsy concluded.

Like Joe, while Gypsy was in the higher security prisons he was jailing, living each day as a prisoner, and not thinking about the outside. As he moved to lower security, however, he adapted the role of a gleaner.

Candy, the Mexican Delight Candy is 31, stands about 5'7", and has a slight build. With shoulder-length blond hair, effeminate ways, and a gaunt face, Candy would be an obvious target for sexual predators in a higher security prison. At Fort Dix, on the other hand, Candy says that he has never been abused sexually.

When I asked Candy about his crime, he told me freely that he is serving a two-year sentence for child pornography. In a higher security prison, this fact alone would have brought censure and abuse upon Candy, but at Fort Dix he saw no reason to conceal what he had done. No one seemed to care about his offense. People were interested in Candy for other reasons.

Candy says that he met Juan, his first boyfriend, when he was a holdover at Lewisburg. They both were transferred to Fort Dix, where they continued their homosexual relationship. When I asked Candy whether Juan considered himself a homosexual, he said no. "Juan was just adapting to his environment. Since there were no women around I became a substitute. It was a relationship where he used me and I used him," Candy said.

But it wasn't a possessive relationship. Juan began inviting his friends to meet Candy, and Candy said that he would engage in sexual relations with those people, too. Everything was consensual, Candy said. There was no pressure being placed upon him. There were times when he had as many as five sexual partners in a single day, many of whom he didn't even know. This promiscuity, Candy says, earned him the nickname "Mexican Delight" on the Fort Dix compound. I asked Candy whether he was concerned about the AIDS virus.

"Of course I'm concerned," Candy said, "but I'm not going to stop having sex because of fear. There aren't any condoms around. If I catch it I catch it. Besides, I mostly only give blow jobs."

"Aren't you aware that the AIDS virus can be transmitted through oral sex?" I asked.

"Well," Candy paused, "it's not as likely."

Besides being a holdover, he has never served time in a higher security prison. When I asked whether he had any concerns about being transferred to a medium-security prison or a penitentiary, he said that he would probably enjoy it more. He says that the people with whom he has sex at Fort Dix are too secretive. Candy flaunts his homosexuality and says that he has never felt threatened since he arrived at Fort Dix.

When he first arrived, guards frequently stopped him and told him that if anyone gave him any problems or pressured him in any way that he could come to them for assistance. "But there have never been any real problems," he said.

"On three separate occasions guys came into the shower with me and wanted to have sex. When I told them no, that I wasn't interested in them, they left. If I'm not interested in someone I can tell them no and they're willing to leave," Candy concluded.

"Do people who represent themselves as heterosexuals sometimes approach you for sex?" I asked.

"They do it all the time," Candy said. "Sometimes they do some really freaky shit. One guy showed me his dick and begged me to have sex with him. He was one of those guys who had used a razor to slice the head of his dick open so he could slide a bead under the foreskin. The foreskin on his penis grew over the bead, and he said that it was going to enhance his sexual performance on girls when he got out. He wanted to try his new tool out on me. But I declined."

"What do you mean 'he was one of those guys?' Do a lot of guys insert beads into their penises?" I asked.

"A lot of guys in prison do," Candy said. "I've seen it a bunch. They always ask me if I like it, but that shit's even too freaky for me. It's always the so-called straight guys who are mangling themselves up like that.

"Heterosexuals always want to be real discreet about their relationships with me. One time I was in bed with a guy in a two-man room and an orderly walked in on us. I just started laughing but the other guy got so embarrassed. He ran after the orderly and offered him money not to tell anyone. I didn't care at all."

"You don't feel any stigma for being a homosexual?" I asked.

"No. That's who I am," Candy said.

I asked Candy whether the guards and administrators knew of his promiscuity.

"Well of course they know I'm gay," he said. "It's in my file. Besides my record, everyone here pretty much knows who I am. But that doesn't really matter. I've never been caught in the act by a guard. And if I were caught I wouldn't really care. All that would happen is that I'd go to the hole for a week or so."

"Does being a homosexual lessen the punishment of confinement?" I asked.

"I don't feel like I'm being punished at all," Candy said. "I'm living free, eating free, and having as much sex as I want. If things prove too tough outside, I won't have any objections to violating parole and coming back."

Candy is willing to continue jailing.

Carlos, a Fish Not everyone in Fort Dix is serving an easy sentence. Carlos, a 30-year-old drug offender, is in his second year of a fourteen-year sentence. As a newly confined prisoner, he's known as a fish in prison vernacular. Carlos is having a difficult time adjusting and finds the stress level unbearable.

Carlos tells me that he can't stand the lack of privacy. "There is never a moment's peace around here," Carlos said. "I'm not used to living around so many people, all the noise, all the filth."

In particular, Carlos complained about having to share the bathroom with so many strangers. Each housing unit requires the 350 assigned prisoners to share a total of twelve showers.

"The sinks, toilets, and shower areas are always filthy," he says. "I can't even take a shit in peace. I'll be using the toilet and somebody from the next stall will start talking to me. I don't want to have a conversation with a stranger when I'm using the toilet.

"Or how about when I'm brushing my teeth," Carlos continued. "Some guy using the sink less than 2 feet away from me will start blowing bloody snot out of his nose into the sink. I don't know what kind of disease he's got. But I have to live with him. Besides the people, the stench of piss and shit contaminates the whole floor, and the warden blocked up half the windows in the unit so we can't get enough fresh air. There's just no respect here. The guards treat me like shit. They kick my bed at night, shine flashlights in my face when I'm sleeping. And I miss my family."

Carlos is from Miami. He left behind a 27-year-old wife, a 1-year-old daughter, and a 6-year-old son. He supported his family as the owner of a small business, but since he's been incarcerated his business has deteriorated, his wife has been suffering from depression, and he's helpless to contribute.

"The phone system is driving me crazy," Carlos said.

In April 2001, prison administrators enacted a rule that limited federal prisoners to 300 minutes of phone time per month. Prisoners can make phone calls in 15-minute intervals, but once they have exhausted their 300-minute allotment, they are denied access to the prisoner telephone system until the first day of the following month. Carlos has been unable to manage his phone time.

"I call home and my 6-year-old son is crying on the phone to talk with me. How can I cut him off? When I first came in, we didn't have these phone limits and I used to hold my family together through long and regular phone conversations. They live over a thousand miles away, so regular visits aren't practical. But now I can't even talk on the phone. Last month I had used up my 300-minute limit by the twelfth of the month. I couldn't call again until the first of the month. Now it's the fifth and I've already used up 115 minutes. I'm sick."

"Why do you continue using so much of your phone time if you know you've only got 300 minutes available per month?" I asked.

"You don't know what it's like to have children in here," Carlos said. "After I didn't call for the last two weeks of last month my son cried for days. When I was finally able to call again this month, he kept insisting that I call him back. He's telling me that I must not love him anymore because I no longer call like I used to call. It breaks a parent's heart. And it's not only the children. My wife, my mother, everyone in my family tries to keep me on the phone. This is tearing my family apart."

"How is it affecting your own adjustment to prison?" I asked.

Carlos shrugged. "I can't sleep at night. I'm depressed all the time. When I couldn't speak with my family last month I wrote a request to the warden asking for additional minutes. The warden told me I didn't have a good enough reason. Sometimes I don't even feel like living. I'm tormented every day. Guards talk to me like I'm an insect, like I don't even matter. I don't know how they can treat people like this. And I can't say anything back. These people don't even allow me to be sick, to experience my depression. I can't sleep at night and so I'm tired during the day. But if I'm late for work I get an incident report. Life in here is just too hard. I have a life outside, but they're tearing my family apart." Carlos concluded.

"You know," I said, "the problems you're describing have more to do with your adjustment to confinement itself. Things might even be more difficult for you in another prison."

"I don't know about any other prisons," Carlos admitted. "I only know that hell couldn't be worse than my life in Fort Dix."

As a fish, Carlos doesn't really fit into any of the Irwin categories. He hasn't yet adjusted to his confinement; he hasn't found a routine to help him pass his time. He has no sense of direction, is unable to find peace within the prison, and is unable to connect with the world outside. Until he adjusts, he can expect to serve a difficult term.

CONCLUSION

Being confined in Fort Dix, a low-security prison, is better than being confined in medium or high security. This prison lacks tension. There are no gangs threatening the safety of others, and during the five years that I've been confined at Fort Dix, there have been few disturbances that resulted in institution-wide lockdowns.

These profiles are hardly exhaustive, yet they show that men at Fort Dix can serve their time in the manner they choose. Most people find ways to adjust, but some—like those who have not been incarcerated elsewhere—have difficulty. Nevertheless, I've met no one in this low-security prison who feels compelled to belong to any particular group. Few fear for their safety. Most are free to serve their sentences without interference from others. As Gypsy said, people at Fort Dix complain a lot, but everyone overlooks the violations of prison etiquette that could bring serious consequences in other institutions.

For example, in other prisons, known sexual offenders would be abused regularly or forced to live in protective custody; at Fort Dix, on the other hand, Candy lives without shame. Hustlers like Carnalito might have to deal with extortion artists. Poker Joe wouldn't be writing but instead looking for action; in Fort Dix's easy atmosphere he's focusing on skills that he hopes will help him succeed upon his release. And Gypsy, a former leader of a nationally recognized violent group, is "decompressing" and learning to live without a sword.

This isn't to say that Fort Dix is without its problems. The pressures on the prisoner population, however, are far less severe than in higher security prisons. Whereas some people are able to use the less intense environment to accomplish their own goals behind Fort Dix's fences, others complain that they would prefer to be doing time in a "real prison," a place where they would find more respect. Like Gypsy, I remain skeptical about such assertions. If a man is after respect in prison, he'll get it just as easily at Fort Dix as he would at Lewisburg, Atlanta, or Leavenworth.

Some citizens resent prisons like Fort Dix, where prisoners aren't enmeshed in tension. I have heard guards say that every prisoner should be held in a penitentiarylike environment. They favor the tight controls and harsh living conditions.

Higher security prisons, however, are much more expensive to operate. They use much higher guard-to-prisoner ratios. With 2 million people currently serving time in American prisons and jails, administrators choose to hold prisoners in the least-restrictive environment possible. This is an economic decision. Prisons are limited resources. Administrators who work with budgets must reserve the more costly penitentiary space for those prisoners who can't function in lower security facilities. Those who remain in the higher security facilities are more inclined to participate in the prison subculture; these men are doing time or jailing. As the men move into lower security, like at Fort Dix, they frequently change their patterns of behavior. They're more inclined to spend time gleaning. In the next chapter, I'll describe my own adjustment.

10

Choosing to Survive

When I was confined initially, in 1987, I was 23 and not educated formally much be-
yond the high-school level. In fact, I had been an adult for only five years when I re-
ceived the forty-five-year sentence I am serving currently. After trial, conviction, and
sentence, while waiting in the solitude of my jail cell, I began to accept the reality that
I would serve a significant portion of my life in prison. This chapter describes how
I serve my time.

THE COST OF BAD DECISIONS

I had no excuse for the hole I had dug for myself. Knowing that I was the
one who chose to sell cocaine, there was no one but myself to blame for the
problems I had created. Although, initially, I thought the sentence excessive,
the more time I spent confined, the more I realized how common that feeling
of self-pity was among the prisoners around me. Everyone complained as if
they were victims of a corrupt legal system. They were incarcerated because
of rats who had snitched them out. Or their prosecutors had a personal
vendetta against them. They weren't guilty. It was as if I were one of the few
people in the entire prison who was actually guilty.

I felt really out of place. Not only was I confined, I couldn't shake my
feelings of guilt for the humiliation I had caused my family and community.
By then, it was early 1988 and America's problem with drugs was front-page

news. Every day. As I read articles about steps the government was taking to respond to the presence of drugs everywhere, I felt dirty for being associated with this wave of crime.

I knew that I had made bad decisions. Those decisions, I began to realize, had shaped the ways in which my community thought about me. Being convicted of a crime, I was a criminal. Still, I didn't identify with the other prisoners around me who were openly embracing the *criminal* label. Ironically, I identified with the community members outside who loathed me for the crimes I had committed. Those guilty feelings tormenting my thoughts rendered me incapable of identifying with the others around me. I had an obligation to make things right. In other words, I could decide how I would serve my time.

I didn't really care about an appeal or winning relief through the judicial system. It was far more important for me to find ways to reconcile with my community, to make amends. Because of my convictions, society perceived me as vermin—a predatory animal. I wanted to change those perceptions and to explore steps I could take to build character and integrity during the years ahead of me—virtues that I then recognized had been missing from my life prior to my conviction. I didn't want to be known as one who complained about his sentence. Rather, I hoped to demonstrate through my actions that I was committed to earning freedom. Earning freedom. Those words still have a radical ring in my environment. But what kind of freedom was I seeking? Freedom from incarceration? from ignorance? from shame? from indignity? Perhaps all of these.

EARNING FREEDOM

In the darkness of prison, finding ways to compensate society for my crimes wasn't easy. As I wrote in earlier chapters, I committed myself to a ten-year plan. During my first decade, I hoped to build a record that would not only demonstrate my remorse for breaking the law but give members of my community reasons to see me as more than one who lived outside the law during his early twenties. I hoped that my response to the punishment inflicted upon me would help my community accept me once again.

Looking for opportunities to educate myself was my first step in working toward acceptance. I was fortunate in that when I began my term, federal funding was available to help prisoners participate in higher education programs. Soon after I arrived in USP Atlanta, I enrolled in Ohio University's correspondence study program. A few months later, Mercer University began offering courses inside the prison itself. Studying lifted me from depression and helped me feel as if I could become more than simply a prisoner. I read about concepts that helped me see beyond the penitentiary's walls.

Finding ways to reach out of the penitentiary was important for me. The 40-foot wall surrounding the prison limited my ability to see. Anywhere I turned I saw closure, permanence, as if I were in my own tomb. The only escape was looking up while standing outside. Although it was beyond my reach, at least I could see the openness of the sky. It gave me a little hope, in contrast with the despair I felt whenever I looked at eye level—all horizontal vistas were blocked by the gray-beige ugliness of the wall. The wall was a constant reminder, a message appearing whenever my eyes were open that I wasn't welcome outside. Like an animal unfit to live among civilization, my community had determined that I needed to be contained.

Reading and learning helped me conquer these feelings of containment. Each course I completed felt like a step to a ladder I was building that would lead me over the wall. The more I learned, the more confident I became that I could surmount the bad decisions I had made that had led me to prison in the first place. Despite the walls around me, books and college studies were opening my mind, freeing a spirit within me that helped me feel more complete as a human being.

But there were a lot of obstacles to my studies. Voices were constantly screaming around me. Guards were always slamming the heavy steel doors, and strife among my fellow prisoners was constant. The atmosphere behind prison walls isn't conducive to studying in higher education. On the contrary, prison provides a constant tension, a power struggle between guards and prisoners as well as among the prisoners themselves. Despite the goals I wanted to achieve, I constantly had to observe the potential dangers around me.

In response to the intensity—the charged atmosphere, the weapons, the violence, the frustrations—I developed a structured schedule that kept me busy and out of harm's way. In the beginning years, I took every opportunity to make certain my schedule was full. I would rise early to study in my room. At 7:30 A.M., I'd attend my job as a clerk for the UNICOR factory, where I'd remain until 3:30 P.M. During the count I would nap or read. As soon as the unit was released, I would attend my classes in the education building. After class I exercised with weights, then returned to the unit. I was obsessed with my schedule and building a stellar prison record.

I calculated every hour of the day, always struggling to find a balance that would limit my exposure to potential problems while at the same time giving me the latitude to achieve my goals. Staying focused and working toward independent projects was my way of dealing with the environment and keeping a degree of control for myself.

Besides managing my time, I found it essential to find a good cellmate and a good job. A good cellmate, for me, meant finding someone who had some stability in his life, someone who wasn't cooking hooch, smuggling drugs, or preying upon others in the penitentiary. The room was important because it was a kind of sanctuary from the madness. Even though I was active in work, school, and exercise, leaving me little time in the room itself, a bad cellmate, one who enmeshed himself in the prison's chaos, would have made my time much more difficult. I didn't want the anxiety of dealing with overzealous guards who would be shaking down my cell each day in search of a problem, a cellmate who was drunk all the time, or a guy who stores drugs in the room.

The right prison job, too, was essential. If I had been assigned to one of the maintenance, landscaping, or food-service jobs, for example, I wouldn't have had opportunities to work so much on my academic projects. I held a clerical job in UNICOR while I was studying toward my undergraduate degree, and my supportive detail supervisor gave me a tacit authorization to study after my assigned duties were completed. Because of her support, I was able to complete the requirements for my undergraduate degree before the U.S. Congress eliminated access to federal funding for prisoners working to educate themselves. Providence, therefore, played a role in my adjustment to prison.

Factories with Fences

While reading a criminal justice book, I came across a speech by Warren Burger, the conservative former chief justice of the U.S. Supreme Court. Justice Burger delivered his speech "Factories with Fences" during the commencement ceremonies at Pace University on June 11, 1983. In that speech, he observed the relationship between education, hard work, and success. Then he urged prison administrators to initiate programs through which "the inmate could earn and learn his way to freedom and a new life." Justice Burger's speech inspired me. I began looking for further opportunities to contribute to society, to make compensations for breaking the law. Indeed, I looked for any opportunity to demonstrate that I was working to "earn and learn my way to freedom."

Although the nature of my conviction prohibited me from being considered by a parole board, I knew the U.S. Constitution gave the president authority to commute the sentence of any federal prisoner. President Bush, the elder, had just been elected to the White House though, and he stepped up America's War on [people associated with] Drugs. Even so, how does a federal prisoner bring himself to the attention of the president of the United States of America? That was the question I had to answer.

Mentors

During my second year in Atlanta, I met another prisoner, Mark H. Through one of our conversations, Mark mentioned a family friend, Dr. R. Bruce McPherson, who was a professor of education from Chicago. When I heard about Bruce, I implored Mark to introduce me. I instinctively knew I needed a mentor, and the more I heard about Bruce, the more convinced I became that he could help me grow during my confinement.

Mark gave me Bruce's address, and I wrote him an introductory letter. Bruce welcomed me into his life. He began visiting me regularly, graciously introduced me to his family, and immediately began helping me improve my writing skills. He also helped me formulate a plan that we hoped, in time, would prove me a worthy candidate for executive clemency.

The plan comprised three parts. First, I would need to continue my efforts to educate myself. At a minimum, I would need to complete the requirements of an undergraduate degree. Then, if possible, I would need to find a university that would allow me to complete a graduate or professional degree.

Besides educating myself, I also would need to create opportunities to contribute to society. It wasn't so important whether my contributions were made inside or outside of prison walls. What was important was that I built a record demonstrating my commitment to compensating society for breaking its laws. The third part of the plan was that I needed to prove discipline by keeping a record that was free of disciplinary infractions during my period of confinement.

The plan became my compass. It gave me constant direction. With the plan, and the long-term goals that I hoped to achieve with it, I was motivated to rise early every morning. And whenever I came close to a potential problem, I could think about the overall plan and question whether the problem was worth threatening the goals that Bruce and I had established.

When ten years passed, I wanted to have earned a graduate degree, to have built a long record of community contributions, and to have a disciplinary record free of any infractions. With that, I hoped, I could begin a campaign for commutation of sentence. On the other hand, a problem in the penitentiary could derail my hopes for relief; every problem in prison has the potential of escalating to monumental proportions.

By keeping a structured schedule, though, I was able to make progress. I completed my schoolwork, stayed out of trouble, and looked for opportunities to contribute to society. As a prisoner, I began looking for opportunities to work inside the prison as a volunteer.

One of the first opportunities I found was as a volunteer in the suicide-watch program. At any given time, up to ten prisoners in Atlanta's population were being held in special individual cells reserved to hold prisoners whom staff members consider suicidal. Prisoner volunteers worked together with the prison's psychologist to help those under observation. My responsibilities were monitoring the prisoner, recording his behavior, and conversing with him when he felt like talking.

Later, as I moved further along into my academic program, I began working with the prison's education department as a volunteer to help illiterate prisoners learn the fundamentals of reading and writing. Eventually, administrators in the education department allowed me to organize and teach classes on my own through the Adult Continuing Education Program.

By early 1992, it became apparent that I was going to have accumulated enough credits to earn my degree by the summer. Academic programs by then had become such an integral part of my life in prison that I began to worry about what to focus on next.

I wanted to earn a law degree. My goal wasn't to join the bar and become a practicing lawyer. Rather, I wanted to learn as much about the law as possible so that I could contribute to some of the people around me who were struggling with legal issues. I began a letter-writing campaign to law schools to see whether correspondence studies were available. Bruce helped me by contacting the American Bar Association and obtaining a list of addresses for all accredited law school programs.

I wrote to over a hundred law schools, but each response came back the same. They told me the American Bar Association doesn't authorize the study of law through correspondence, because the interaction of minds is an integral part of an education in law. The dean of Hofstra University, however, was intrigued with my letter and passed it along to Professor Al Cohen, the dean of Hofstra's graduate school. Professor Cohen wrote me back and told me that although Hoftsra couldn't admit me into its law program, the school might consider waiving its residency requirement and permit me to earn a master's degree.

The news really encouraged me. I began writing letters to members of the graduate committee in an effort to persuade them that despite my incarceration and inability to fulfill the residency requirement, I would work hard and consistently through the program. Eventually, Hofstra agreed to admit me. Through course work in political science, cultural anthropology, and sociology, I was going to study the Federal Bureau of Prisons and the people that it holds. It was to be an interdisciplinary program that would culminate with a Master of Arts degree. My family supported me by providing the tuition costs at Hofstra.

A New President

In June 1992, Mercer University awarded my undergraduate degree, and I began preparations to study at Hofstra. At the same time, a then hardly known governor from Arkansas was getting a lot of media attention in his bid to win the White House.

President Bush recently had declared victory in the Gulf War with Iraq and enjoyed rather high approval ratings. He had cultivated a reputation as being a tough-on-crime politician, and I saw little reason to submit a petition for clemency under his administration; I needed to serve more time and distinguish myself in the prison system.

But the economy was suffering during the summer of 1992, and Bill Clinton's call for change was striking a chord with American voters. The fact that his own brother had served federal time for cocaine trafficking, and that he appeared receptive to calls of eliminating long sentences for nonviolent drug offenders, encouraged thousands of other prisoners and me.

Expecting that I would be submitting a petition for clemency sometime during the next presidential term, I kept a close eye on American political events during the 1992 election. I was especially encouraged as the election proceeded into its final months. Bill Clinton was gaining in the polls and making overt attempts to reach young voters; he was the first serious presidential contender to appear on the MTV network. When confronted with accusations about Clinton's use of marijuana and draft dodging, his defenders argued that none of us would want to be judged for the bad decisions we made when we were in our early twenties; society should judge us for the growth we have made since then. For obvious reasons, such words were welcome to me.

Besides watching politics, in the summer of 1992 I was doing what I could to prepare for my upcoming studies with Hofstra by reading books on corrections and doing what I could to cultivate my network of support. By then,

Bruce had been working closely with me for over two years. I realized how valuable his friendship had become to me and began a project to find more mentors, particularly ones who could help me confront the challenges of studying the criminal justice system through correspondence.

Most of the books I was reading to prepare for my studies focused on corrections, and the authors were all professors. After reading each book, I wrote a letter of introduction to the book's author. Through the letter I explained how the book helped my understanding of our nation's prison system. I also explained that not only was I a federal prisoner, but that I had recently completed my undergraduate degree and was about to begin studying the federal prison system at Hofstra. I asked the authors if they would help guide me through my studies.

I was surprised that so many of these professors responded to my requests for assistance; I began developing relationships with some of America's leading penologists, including Norval Morris, George Cole, John DiIulio, Marilyn McShane, Frank Cullen, Tim Flanagan, and Leo Carroll. They encouraged my studies and generously agreed to help by critiquing my papers and providing me with reading materials. In fact, several of these professors have visited me in prison.

The professors also opened opportunities for me to begin making contributions to the community outside of prison walls. Indeed, as I progressed through my studies, some of them allowed me to contribute chapters to scholarly books they were writing, make presentations (vicariously) to their professional conferences, and even participate in their course work. Mentors became a key to my development in prison and brought meaning to my life.

In the fall of 1992, Bill Clinton was elected the 42nd president of the United States. On election night, every television in USP Atlanta was tuned in to one of the networks covering the election. Thousands of drug offenders were hoping that a new administration would provide some relief to a crowded and growing federal prison system. To me, Bill Clinton seemed like he would be receptive to the concept of "earning and learning" one's way to freedom. With his victory on election night, I was infected with his message of hope.

The Clemency Petition

By early summer of 1993, I was completing my sixth year in prison. I hadn't originally planned on submitting a petition for clemency until I had served ten years of my sentence, but the new president's agenda for change really inspired me. I consulted with my mentors, and all with whom I spoke encouraged me to submit my petition. I requested the application for clemency from Ms. Forbes, my case manager at USP Atlanta.

The petition itself was rather straightforward. I provided information about my background, about my criminal conviction, and about the reasons I believed myself worthy of a commutation by the president. In July 1993, I submitted my petition to the Office of the Pardon Attorney; the pardon attorney is responsible for accepting and reviewing clemency applications and preparing recommendations for their disposition.

Once my petition was on file, I continued with my studies, my efforts to redeem myself, and my efforts to expand my network of support. I prepared a portfolio that described my growth in the prison system and sent it to potential sources of support that I saw in the news or read about through books; I asked those people to write to the pardon attorney on my behalf and express their support for the concept of earning freedom.

Every few months I would write to the Office of the Pardon Attorney and inquire about my petition. Each time I wrote I received a form letter back telling me that my commutation remained under consideration but hadn't yet been acted upon. My hopes remained high.

In 1994 I transferred to McKean, and in the summer of 1995 Hofstra University awarded my Master of Arts degree. I really expected that degree would make a difference in my case and quickly sent a copy of my degree to the pardon attorney. I asked her to attach it to my petition. Later that year, however, during the Christmas season, my case manager gave me a letter informing me that my petition for clemency had been denied. No reason was given.

The news depressed me. When I received it I was in my eighth year of my sentence. The goals I had set for myself to complete in ten years had been completed in eight. At the time, I had about nineteen years remaining to serve on my sentence. It was time to begin making plans for my next decade.

The news from the pardon attorney clouded my thinking. I had built my sentence around education projects, but now I wondered whether there was something else I should be doing. The only thing that seemed to matter was the passing of time. I did some research on commutations and learned that presidents in recent decades had severely lessened their use. Indeed, during President Roosevelt's administration, he granted 491 commutations; President Kennedy granted 100 commutations during his term; and President Johnson granted 227 commutations. But after President Nixon, who granted 62 commutations, the use of sentence commutations began to decline. Through the summer of 1999, after seven years in office, President Clinton had granted only 3 commutations.

The irony, of course, is that while recent presidents have declined to exercise their power to grant mercy, the federal prison population has soared. The government had become less merciful. After I was denied clemency in 1995, I chose to wait several years before I would file a second petition. I would use that time to strengthen my record of contributing to community projects and working to build my growing network of support.

PRISONERLIFE.COM

Friends in my network of support sponsored a personal Internet site for me at PrisonerLife.com. I've found this project extremely helpful in interacting with the community and learning more about what taxpayers expect of federal prisoners. Although federal prisoners don't have direct access to the

Internet, my supporters help me publish information on a personal web site at *www.PrisonerLife.com*. The Internet has been more than a tool for me; it also has proven itself extremely therapeutic.

Through my personal web site I have a forum to reach outside of these fences, to connect with the world. As a long-term prisoner, I find it extremely important to initiate contacts with law-abiding citizens. If I didn't reach outside, my associations would be limited to the felons with whom I'm confined. Such relationships can't be conducive to leading a law-abiding life as a taxpaying citizen upon release.

My Internet site gives me the privilege of expressing my views to the public, and it encourages Internet users to respond. I write about the prison system, the people that it holds, and the efforts I am making to atone for the criminal behavior of my early twenties: The site offers a message board and e-mail services, so Internet users who find my site are able to express their opinions about what I have written. The web site has helped me expand my network of support, allowed me to make many new friends, and given me a life outside of these walls. Through it, I am able to interact with citizens and learn more about what taxpayers expect of the criminal justice system. Further, the discussions generated by my Internet site at *PrisonerLife.com* are helping me learn more about concepts of forgiveness in the law.

ATONEMENT

As years passed, I began to study the literature on acceptable ways of seeking forgiveness. Cornell University's Professor David Garvey's writings helped me understand that atonement is both a goal and a process. As a goal, atonement seeks the reconciliation of the wrongdoer and the victim. It also seeks the reintegration of the wrongdoer back into good standing as a member of the community. As a process, Garvey explains that atonement has several steps; and the successful completion of those steps should ideally lead to atonement—the goal.

As one who has broken society's laws, I have had it in my power—and I continue my struggle—to repent for my wrongful conduct, to apologize openly to society, to make reparations, and to serve penance.

I began these efforts to atone upon my conviction and continue working to build a record that demonstrates my commitment to leading a law-abiding and contributing life upon my release. These represent my efforts at *expiation*, which Garvey calls the first stage of atonement. *Reconciliation*, which Garvey calls the second and final stage in the process of atonement, requires the victim's forgiveness. That, obviously, isn't within my sphere of control.

I'm guilty of organizing a group of people who participated in a scheme to distribute cocaine. It was wrong for me to break the law, and ever since I was convicted, I have worked to atone for the humiliation I caused my family and for the disappointment I brought to my community. Now that I am more than halfway through my second decade of incarceration, I'm much better able to appreciate the need to seek society's forgiveness, and it's the reason

I have offered my fellow citizens my categorical and unequivocal apology for the crimes I committed as a younger man.

Although I'm convinced that I'm as ready now as I ever will be to live in society, as of this writing, I haven't filed a second petition for executive clemency. I won't file again unless I receive conclusive proof that citizens from my community accept my efforts to atone, forgive me for the crimes I committed during my early twenties, and support the efforts I have made to earn freedom. Why? Because as Professor Garvey explains, "identifying with one's fellows is in large measure what makes a community." And someday, whether in 2013 when my scheduled release date comes, or sooner if my fellow citizens and the president deem me worthy, I want to participate in my community again. I will continue my efforts to earn freedom, but if support from American citizens isn't forthcoming, I'm mentally prepared to remain in prison until 2013. Either way, I will continue using every day that I remain in prison to prepare myself to lead a law-abiding, contributing life upon release.

CONCLUSION

I have used goals to help me hold onto my sanity and grow during my period of incarceration. By working toward something more than a release date that seemed like light-years away when I began serving this sentence, I established a ten-year plan that I hoped would help me advance my date. My commitment to following that plan gave me the reasons to sidestep the strife and conflict through which I've lived during my entire adult life.

Although my efforts haven't yet resulted in any advancement of my release date, I'm confident my efforts have helped me grow as a human being during the time I have been confined. Over two hundred years ago, Voltaire wrote that if one doesn't want to commit suicide, one must stay busy. I've stayed busy, and it has helped.

Despite living without female intimacy, my inability to enjoy the pleasures of fatherhood, the joys of building a career, or participating in family events, my spirits remain high. I exercise religiously and enjoy a frequent correspondence with people who accept me and whom I respect. My life is behind prison fences. Because of my ability to reach outside, however, to enjoy the support of a strong support network that I have cultivated for years, I'm rarely melancholic. And no one will ever hear me whine about the sentence I continue to serve. As Tim Ufkes, a beloved family member has helped me realize, I'm not a victim. Rather, like everyone, I have the choice of how to respond to adversity. And I'm choosing to survive, and eventually, to prosper as a member of my family and community.

11

A Prisoner's Suggestions

As a prisoner, I often wonder about the purposes of long-term incarceration. Taxpayer dollars fund federal and state prisons, so it follows that these institutions should respond to the needs of society. Citizens, therefore, have a right to know whether the federal prison system (and the various state systems) is succeeding or failing. But what is a successful prison system? What do citizens expect offenders to accomplish during the years they serve? And how much do such expectations shape and influence prisons and the way administrators manage them? In this concluding chapter, I'll look at these issues.

THE GOALS OF INCARCERATION

Over the years, when opportunities arose, I sought answers to the questions above from prison administrators. Predictably, most told me this is a need-to-know business, and, that as a prisoner, I don't need to know. The prototypical administrator views all prisoners as cogs in the criminal justice machine, a machine that continues expanding with only marginal accountability for its success or failure. Continuing my efforts to connect with the broader American society, its needs and expectations, I sought answers elsewhere.

I looked to criminal justice theorists who write about the four stated goals of incarceration: incapacitation, retribution, deterrence, and rehabilitation. My sixteen years of experience living behind walls and fences suggests that although these goals frequently appear in the criminal justice literature, administrators don't emphasize each goal equally. In fact, I have concluded that administrators succeed in achieving only one of these goals.

Incapacitation

As a system of incapacitation, the Federal Bureau of Prisons should receive high marks. People confined within these fences certainly are incapacitated, prevented from participating in communities. In all the years I've been confined, only one prisoner has escaped from a prison where I was held. As a system of incapacitation, one designed to physically separate people from their communities, federal prisons succeed brilliantly.

Prisons also succeed in erecting barriers to separate prisoners mentally from their families and communities. Rules now prohibit federal prisoners from using the telephone for more than 300 minutes per month; they prohibit prisoners from visiting with anyone they didn't know prior to incarceration; and most federal prison wardens prohibit prisoner access to word processors to facilitate writing. It's with a degree of duplicity that administrators say they encourage prisoners to maintain close family and community ties. The rules they implement belie such assertions and stifle prisoner interaction with anyone outside prison fences.

Although the prison system succeeds as a great design for incapacitation, I wonder why so few citizens question the validity of this goal as a public policy, at least in terms of extended sentences. Historians tell us that early prisons were designed to remove offenders from society in order to encourage their penitence. Somewhere along the way, legislators abandoned thoughts about inducing prisoner penitence and reformation. They just began passing sentencing laws that incarcerate people for longer periods of time.

In the beginning years of the penitentiary system, people who entered the prison's gate were blindfolded, led to a single cell, and cut off from all forms of communication with the world. A prisoner's only companion was a Bible, as administrators had hopes that the Good Book combined with incapacitation would inspire the wrongdoer to repent. But at that time, average prison sentences didn't exceed two years. An individual served his time, but then rejoined his community. Perhaps one to two years of total incapacitation was an effective response to crime.

Total incapacitation, however, isn't an effective response when offenders are serving decades at a time. And today, the federal prison system is so crowded that officials consider those with fewer than ten years to serve as short-term prisoners; many more are serving longer sentences. The proliferation of longer sentences argues for a reevaluation of the goals of confinement. Ideally, incarceration shouldn't only protect society, it also should help offenders identify and embrace the values of communities outside of prison fences.

As prisoners serve longer sentences, incapacitation ceases to work as a tool for personal reform. Without opportunities to participate in outside communities, prisoners tend to become absorbed by the prison subculture. As I have tried to demonstrate in this volume through vignettes and profiles of men I have encountered in prison, it's a subculture that diametrically opposes the larger culture outside of prison walls. Instead of helping the incarcerated focus on steps they can take to lead contributing lives upon release, the total separation of prisoners from their communities encourages just the opposite. Many prisoners form even closer alliances with the world of crime. Relatively few prisoners become serious about steps they can take to succeed outside; instead, they simply focus on living inside the walls.

Prison is a place where men cheer when representatives of government or law enforcement are attacked. Just yesterday I heard a man cheering for Timothy McVeigh. "We have to cheer for McVeigh," the prisoner said. "Fuck society. Those people don't care about us or our families."

By definition, placing a man in confinement separates him from the community. There's no question that to protect society, those men and women who are irrevocably criminal need to be incapacitated by the criminal justice system. Evil does exist in the world, and some people insist upon preying on society, refusing to respect or abide by the rules that hold communities together. The prison system must protect society by confining dangerous offenders. But is it wise to separate all offenders for generations, to engender a persistent hatred in them and their families? Leaving people with no hope to participate in outside communities for multiple decades doesn't encourage prisoners to prepare themselves for release. Instead, they focus on living in the predator-versus-prey or us-versus-them world of prison. Such conditioning doesn't bode well for society when these people's release from prison comes.

The Bureau of Justice Statistics says that in 1980, over 156,000 people were released from prison; in 1990, nearly 424,000 people were released from prison; in 2001, 614,000 people were released from prison. With the drastic cuts in funding for educational programs, the abolition of parole boards, and further movement toward total separation from mainstream society, many of those prisoners rejoined their communities with little else besides an expanded repertoire of how to commit crimes more efficiently and a more extensive network of criminal associates. Warped value systems developed through years of incarceration render most long-term prisoners incapable of finding legitimate places for themselves in the communities that most inevitably will join.

Prison staff members who consider themselves correctional professionals might serve society better by designing programs that encourage individuals to identify and reintegrate with law-abiding communities. This is especially important if politicians persist in increasing the length of sentences. These are communities to which hundreds of thousands of prisoners return each year. By advocating policies that completely alienate offenders for decades at a time, some administrators, perhaps inadvertently, actually are encouraging high recidivism rates.

In summary, I would give prison administrators high marks in reaching their goal of incapacitating prisoners. The value of such a goal to the community has merit; however, as the goal is currently pursued, it becomes dubious at best. It's self-defeating.

Retribution

The federal prison system doesn't earn such high marks as a system of retribution, at least not for long-term offenders. After about five years of confinement, prisoners begin growing accustomed to the fences and walls. The formerly ill effects of punishment begin to subside. By the time ten years pass, prisoners have developed routines inside the fences and have become used to harassment from petty bureaucrats. Life becomes normal and predictable, although within a restricted, harsh, and sometimes inhumane closed society.

I've spent virtually my entire adult life in prison. It has become a way of life for me, and at this time I don't feel like I'm being punished at all. I broke the law when I was in my early twenties, and I am remorseful for disappointing my family and community. The arrest, the conviction, the first several months of separation from family and community were definitely punishment. Retribution hung on my shoulders like a lead coat. But as the months turned into years and the years turned into decades, as I progressed from my early twenties to my late thirties, it became much more difficult for me to reconcile my time behind these fences with the crimes I committed during the Reagan presidency.

The prison system has grown more crowded over the years. As it expands, budgetary restraints cause administrators to cut programs that benefit prisoners directly—and society indirectly. This has made life more onerous in prison, but tighter living conditions and more rules aren't retributive acts. They're management decisions that in no way are connected to the crime for which prisoners are serving their sentences. In fact, administrators who make these management decisions aren't even familiar with individual prisoners, much less the crimes for which they're serving time.

After prisoners pass the five-year mark, rule changes and mean-spirited policies no longer bear a relationship to the original crime. They're just a change in the atmosphere, something new to which the prisoners must adapt. They're aggravating, but virtually no prisoners connect these frustrations as resulting from their particular crimes. Not after several years have passed.

As time goes by, any connection between the original crime and punishment-type policies in prison diminishes. I was punished for wrecking my mother's car when I was 16. If she were to stop speaking to me now as further punishment for that act, the connection would be incomprehensible to me. Similarly, I see no connection between tougher prison policies and my criminal behavior of 1987. How can prison policies be punishment when individuals on the receiving end don't know the reason for their punishment or that they are being punished at all? Once prison becomes a way of life, retribution—punishment—ceases to exist.

Warden Luther used to say that people are sent to prison as punishment, not for punishment. There's no question that one's original removal from society represents a punishment. That dramatic action is immediate and closely connected with the criminal conviction. As decades pass, however, the relationship between the original crime and the life one is leading in confinement becomes less clear.

If one is sentenced to a thousand lashes, after he has received the first couple hundred, he becomes numb to the rest. I've become numb to my punishment. Now that I've passed fifteen years behind these fences, I wonder how my continued incarceration serves the public interest. What's to be accomplished? If it's punishment, retribution, then I would give administrators low marks for failing to keep me cognizant of the relationship between their punishment and my crime.

Plato, one of the great Greek philosophers who helped shape Western civilization, rejected retribution. In fact, he considered such a goal barbaric and didn't believe it had a place in society. After an amount of incapacitation and retribution appropriate to one's crime, responses to crime should focus on the future rather than the past. Professor Jeffrie G. Murphy described Plato's theory of punishment as moral improvement. Instead of striving to punish offenders interminably, society ought to look for opportunities to transform the character of the criminal from a state of vice to a state of virtue; Plato suggests society should help individuals do the right thing for the right reasons. Punishment for the sake of vengeance serves no purpose in an advanced society.

Deterrence

As a system of deterrence, the prison system clearly fails. The federal prison population has increased from fewer than 40,000 prisoners when I began serving my term in 1987 to more than 160,000 prisoners in 2002. With more people being sent to prison every day, it's hard for me to understand and concur with the argument that long prison sentences are an effective deterrence to crime.

To be certain, the possibility of an initial arrest is a deterrence to crime. Contemplation about one's humiliation in the community is a deterrence to crime. Thoughts about an initial separation from one's family and community are deterrences to crime. I am skeptical, however, that a twenty- or thirty-year sentence is more of a deterrence than the prospect of ten years behind bars.

After ten years of incarceration pass, one loses much of the perspective of time. Would a man calculate that it's okay to commit a crime if he were to receive a sentence of ten years but not a sentence of twenty years? I doubt it. Few criminals calculate the possible consequences of their actions in such ways. Swift and certain punishment, humiliation in one's community—these acts represent effective deterrences to crime. Prolonged incarceration, however, is more like an exile. And when one is in exile, one learns to live with his environment—especially when barriers are erected to sever ties between the individual and the home community.

Rehabilitation

If rehabilitation remains a goal of the prison system—and I doubt whether more than a few of those in authority pay anything more than lip service to this goal—then administrators are failing miserably. Federal prisoners convicted of committing crimes after November 1987 haven't been eligible to advance their release dates through petitions to parole boards; the only body in the criminal justice system to evaluate rehabilitation and act to reward its achievement in the life of a prisoner has been dismantled. Educational programs also have been cut, so individuals striving to develop meaningful skills face higher hurdles. Although a prisoner may behave in an infinite number of ways to lengthen his sentence or make his time more difficult, he has zero opportunities (with regard to prerogatives controlled by prison authorities) to distinguish himself in a positive way, to advance his release date, or to improve his living conditions.

Prison administrators offer few incentives to encourage prisoners to grow during their terms in confinement. Nor do they formally recognize prisoners who make consistent efforts to grow. During the semiannual meetings a prisoner has with his unit team, there's no mention of "rehabilitation" as a goal (by that or any other name) and no formal recognition given to prisoners who make strides toward an undefined (and perhaps nonexistent) goal of rehabilitation. In fact, when I asked my unit team recently what I could do to distinguish myself positively, they had no answer. "Just do your time."

Administrators make it patently clear that custody and security are their primary missions. The threat of being transferred to a higher security prison or the loss of privileges hangs over the head of the prisoner like the sword of Damocles. Rehabilitation may be a spoken or written goal, but, in practice, minimal efforts are made to encourage prisoners to develop skills and values that will help them succeed as law-abiding citizens upon their release.

Researchers say that two-thirds of all prisoners are likely to be re-arrested within three years of their release. Although I don't claim to be a statistician, such figures suggest to me that if rehabilitation is an actual goal of prison administrators, then evaluators ought to award an F to the prison system. On the other hand, if the goal is to disenfranchise permanently all who come through prison gates, then administrators are doing well. With over 66 percent of the people leaving prison being arrested again, it's difficult to conceive of a better plan to render people incapable of living in society than isolating them in the abnormal world of high-security prisons.

WHAT IS A SUCCESSFUL PRISON SYSTEM?

A decade ago, 1 in every 218 persons in America lived in a prison. Today, 1 in every 142 persons is in prison. This is more than a 60 percent increase in our per-capita incarceration rate over a ten-year period. If this trend continues, in ten more years more than 1 in 100 will be incarcerated; in twenty years, 1 in 60 human beings in this country will be a prisoner. Our nation will have evolved from the land of the free into the land of the incarcerated.

But is a prison system growing at this rate a success, especially when repeat offenders fuel its growth? Prison administrators now are spending $40 billion each year in taxpayer funds to keep offenders incarcerated. It behooves Americans, therefore, to establish criteria that would define a successful prison system.

Again, if taxpayers don't expect a prison system to do more than isolate people from their communities for prolonged periods of time, then the prison system as it currently operates is succeeding. A relatively enlightened society, however, should expect more. Indeed, over the past 200 years our country has made significant developments in education, science, and technology.

Locking people in cages for decades at a time, however, is an eighteenth-century response to crime. As a culture, we need to move forward.

The prison system certainly should be equipped to confine offenders. Instead of isolating all prisoners completely, however, administrators ought to encourage them to identify with their communities. Rehabilitating. Correcting. Prisoners then would recognize their own real interests in working toward becoming fully participating and contributing citizens—and this time in a law-abiding manner. A successful prison system would work to lessen the quantity of repeat offenders.

Administrators ought to embrace the advances made through the psychology of behaviorism, and use the promise of rewards instead of the threat of punishment to shape behavior. In essence, as the former Chief Justice Warren Burger suggested, administrators ought to initiate policies that encourage prisoners to earn and learn their way to freedom.

With so many people returning to prison after their release, I have come to the conclusion that prisons lead people to fail further in their lives. They make bad men worse; there's nothing "correctional" about prisons. In the 1970s, when rehabilitation programs were in vogue, it might have been appropriate to consider prison guards as correctional officers. Surging populations coupled with the emphasis on removing educational programs and parole boards, however, have transformed correctional officers into warehousing officers. They are storing and counting humans.

Too many people leave prison without skills and with a distorted value system. A successful prison system, on the other hand, would reverse such trends. It would use incentives to encourage prisoners to grow and to develop good character, temperance, and integrity. Programs shouldn't necessarily focus on helping prisoners get out of prison sooner. Rather, they should focus on helping prisoners understand why they should make different decisions so they can and will contribute to their communities. Administrators ought to help prisoners appreciate the virtues of self-reliance and hard work. Many need a social reconditioning, as they now embrace the values of the criminal world rather than society's. They need help to see a connection between community contributions and a better quality of life. A successful prison system would recognize prisoners who work to redeem themselves. It would offer opportunities instead of barriers to those struggling to develop skills that could help them participate in their communities.

Many prisoners see no reason to prepare themselves for release because they don't understand anything besides immediate gratification. They find that gratification by distinguishing themselves with their peers by becoming more involved with the prison's subculture or underground economy. They don't find it by completing self-improvement programs or educating themselves.

A system that distributed privileges according to merit, on the other hand, where individuals experienced an immediate incentive for appropriate behavior, would encourage prisoners. It would give them a dimension of control over their destiny that myopic prison policies don't address presently. As things stand now, prisoners can do an infinite number of things to make their life worse, but only the turning of calendar pages formally changes their status for the better in the eyes of prison administrators.

When administrators are able to lessen the number of people returning to prison after release, they then will lead successful prison systems. But as long as the population levels of the prison system continue growing at the rate of wild weeds in an unkempt field, and as long as researchers predict that two out of every three prisoners will be arrested again within three years of their release, then citizens must come, however reluctantly, to the conclusion that prisons are great instruments for incapacitating offenders, but they aren't effective for much else.

So, what do citizens expect offenders to accomplish while serving their sentences? How can administrators help? How can citizens help?

What Do Citizens Expect Offenders to Accomplish?

From the beginning of my prison term, I've tried to understand the expectations of my fellow citizens. What do citizens want offenders to accomplish during the terms they serve? Prison administrators and policies have provided me no answers to this question. Bureau of Prisons personnel only want prisoners to abide by prison rules, and they threaten sanctions and tighter controls to keep prisoners in line. But I've always suspected that citizens want more.

I've sought advice through my mentors, through my readings, and through those who visit my web site at *PrisonerLife.com*. In the process, I've learned that my suspicions are accurate—citizens want offenders to do more than simply serve their time.

Citizens expect offenders (except for the relatively few whose behavior demonstrates that they're unwilling to live according to society's rules) to identify with the goals of the larger community. They want offenders to express remorse for breaking society's laws. They want offenders to understand why laws are necessary to hold society together, and that it's every citizen's responsibility to abide by all existing laws and work to change unjust laws through the democratic process. Citizens want offenders to accept responsibility; to redeem themselves; and, eventually, to work their way back into the community as law-abiding, taxpaying, contributing citizens.

My experience of living in prison, however, suggests that few offenders even hear of these goals, much less understand them. Many come from backgrounds rendering them unfamiliar with such basic concepts as citizen responsibility or accountability. They feel that all control over their lives has been taken from them. During the terms they serve, such prisoners reject the values of a society they feel has rejected them. Instead, they participate more fully in the subculture behind prison fences and find barbaric behavior acceptable. Prolonged exposure to the abnormal world of prison makes it reasonable for these prisoners to live as unproductively as possible and to accept violence or the threat of violence as the appropriate response to any form of disrespect. After decades pass of living in the abnormal subculture behind fences, it's no wonder that so few succeed upon release. Prisons condition prisoners to fail.

How Can Administrators Help?

Administrators can reverse this worsening cultural condition by discouraging, or undercutting, the abnormal subcultures that currently flourish behind the walls of all coercive prisons. Instead of completely alienating prisoners from communities to which they'll return eventually, administrators ought to design programs that will inspire prisoners to identify with those communities. Administrators ought to look for opportunities to provide offenders with goals toward which they can work. And when offenders achieve those goals, administrators ought to reward them with privileges. It's not a terribly complex strategy.

Because prisons are total institutions, with administrators controlling (or attempting to control) prisoner activities at every hour of the day, they are ideal for introducing a gradual system of incentives designed to encourage the principles of good citizenship. Administrators working to meet the needs of society should look for opportunities to help offenders choose patterns of behavior that will help them stay out of prison—not simply leave prison sooner.

Such a goal isn't unattainable, and achieving it would in no way increase the costs of incarceration. Administrators would only have to begin by managing their prison systems through an objective promise of rewards for hard work and accomplishment; these rewards could work together with the current system of punishment for misbehavior. By initiating programs through which prisoners could earn privileges, administrators would help them connect with the reasons to participate.

Privileges don't have to inflate budgets. Staff can begin with simple privileges. In these bastions of deprivation, even the smallest incentives have meaning. Access to personal clothing, access to preferred housing, access to better visiting privileges, access to more learning opportunities, access to higher earning opportunities, access to community programs. As prisoners come to realize that through appropriate behavior they could enhance their quality of life and work their way toward freedom, they would be less inclined to engage in the subversive subcultures that exist and dominate in all prisons.

Further basing the prison system on merit, where prisoners could develop an objective plan through which they could earn their freedom, would inspire more of the 2 million people living behind bars to develop habits of good citizenship and identify with law-abiding communities. By encouraging prisoners to establish short- and long-term goals, and recognizing those who achieve their goals, administrators simultaneously discourage prisoners from participating in subversive subcultures. A merit system would prove infinitely more effective than a prison system based on time. Instead of trying to ingratiate themselves into the subculture of prison, a culture of failure, more prisoners would learn to identify with behavior that leads to success.

Under Warden Luther's management principles at McKean, which embraced such a system, prisoners were less inclined to participate in disruptions. When he left the institution, however, and the incentives system he had established disappeared, prisoners soon responded with violence that caused over $1 million damage to government property.

Even today, the differences in prison environments have a demonstrable impact individual prisoners. While being held in higher security prisons, Gypsy always kept a weapon nearby and responded to all forms of disrespect with violence. Since he transferred to the less coercive environment at Fort Dix, however, he has begun to decompress, to prepare himself mentally for the challenges he knows he'll face upon release. Even Joe B. has given up the hustles that carried him through his first decade of confinement. Now that he's at Fort Dix, he has left the prison subculture behind and focuses on developing skills he believes will contribute to his success upon release.

Until prison authorities, from the top down, make efforts to change the prison culture, the similar efforts of other parties—prisoners, their families, reform-minded politicians, interested citizens—will be futile.

How Can Citizens Help?

Citizens have an interest in supporting programs designed to help offenders succeed upon release. They can help by working as mentors to people in prison. I attribute much of my own growth behind prison walls to the help I received from mentors. As sources of support, mentors have a significant impact on offenders. They help offenders establish meaningful goals, then help them evaluate their progress as they work toward achieving those goals.

While there are a few BOP-sponsored mentoring programs, generally it's difficult for a concerned citizen to establish a support system for an incarcerated man or woman—not impossible, but difficult. Certainly prison officials aren't spending much time recruiting mentors in the wider community. And particularly onerous is the BOP regulation that attempts to cut the prisoner off from new sources of assistance. A prisoner, supposedly, can work only with the support system that existed when he or she was arrested and incarcerated. The illogic of such a regulation wouldn't be lost on the average 10-year-old.

Exceptions to the current policy (which may well have logical dimensions) should be made to encourage one-to-one tutoring and mentoring relationships and programs, prison by prison. When nations with illiterate populations have been successful in raising literacy levels, it has been with such a strategy. Prisoners in the United States today can be characterized as undeveloped or underdeveloped "nations" in terms of literacy, education, and competence to succeed in the society outside of prison. Citizens will help, if welcomed.

Any type of community interaction with prisoners discourages participation in prisoner (or criminal) subcultures. And in order to lessen the likelihood of future criminal behavior, nothing can be more effective than helping offenders identify with and embrace the goals and values of the larger community. Programs that allow offenders to interact with members of the community go a long way in helping them choose to develop good character, integrity, and discipline.

Despite the years offenders serve, at least four out of five return to their communities. That's a reality. That's a figure that American citizens should memorize. These communities, and indeed the entire national community, therefore, have an interest in helping these offenders become better citizens.

CONCLUSION: HOW CAN I HELP?

I will serve my remaining years in prison working to help others around me understand the importance of setting goals and then creating personal plans that help them achieve those goals. I will continue my own efforts to open new relationships with people in the community, and I will continue work to help others develop strong networks of support. I also will look for opportunities to educate citizens about the prison system and the people that it holds, and I will encourage voters to support the concept of allowing offenders the opportunity to earn freedom. Such a commitment led to my writing this book.

Two organizations to which I will try to contribute include Families Against Mandatory Minimums (FAMM) and the November Coalition. Both of these groups are grassroots organizations designed to change the mandatory-minimum sentencing laws that have resulted in our nation's having one of the highest incarceration rates in the world. Prisons alone aren't the solution to crime. The absurd number of people serving multiple decades for nonviolent offenses alone is a valid reason for legislators to reconsider mandatory-minimum sentencing laws and to create early release valves for people who demonstrate their commitment to earning freedom.

Through FAMM, the November Coalition, and my web site at *PrisonerLife. com*, I will continue my own efforts to earn freedom. I also will work to help others behind these fences develop strategies that will lead to their success upon release. As a federal prisoner, what else can I do? That's not a rhetorical question. I want to be both a problem finder and one who helps solve problems.